FOXFORD *cafe*
COOKBOOK

Kathleen Flavin has been head chef at the Foxford Cafe since 2010. She is a native of Tourmakeady, or Tuar Mhic Éadaigh, a small Gaeltacht area in south Mayo, where she lives with her husband, Barry, and two teenage children, Oisin and Sophie, and their beloved dog, Buddy. She trained as a chef in GMIT Galway and has spent over twenty-five years working in commercial kitchens, from five-star hotels to fine dining restaurants – food is at the heart of everything she does. Her philosophy, and that of Foxford Cafe, is to cook nutritious, simple and versatile dishes, with an emphasis on seasonal and locally sourced vegetables, meat and fish. She appreciates the hard work and dedication of local producers and farmers and believes that they, alongside our Irish butchers, cheesemakers, local growers and suppliers, need to be supported and cherished, as they support and enrich our local communities. 'Ar scáth a chéile a mhaireann na daoine' – we all live in each other's shelter.

FOXFORD *cafe* COOKBOOK

Kathleen Flavin

THE O'BRIEN PRESS
DUBLIN

CONTENTS

Foreword *Joe Queenan*   page 7

Introduction   9

SALADS

Fresh Fig and Pickled Pear Salad with Cashel Blue Cheese   13

Cucumber Pickle   14

Garlic Roasted Broccoli with Romesco Sauce and Toasted Almonds   17

Bombay Roast Potatoes   18

Watermelon Salad   21

    Mint and Lime   21

    Honey and Pink Peppercorn Dressing with Feta   21

Roasted Cauliflower with Parmesan   22

Seasonal Leaf Platters   25

    Mixed Leaves with Maple-Glazed Peach or Nectarine, Toasted Pecans and Cashel Blue Cheese   25

    Rocket with Pickled Cherries, Orange and Crumbled Goat's Cheese   25

New Season Baby Potatoes with Lemon Caper Aioli   26

Tomato and Strawberry Salad   29

Pappardelle Pasta with Pesto   30

Winter Slaw with Ginger and Sesame Dressing   33

Curly Kale with Maple Tahini Dressing and Pickled Red Onion   34

Roast Cauliflower Salad with Pearl Couscous and Zhoug   37

Diced Beetroot and Orange Salad   38

SOUPS AND BREADS

Carrot, Ginger and Coconut Soup   43

Creamy Mushroom and Spinach Soup   44

Tomato and Roast Pepper Soup   47

Curried Cauliflower and Coconut Soup   48

Seafood Chowder   51

Broccoli, Potato and Spinach Soup   52

Carrot and Parsnip Soup   55

Cauliflower Cheese Soup	56
Minestrone Soup	59
Brown Soda Bread	60
Brown Treacle Soda Bread	63
Fruity Soda Bread	64
Focaccia	67

CAFE FAVOURITES

Spiced Lamb and Potato Parcels	71
Frittata Three Ways	72
Pork and Apple Sausage Rolls	75
Beetroot Patties with Roast Carrot Hummus	76
Lamb Koftas with Tzatziki	79
Falafels	80
BBQ Smoked Salmon Fishcakes	83
Cauliflower Tacos	84
Free-Range Egg Quiche Three Ways	87
Roast Carrot and Chickpea Rolls	90
Goat's Cheese Tartlets with Red Onion Marmalade	93

SOMETHING SWEET

Scones Three Ways	99
Fruit or Plain Scones	99
Iced Lemon Scones	100
Brown Treacle Scones	101
Date, Coconut and Dark Chocolate Powerballs	102
Iced Lemon Loaf	105
Chocolate Chip Cookies	106
Gluten-Free Millionaire's Shortbread	109
Rich Fruit Loaf Cake	112
Chocolate Brownies	117
Apple Bakewell Slices	118
Rocky Road	123
Peanut Butter and White Chocolate Powerballs	124

CAKES AND TARTS

Simple Sponge Cake	129
Maple and Pecan Pie	132
Orange, Polenta and Early Rhubarb Cake	135
Blueberry and Lemon Polenta Cake (Variation)	136
Chocolate Cake with Real Chocolate Frosting	138
Lemon Meringue Pie	143
Coffee Cake	144
Brown Sugar Meringue Roulade	148
Rhubarb and Custard Tart	153
White Chocolate and Cranberry Cheesecake	156
Baked Chocolate and Mint Tart	161

FOXFORD CAFE PANTRY

Foxford Cafe Christmas Pudding	165
Foxford Jams	166
Beetroot Orange Chutney	169
Homemade Granola	170
Cranberry Orange Biscotti	173
Dehydrated Orange Slices	174
Pickled Beetroot	177
Pickled Pears	178
Pickled Cherries	181

DRESSINGS

Honey and Pink Peppercorn Dressing	184
Maple Tahini Dressing	184
House Dressing	184
Ginger and Sesame Dressing	185
Buttermilk Dressing	185

Our Suppliers	186
Acknowledgements	187
Index	188

FOREWORD

'... and our Foxford tweeds ... nothing like it in the whole wide world.'
James Joyce, *Ulysses* (1922)

On 2 May 1892, the sluice-gates on the mill-race in the River Moy were opened and the looms of Providence Woollen Mills began weaving. The establishment of the mill has left an indelible mark on the town of Foxford. The enterprise, the brainchild of Mother Agnes Morrogh-Bernard, a member of the Sisters of Charity, was established with the primary aim of improving the lives of people in a very poor region of County Mayo.

Employment was provided and a brand was created. Foxford blankets and tweeds entered the lexicon of Irish life. Families were wrapped in Foxford blankets and occasions were lovingly marked with gifts created in Mayo. The brand continued to thrive until the 1980s, when the Sisters of Charity decided to exit the commercial world and called in the receivers. I was a young accountant at the time and became fascinated by the mill, its story and its potential. With the help of a group of investors, we bought the business and kept the story alive. Today FOXFORD is a lifestyle brand offering homewares, bedlinen and food. Still rooted in our history, we continue to weave FOXFORD throws and scarves here in our County Mayo mill.

When I was growing up in the 1960s on a small farm in Lahardane, north Mayo, 20 kilometres from Foxford, the mere suggestion that I would be associated with the publication of a FOXFORD Cafe cookbook would have been seen as highly unlikely. There is an old saying about how to make the gods smile: 'tell them your plans'! My love of food was a gift from my mother, a lady I owe a lot to, and the cafe has gone from strength to strength since it opened in 2010.

I owe a huge debt of gratitude to my wife, Claire, our family, staff and customers who, through their hard work and support, have enabled FOXFORD to grow and thrive. I would also like to acknowledge the contribution of Tom O'Mahony, who was our chairman, a colleague and a friend since we took over the business in 1988. Tom passed away on 30 April 2024 and we miss him greatly. I wish he were here to turn the pages of this book, as he was always a great fan of FOXFORD Cafe.

I hope you enjoy trying out the recipes and that they taste just as good as when you visit us.

Joe Queenan
Managing Director
FOXFORD

INTRODUCTION

FOXFORD Cafe is situated on the first floor of the home of the FOXFORD brand on the banks of the River Moy in County Mayo. It is a bright, airy space filled with natural light, where on weekdays the rumbling of the looms in the working mill can be heard beneath the floorboards. Cafe seating meanders through spacious rooms: the original Manager's Office, the Pattern Room, the Patio, and the Design Office – all with nods to the Woollen Mills' rich history. The walls are adorned with historical artefacts and photographs documenting the history of the mill, originally called Providence Woollen Mills, since its inception in 1892. The motto of our founder, Mother Agnes Morrogh-Bernard, was 'Providence Will Provide'. As custodians of her legacy, I hope we have lived up to her expectations.

The cafe is hive of activity seven days a week and has been since it opened in 2010. Our food philosophy here is simple: cook great-tasting, local, nutritious and seasonal food for our customers, and serve it in a welcoming, friendly space. Our counter is packed with giant platters of seasonal salads, quiches, tartlets, sausage and veggie rolls and fish cakes, to name a few, alongside soups, breads, cakes, bakes and coffees, all prepared daily by our talented cafe team.

Our pantry shelves are stacked with tastes of the cafe to take home: jams, marmalades, dressings, chutneys, pickles and granolas, all made in-house. When I started in the cafe, there were two full-timers, myself as head chef and Rachel the restaurant manager, and three part-timers. It's a far cry from the up-to-twenty full- and part-time team we have now, but Rachel, my partner-in-work-crime, is still here too! That first winter, we decided we would make and jar our own products, as our customers had been asking for them and our part-time staff needed hours. So we filled our pantry in the off-season and sold out every Christmas and summer. Each product was hand poured in our kitchen and labelled behind the cafe counter between serving customers. Ten years on and our retail range is an integral part of our cafe business – we have a dedicated production kitchen and we produced and sold 40,000 products in our own stores in 2024 alone.

This book is filled with recipes that we use every day in the cafe kitchen, all tested and tasted by our team so that you can replicate them at home. These recipes have many stories; some have been with me since my early twenties. They have been collected, nurtured, tweaked and, most importantly, made thousands of times since. I trust you will enjoy this book, reading the recipes and looking at the beautiful photography, but most of all I hope it ends up with turned-down pages, smudges of batter and drizzles of oil. I hope you find it useful and practical and that you can recreate a little bit of our beloved Foxford Cafe at home.

Kathleen Flavin
Head Chef
Foxford Cafe

SALADS

Our salads are a huge part of our menu. They change every six weeks or so with seasonal availability. We are advised to eat the rainbow, and our salad counter ensures you can do that all year round. I love using fruit in salads and use pickling techniques to ensure we can have it out of season too.

Preparation and planning are the key to being able to make fresh salads daily, and you can elevate them using dressings, pickles, nuts, seeds, fresh herbs and spices. Cooking techniques help immensely when varying your vegetables and fruits for salads. Shredding kale makes it instantly more palatable, and popping peaches or nectarines on a griddle intensifies their natural sugars if they are under-ripe. Roasting cauliflower transforms it entirely. Simple pestos, using wild garlic, basil or even rocket, are a great way of prolonging these wonderful herbs or leaves and give an instant lift to a pasta or leaf salad.

Fresh Fig and Pickled Pear Salad with Cashel Blue Cheese

This beautiful salad never fails to impress on our salad counter. We are lucky enough to have a local supplier of figs, Liz Courtie. Our award-winning pickled pears really elevate this simple but impressive salad, so you can buy them or have a go at making them yourself (the pears can be done well in advance).

SERVES 6–8

3 pickled pears (page 178)
6 fresh figs
100g rocket, or other winter leaves, washed and dried
100g Cashel Blue cheese

1. Slice the pears and figs into wedges, and arrange alternately around your favourite platter.
2. Pop the rocket or winter leaves in the centre and crumble the Cashel Blue on top.
3. Drizzle some of the poaching liquid from the pears over the leaves before serving.

Cucumber Pickle

This pickle is a staple on our salad counter – it's been a favourite of mine for years. I like to add chilli, as it gives it a great kick without altering the refreshing taste of the cucumber. It pairs well with so many dishes – like smoked salmon or simple grilled or poached fish – and it's a great addition to a green leaf salad. Make two jars and gift one – or not!

MAKES 2 X 450G JARS

1kg cucumbers
1 red onion
250g granulated sugar
10g salt
200ml cider vinegar
½ tsp chilli flakes

1. Wash and slice the cucumbers as thinly as possible, using a sharp knife, mandolin (just mind those fingers) or food processor.
2. Peel and halve the onion, then slice as thinly as possible, as above, and place in a large bowl with the cucumber.
3. Mix all the other ingredients together and pour over the sliced cucumber and onion.
4. Spoon into clean jars or any container with a lid, and divide the pickling liquid between them.
5. Store in the fridge. Cucumber pickle will keep for 7–10 days in the fridge – it will lose colour as it ages.

Garlic Roasted Broccoli with Romesco Sauce and Toasted Almonds

This vibrant salad is a great centrepiece for any dinner or lunch table. It's great on its own or with grilled or breaded chicken or white fish. The recipe makes a large batch of romesco, which is often served with roast vegetables, like in the cauliflower tacos on page 84. I also use romesco as a dressing for a simple orzo salad with rocket and Parmesan.

SERVES 4-6

2 heads of broccoli
3 cloves of garlic
200ml olive oil
sprinkle of sea salt (I use Achill Island)
150g flaked almonds

FOR THE ROMESCO SAUCE

2 cloves of garlic
350g roasted peppers
40g toasted bread (GF or regular)
2 tsp paprika
2 tsp balsamic vinegar
sea salt and cracked black pepper, to taste

1. Preheat your oven to 170°C fan/190°C/gas 5.
2. Use a sharp knife to cut the broccoli florets as close as possible to the stalk. Cut them into 3-4cm pieces.
3. Mince the garlic, then mix with the oil.
4. Place the broccoli in a large bowl. Pour the garlic oil over the broccoli, with a generous sprinkle of sea salt, and mix well until all the broccoli is coated. Spread evenly on a baking tray.
5. Place in the oven and roast for about 9 minutes. Check it's cooked by piercing with a sharp knife – it should be tender but have a slight bite. Remove from the oven and allow to cool.
6. Turn the oven down to 160°C fan/180°C/gas 4. Place the flaked almonds on a baking tray and cook for about 10 minutes, tossing a few times during cooking so they toast evenly. (You can always do extra, cool well and place in a Kilner jar for using another day or to sprinkle on a breakfast or salad.)
7. For the romesco sauce, first mince the garlic. Then place all the ingredients, as well as 50g of the toasted flaked almonds, in a food processor – or a jug if using a hand blender – and pulse until everything is fully incorporated. It doesn't need to be completely smooth.
8. Spread a thick layer of the romesco on a large plate, dot the roasted broccoli over it, sprinkle with toasted almonds, and serve.

Bombay Roast Potatoes

This is ideal when using potatoes from storage, not new season. They are best served at room temperature, are great as a side to a curry and are a super addition to a family birthday or BBQ table. They're a staff favourite here in the cafe – bowls of them just seem to disappear.

SERVES 4-6

1kg Rooster potatoes
150ml olive oil
sea salt, to taste

FOR THE BOMBAY SPICE MIX

1 tbsp ground cumin
1 tbsp ground coriander
2 tsp turmeric
1 tsp chilli flakes
1 tsp ground ginger
¼ tsp ground cinnamon
1 cardamon pod (or ¼ tsp ground cardamon)
1 clove (or pinch of ground cloves)

1. Preheat your oven to 170°C fan/190°C/gas 5.
2. Wash and chop your potatoes into approximately 2cm cubes. Leave in a bowl covered in water until you need them.
3. Next, prepare your Bombay spice mix – a food processor or spice blender is handy for this stage, but if you don't have one, just crush the cardamon and cloves with the blade of your knife or use a pestle and mortar. Mix all the spices together.
4. Drain and pat your potatoes dry, place them in a large bowl and toss them in the spice mix. Season with a good sprinkle of sea salt, then add the oil and toss again.
5. Spread evenly on a roasting tray and place in the oven for 25–35 minutes, tossing occasionally, until they are tender when pierced with a knife but crispy on the outside.
6. Allow to cool to room temperature, then serve.

Watermelon Salad

We do two versions of this salad – they're always on our salad counter in summer and are usually requested by customers in advance of their appearance! They are both light and refreshing – the salty feta version contrasts beautifully with the sweetness of the melon, and the mint and lime version is also great on the breakfast table or as a lunchbox snack.

SERVES 6-9

1 small watermelon
2 limes
20 leaves of fresh mint

Mint and Lime

1. Using a sharp knife, slice off the top and bottom of the watermelon. Sit it on one end, then remove the skin in parts with the knife, using a sawing motion, moving from top to bottom and curving around the melon, without cutting too deep into the flesh.
2. Cut the watermelon in half, then slice across at an angle from side to side. Cut each slice into finger-sized pieces and place in a large bowl.
3. Zest the limes using a Microplane or fine grater, then juice them. Finely chop the mint leaves.
4. Mix the lime juice, zest and mint with the melon and place in the fridge. I like to leave this salad to sit for 30 minutes at least before serving, as it allows the flavours to combine.

1 small watermelon
drizzle of honey and pink peppercorn dressing (page 184)
100g feta
a few mint leaves, to garnish

Honey and Pink Peppercorn Dressing with Feta

1. Using a sharp knife, slice off the top and bottom of the watermelon. Sit it on one end, then remove the skin in parts with the knife, using a sawing motion, moving from top to bottom and curving around the melon, without cutting too deep into the flesh.
2. Cut the watermelon in quarters and slice across each quarter to form wedges.
3. Lay the wedges on a big platter and crumble the feta on top. Shake the dressing well to combine then drizzle over the platter and garnish with a few mint leaves.

Roasted Cauliflower with Parmesan

Cauliflower is such a versatile vegetable and has had a real revival in recent years. I wasn't fond of it as a child but am obsessed with it now. Its delicate flavour means it's easy to partner with other ingredients. A head of cauliflower goes a long way!

SERVES 4-6

1 medium cauliflower (for about 500g florets)
50g Parmesan, grated
30ml light olive oil
25g plain flour (GF or regular)
1 level tsp salt
½ tsp chilli flakes
pinch of black pepper

TO GARNISH

flat-leaf parsley or fresh coriander leaves

1. Preheat your oven to 170°C fan/190°C/gas 5.
2. To prepare the cauliflower, use a sharp knife to remove the green outer leaves and then cut the florets as close as possible to the stalk. Next, cut them into 3–4cm pieces. I usually leave the smaller white leaves in.
3. Mix the rest of the ingredients together, except for the garnish, then toss in a large bowl with the cauliflower, making sure the florets are evenly coated.
4. Place the cauliflower on a roasting tray. Cook for 10–12 minutes until the cauliflower is cooked through. It should still have a slight bite.
5. Scrape all the crusty cheesy bits off the tray with the cauliflower, then pile onto a large plate.
6. Best served at room temperature, garnished with some flat-leaf parsley or fresh coriander.

Seasonal Leaf Platters

We have been lucky enough to source our leaves for the past couple of years from Sarah of Willow and Wild, a local flower and vegetable grower. I'm proud to say that, since 2025, we have had our own raised beds and, with Sarah's help, have been growing our own. I like to add fruit, pickled or fresh, a sprinkle of an Irish farmhouse cheese, sometimes toasted nuts or seeds and a drizzle of dressing or herb oil to these platters, changing them according to what's in season.

SERVES 4-6

handful of pecans
2 peaches or nectarines
½ tsp olive oil or butter
2 tbsp maple syrup
100g mixed leaves, washed and dried
100g Cashel Blue cheese

Mixed Leaves with Maple-Glazed Peach or Nectarine, Toasted Pecans and Cashel Blue Cheese

1. Preheat your oven to 160°C fan/180°C/gas 4.
2. Place your pecans on a baking tray and toast them in the oven for about 10 minutes, tossing them a few times during cooking so they toast evenly. You can always do extra, cool well and place in a Kilner jar for using another day to sprinkle on a breakfast or salad.
3. Wash and cut the peaches or nectarines into wedges – not too thin, as they will shrink when cooked.
4. Preheat a small frying pan over a medium-high heat. Add the butter or olive oil, toss in the peach or nectarine wedges and cook until they take colour – about 2 minutes. Toss, add the maple syrup, cook for no more than 30 seconds, then scoop out onto a plate to cool.
5. Arrange the platter with the leaves first, then the fruit. Sprinkle the crumbled cheese and nuts on top, and drizzle any juice from the fruit over the salad, then serve.

1 large orange
100g rocket, washed and dried
100g Irish soft goat's cheese
150g pickled cherries (page 181)

Rocket with Pickled Cherries, Orange and Crumbled Goat's Cheese

1. Peel your orange and slice thinly across the equator.
2. Arrange the platter with the leaves first, then the orange slices. Sprinkle the crumbled soft cheese and pickled cherries on top, and drizzle some pickling juice over the salad, then serve.

New Season Baby Potatoes with Lemon Caper Aioli

Few things are better than steamed new season baby potatoes with salt and real butter, but this aioli comes a close second. The salty capers marry perfectly with the sweetness of the potatoes, and the lemon juice cuts through the creamy mayonnaise. The aioli makes more than you'll need for this salad – use the rest as a dip for battered cauliflower, to accompany a simple poached salmon fillet or in a sandwich with roast chicken.

SERVES 4-6

1kg baby potatoes

handful of flat-leaf parsley, for garnish

FOR THE LEMON CAPER AIOLI

3 cloves of garlic

480g good-quality mayonnaise

20ml lemon juice

30g capers

2 handfuls of flat-leaf parsley, leaves only

55ml light olive oil

salt, to taste

1. Wash and steam your baby potatoes – they will take anything from 15 to 25 minutes depending on their size. Check with a sharp knife. Allow them to cool before slicing in half lengthways.
2. Meanwhile, for the lemon caper aioli, first mince the garlic cloves, otherwise they will be difficult to blend properly. Place all the ingredients in a food processor – or a jug if using a hand blender – and pulse until the capers break up and the parsley incorporates. It does not have to be completely smooth.
3. Scrape into a sealed plastic container and store in the fridge until you need it. It will keep for 3 days.
4. Place the cooled, halved baby potatoes in large bowl and add a few tablespoons of the aioli. Mix using a large spoon until the potatoes are lightly coated – add more if you wish. Taste to check the seasoning – the dressing is normally salty enough because of the capers, but if not, add a little salt to taste. Garnish with a few parsley leaves and serve.

Tomato and Strawberry Salad

There is nothing better than tomatoes when they are in season! This salad can be made all summer long when Irish strawberries and tomatoes are available. The platter makes a beautiful centrepiece to any lunch, party or BBQ. The salad is also delicious served on its own with a semi-soft cheese like burrata and crusty bread.

SERVES 6-8

10 vine-ripened tomatoes
1 large punnet fresh Irish strawberries
sea salt
honey and pink peppercorn dressing (page 184)

1. Gently wash the tomatoes and strawberries, being careful not to bruise them, and pat dry.
2. Using a sharp serrated knife, remove the stalks of the tomatoes, slice a thin sliver off both ends of each tomato, then cut into 0.5cm-thick slices horizontally.
3. Keep each tomato together, before fanning out around your chosen platter.
4. Chop the green ends off the strawberries and cut in half, or into quarters if they are large enough. Pile into the centre of the platter.
5. Sprinkle the tomatoes with a little sea salt.
6. Drizzle with some honey and pink peppercorn dressing and serve.

Pappardelle Pasta with Pesto

This is always popular on our salad counter. It's a very simple salad but you must choose a good-quality pasta. We use a basil and parsley pesto, without the traditional pinenuts and Parmesan, to accommodate our customers with various allergies. I have included a wild garlic version below as well. The pestos are super-versatile, and you'll have some left over for adding to another dish.

SERVES 4

250g pappardelle pasta (I use De Cecco)

pinch of salt

3 tbsp olive oil

100g Parmesan

FOR THE WILD GARLIC PESTO

100g wild garlic (including tender stems)

8 tbsp grated Parmesan

200ml olive oil

sea salt, to taste

FOR THE BASIL PESTO

100g basil (including tender stalks)

50g curly parsley (leaves only)

3 cloves of garlic

600ml olive oil

salt to taste

1. To make the wild garlic pesto, pulse all the ingredients together using a hand blender – it does not need to be completely smooth. Taste before adding salt, as it may be salty enough depending on the Parmesan. To store, place in a clean glass jar and cover with a few tablespoons of olive oil to keep the air out – this prevents discolouration. Your pesto will keep for up to 10 days in the fridge – not that it will last that long.
2. To make the basil pesto, prepare and store as per the recipe above. You may need to mince your garlic before pulsing, depending on your hand blender's power.
3. Place a large saucepan three-quarters full of water over full heat. The pot should look way too large for the job – pappardelle likes space. Season with a generous pinch of salt and a tablespoon of olive oil.
4. Bring to the boil, and when it's bubbling add your pappardelle.
5. Using a plastic or metal spoon, give it a stir to make sure the pasta is not sticking and is completely immersed. Turn the heat down slightly, to a gentle boil, as pasta is delicate. Cook for 6–7 minutes or according to the guidelines for your brand of pasta.
6. Drain immediately, using a colander, and run the cold tap over the pasta until it's completely cooled. Leave for a couple of minutes so all the water drains away.
7. Toss the pasta in the remaining 2 tablespoons of olive oil – this will prevent it from sticking if you're not using it immediately.
8. To serve, place the pasta on a large shallow platter and spoon your pesto of choice over the top, then sprinkle with ground or shaved Parmesan.

Winter Slaw with Ginger and Sesame Dressing

There are so many versions of slaw and ways to dress it. This dressing packs a punch – it takes a bit of preparation time, but it will keep for months. To add this slaw to a lunchbox every day, I'd suggest prepping enough veg for three days and placing each one separately in an airtight container. Then take out what you need each day, mix and add your dressing. A sliced red apple is a great addition to change it up or add some sweetness.

SERVES 4–6

¼ head of white cabbage
¼ head of red cabbage
1 large carrot
2 handfuls of flat-leaf parsley leaves
190ml ginger and sesame dressing (page 185)
sea salt, to taste

1. Secure your chopping board by placing a tea towel or clean dry cloth underneath it. Using a large sharp chopping knife, remove the stalk parts of the cabbages, then slice thinly along the direction of the leaves, or cut into pieces and feed through the slicing attachment on your food processor.
2. Peel and grate your carrot on the largest side of your grater. Roughly chop your parsley leaves.
3. Place all the cabbage, carrot and most of the parsley in a large bowl, keeping back a few leaves for garnish. Add the dressing and mix until all the vegetables are lightly coated. Taste and season with a little sea salt if you wish.
4. Sprinkle with parsley and serve. This will keep chilled in the fridge for the day – it doesn't keep well overnight, so only mix what you need.

Curly Kale with Maple Tahini Dressing and Pickled Red Onion

Kale is a really nutritious vegetable, even more so when eaten raw. The key to making it more palatable is in the prep – I use the slicer attachment on my food processor to do it. Then it's a matter of dressing it with your favourite dressing – I love this maple tahini one.

SERVES 4-6

1 large or 2 small heads of curly kale
maple tahini dressing (page 184)
sea salt
toasted sesame seeds or almonds (optional)

FOR THE PICKLED RED ONION

500g red onion
100ml cider vinegar
½ level tbsp salt
125g white sugar

1. For the pickled onion, first peel and halve the red onions top to bottom, then slice, using a food processor or a sharp knife, as thinly as possible. Add the vinegar, salt and sugar to a large bowl, stir, then mix in the sliced onion. Pack into an airtight container and refrigerate overnight, ideally, or for 3 hours minimum, for the flavours to develop. Use within 10 days.
2. Take the head of kale, turn it upside down and hold by the base in your non-dominant hand. Using your dominant hand, keeping your fingers pinched on the stem, pull the leaves sharply downwards. They should pull off easily.
3. Place the leaves, now without stalks, in a bowl of salted cold water, swish and leave for 5 minutes. This helps get rid of any bugs. Repeat if the kale is dirty. Drain well and pat dry with a clean tea towel.
4. Now shred the leaves, either using the slicer attachment in a food processor or a large sharp chopping knife.
5. In a large bowl, toss the kale in a few tablespoons of the maple tahini dressing and a pinch of sea salt, and mix well. It can be easy to overdress kale, as it seems so bulky at this point, but it softens with the addition of vinegar and the salt will draw the water out, so less is more!
6. Pile the kale onto a platter or into a serving bowl and dress with some of the pickled red onion.
7. Sprinkle with toasted sesame seeds or almonds if you want to add some crunch.

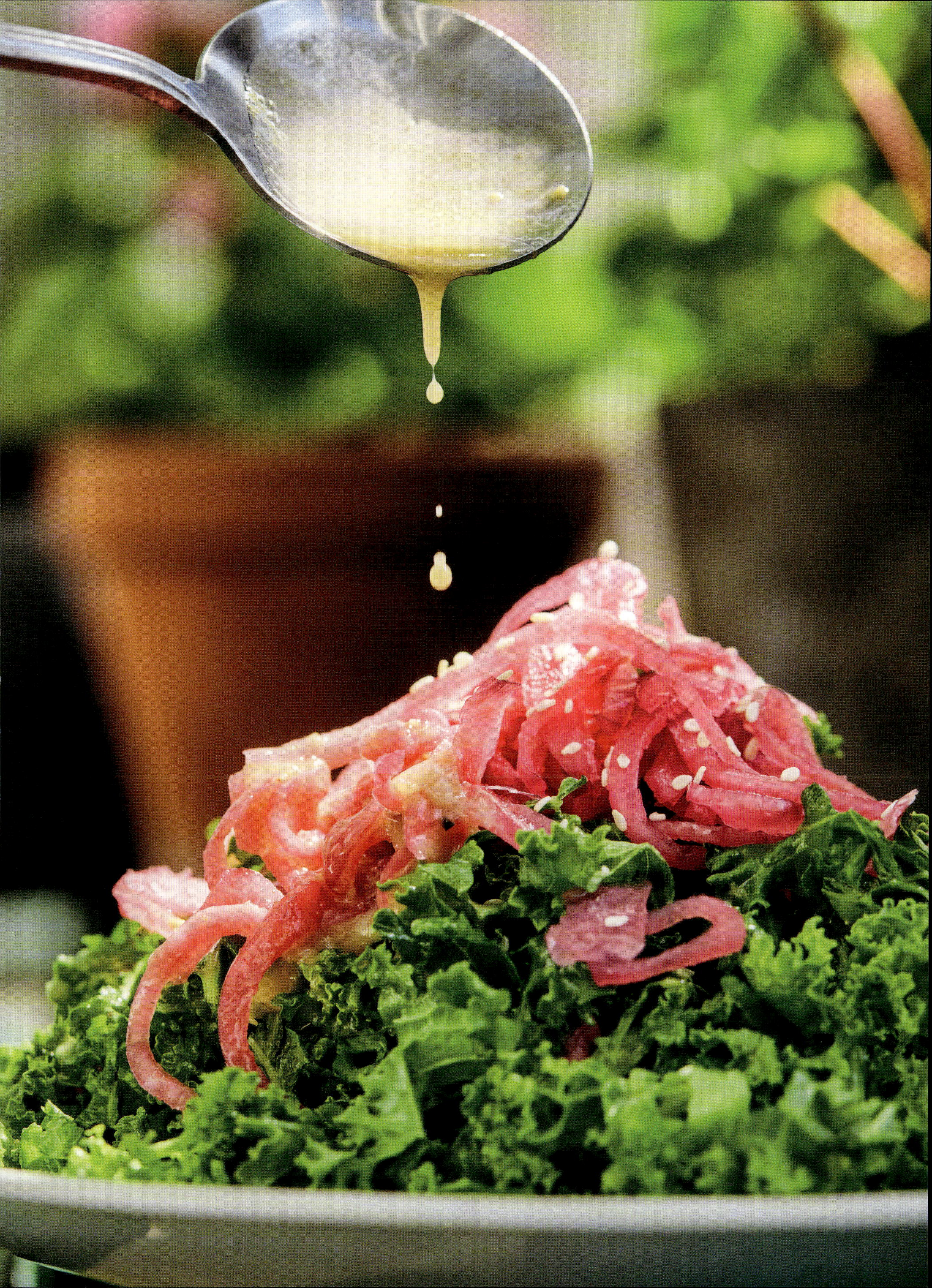

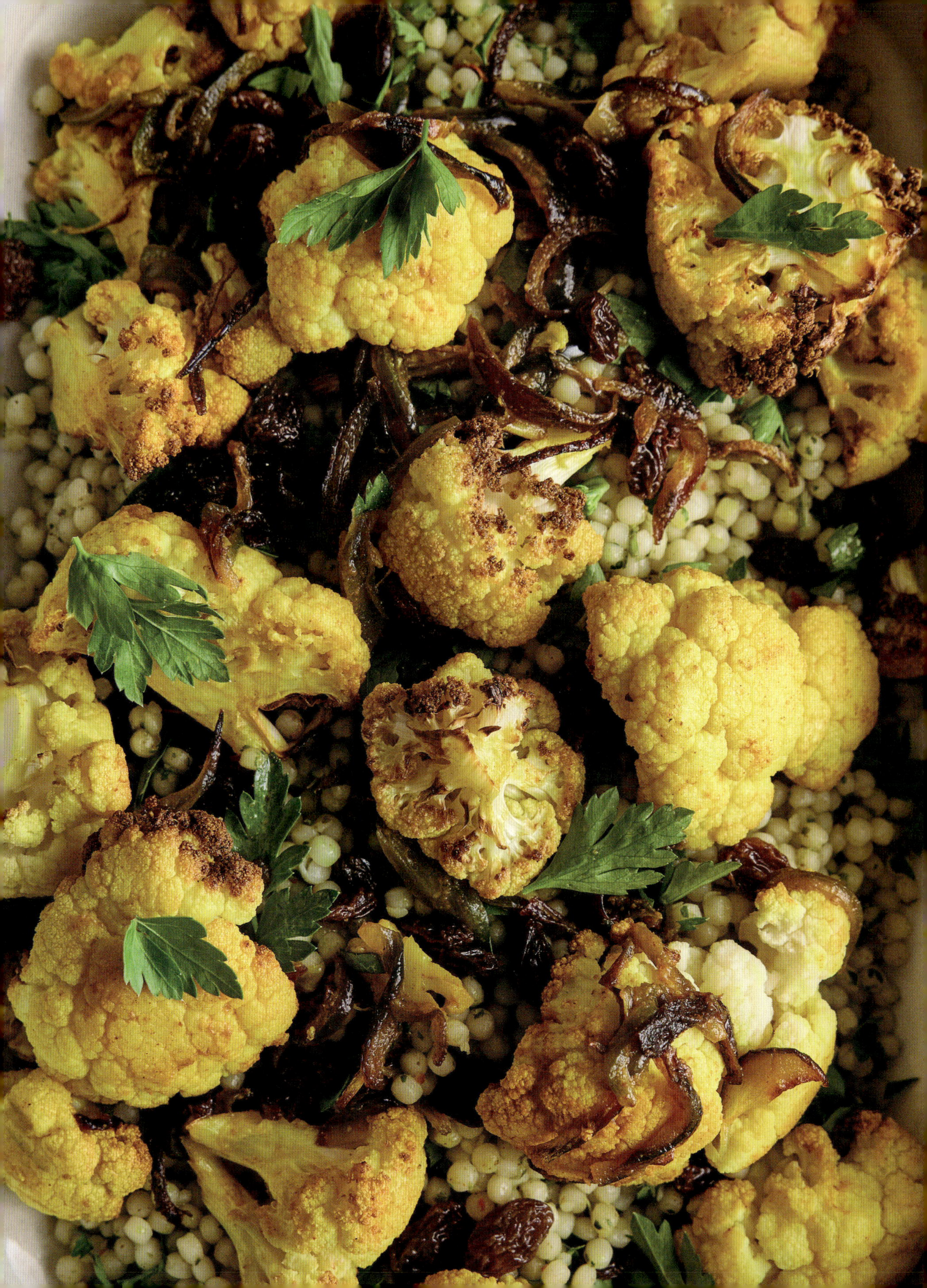

Roast Cauliflower Salad with Pearl Couscous and Zhoug

Pearl couscous is a little harder to find than the regular Moroccan grainy version, but it's worth the effort to search for it. You could substitute orzo pasta, but I prefer the chewier texture of the pearl couscous here. Zhoug is a traditional Middle Eastern sauce – it's fiery, super-herbaceous and the key to the success of this recipe, so don't skip it here. It's a small quantity but it packs a punch.

SERVES 4-6

FOR THE ZHOUG

2 handfuls of fresh coriander
2 handfuls of flat-leaf parsley
¼ fresh red chilli, deseeded
¼ tsp cumin
1 tbsp cider vinegar
1 clove of garlic

FOR THE COUSCOUS

125g pearl couscous
25g raisins
½ clove of garlic
1 tbsp lemon juice
1 tsp zhoug
handful of chopped flat-leaf parsley

FOR THE ROAST CAULIFLOWER

1 medium cauliflower (for about 500g florets)
½ red onion
¾ tsp turmeric
3 tbsp light olive oil
pinch of sea salt

1. Blitz all of the ingredients for the zhoug together in a food processor or blender. It doesn't need to be completely smooth. To store, place in a clean Kilner jar in the fridge, and top with 100ml of olive oil to keep the air out.
2. Cook the pearl couscous according to the instructions on the packet. Drain well and leave to cool.
3. Soak the raisins in a bowl of slightly cooled boiled water.
4. Preheat the oven to 170°C fan/190°C/gas 5.
5. To prepare your cauliflower, use a sharp knife to remove the green outer leaves, and cut the florets as close as possible to the stalk. Then cut them into 4cm pieces – I usually leave the smaller white leaves in.
6. Peel and slice the onion half.
7. Mix the cauliflower and onion in a large bowl. Add the turmeric and olive oil and toss together. Sprinkle with sea salt.
8. Place the cauliflower on a roasting tray. Roast for 5-7 minutes, until the cauliflower is cooked through – it should still have a slight bite. Set aside to cool slightly.
9. Drain the raisins, crush the garlic and add to the couscous with the lemon juice. Add 1 teaspoon of zhoug and mix well. Add the cauliflower, stir through, then scoop out into a shallow bowl or platter. Sprinkle with flat-leaf parsley and serve.

Diced Beetroot and Orange Salad

I was a really fussy eater as a child but, oddly, loved pickled beetroot. My mother and aunties have always grown and pickled their own in various ways, and I always have a jar in the fridge. I love it in all forms now. For those who don't like the sharpness of pickled beetroot but like beetroot itself, this is the salad for you: it's sweet and the orange zest is the perfect partner here.

1kg raw beetroot
150g raisins
1 orange
2 cloves of garlic
1 red onion
45ml cider vinegar
a generous pinch of salt
2 handfuls of coriander leaves

1. Top and tail the beetroot. Wash well, place in a large pot of warm salted water and bring to the boil. Simmer – small beets take about 30 minutes and the larger ones 40–50 minutes. I like them to have a bite. Set aside to cool slightly.
2. Meanwhile, place the raisins in a small bowl of slightly cooled boiled water.
3. Zest the orange using a Microplane or the fine side of a grater. Mince the garlic.
4. Peel and dice the red onion as small as you can.
5. Use disposable gloves for this part. While the beetroot are still warm, begin to peel them – the skin should almost rub off.
6. Dice the beetroot into 1cm cubes, drain the raisins, and mix all of the ingredients together except the coriander, as it will discolour with heat. Allow the mix to cool completely, place in the fridge and chill.
7. Roughly chop the coriander leaves.
8. When the salad is completely chilled, add the chopped coriander to serve.

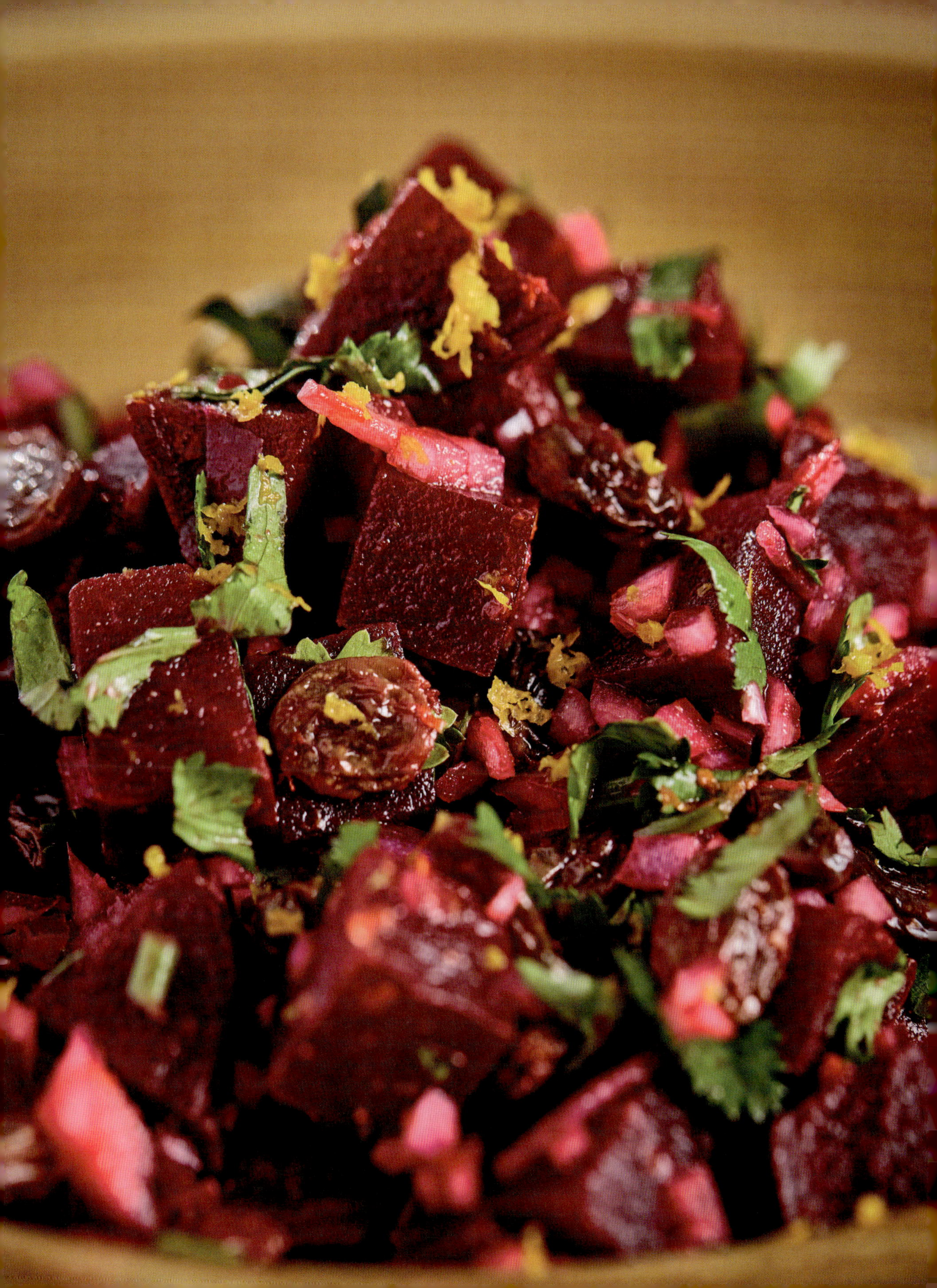

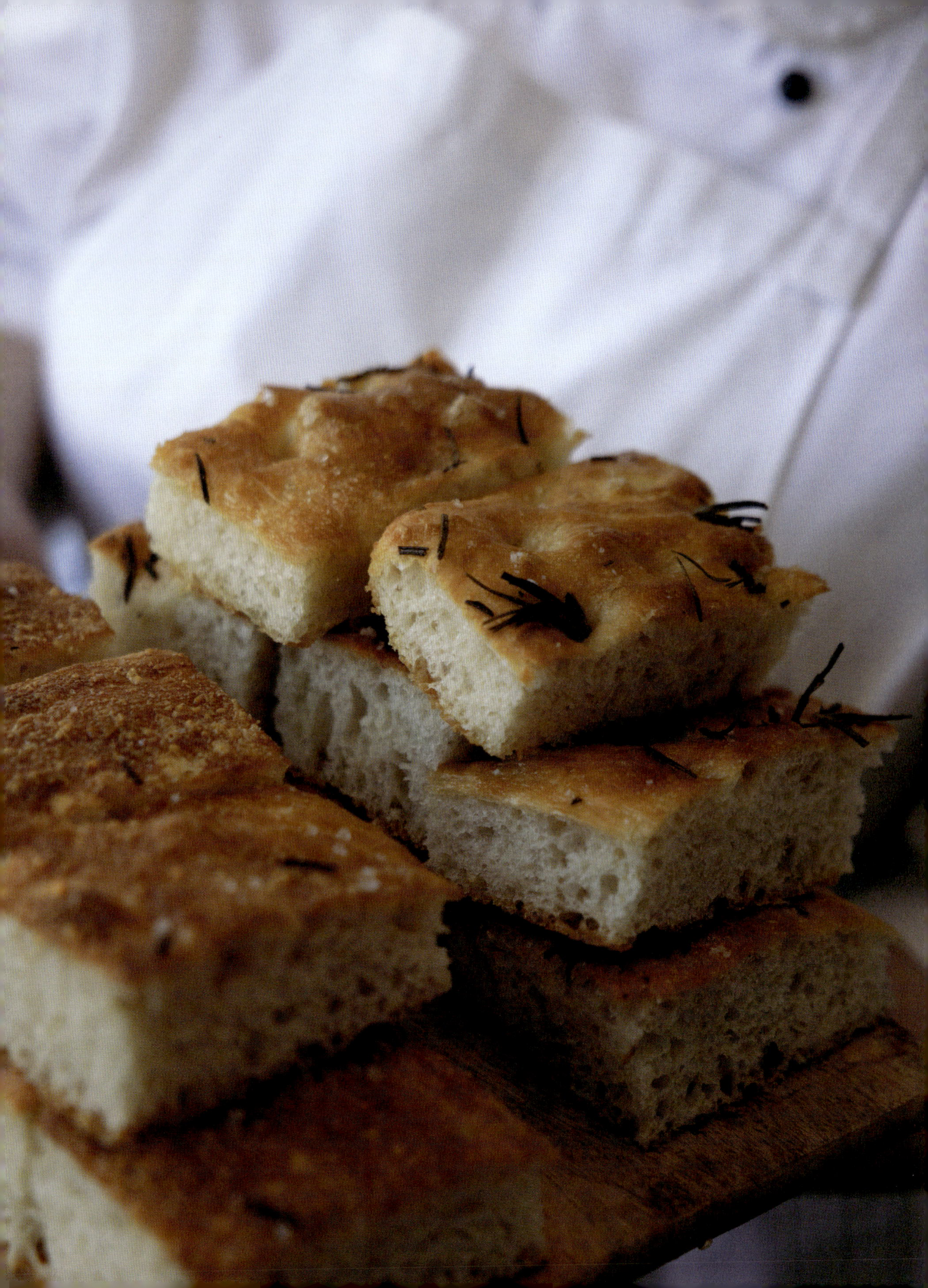

SOUPS and BREADS

A steaming hot bowl of soup can rescue anyone on a cold and wintery day, and the west of Ireland gives us plenty of those. Homemade soup is a constant in the cafe, and we serve it with our own treacle soda bread. My theory with soup is to elevate the single vegetable you are using: if it's a parsnip, make it all about that parsnip. At home, soups are a great way of using up vegetables or pulling together a nutritious lunch on a day when the fridge might be almost empty. Onions, potatoes and garlic are staples in most houses, and that's a good start to any soup. I love to add leafy greens like spinach before blending as a nutritious boost at the end of some soups – it adds great colour and uses up leaves that might otherwise go to waste. All the soups in this chapter feature on our menus and include simple techniques to elevate each one, all easy to replicate at home.

Our breads are baked daily in our kitchen – they're the first thing you smell when you enter the cafe. The recipes here are simple; all you need is your hands and some time. Brown soda bread was a staple on our table as children, with treacle and raisins added sometimes as a treat, and cups and fists were used as measures – it was such a practised habit that they didn't need scales. However, I recommend you use scales in all your baking endeavours!

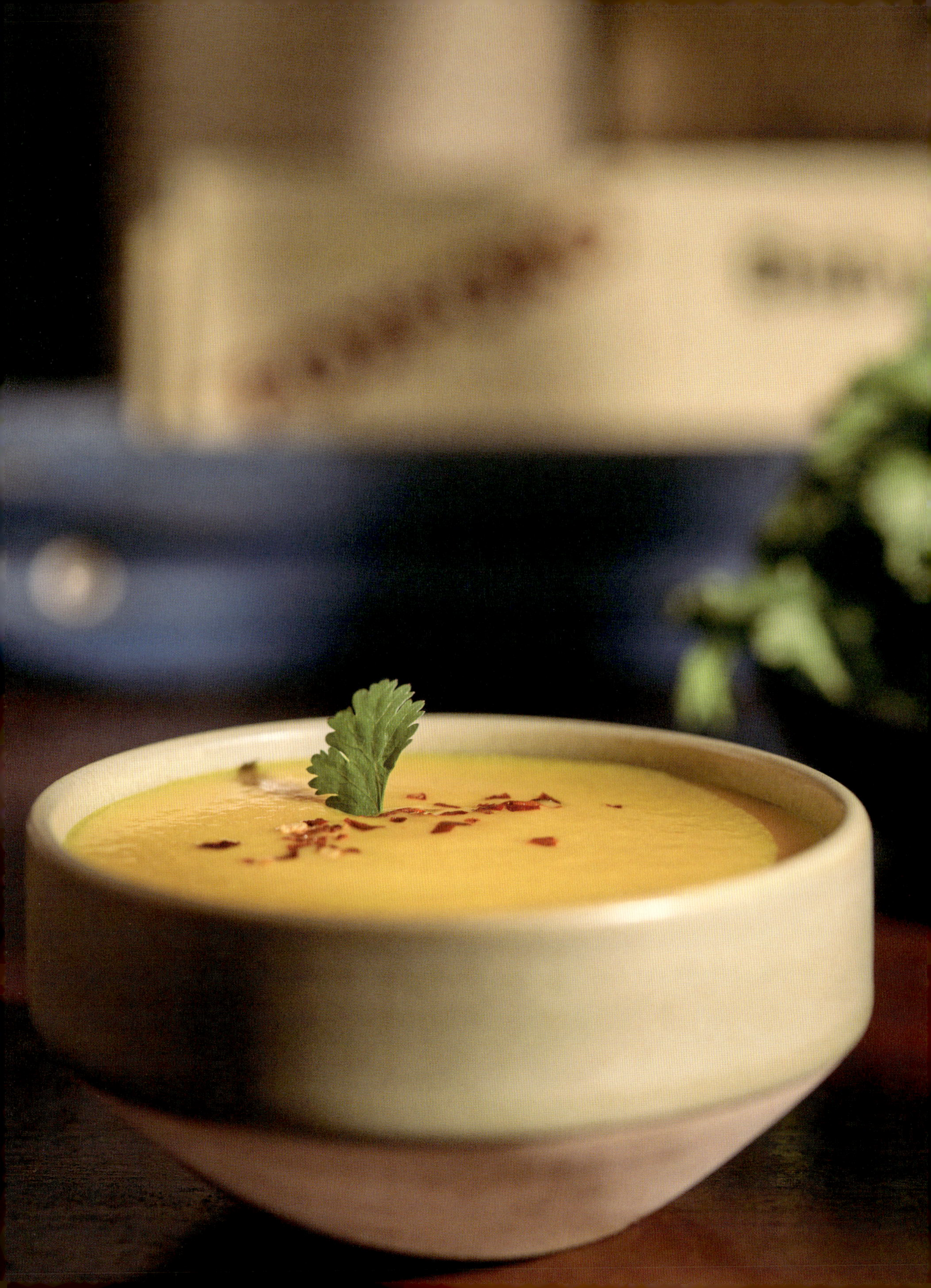

Carrot, Ginger and Coconut Soup

Carrot and ginger is a delicious soup in its own right, but the addition of coconut milk here really elevates it, while being delicate enough not to take over. This recipe is also perfect if you're avoiding dairy.

SERVES 6

1 medium white onion
2 cloves of garlic
1.5cm piece of fresh ginger
2 tbsp olive oil
700g carrots
1 tsp turmeric
1 litre vegetable stock
400ml coconut milk
3 tbsp chopped coriander
pinch of chilli flakes (optional)
sea salt and cracked black pepper

1. Peel and roughly chop your onion and peel and mince your garlic and ginger.
2. Heat the olive oil in a large saucepan, add the onion, ginger and garlic, and cook until they begin to soften but not brown – keep the heat low. It should take 5–6 minutes. Stir occasionally. Meanwhile, peel and chop your carrots.
3. Add the carrots to the saucepan, and continue to cook for 5 minutes, stirring occasionally. Add the ground turmeric, stir to coat the carrots, and allow the spice to cook for 1–2 minutes to release its flavour.
4. Add the stock. Bring to the boil and simmer for 15–20 minutes or until the carrots soften.
5. Remove from the heat and blend using a hand blender until smooth. (You could cool and freeze at this stage if you wish.)
6. Add the coconut milk and gently reheat the soup.
7. Remove from the heat, sprinkle with the chopped coriander and a pinch of chilli flakes, if using, and leave for a minute to allow the flavours to infuse. Season to taste with salt and pepper, then serve.

Creamy Mushroom and Spinach Soup

Mushroom soup is often overlooked, as it's not as colourful as some of its counterparts, but it's so flavoursome. I add spinach at the end here for a boost of colour and nutrients.

SERVES 4

2 medium white onions
2 cloves of garlic
500g mushrooms
90g butter
2 medium (about 100g) potatoes
1 litre vegetable or chicken stock
2 handfuls of spinach
4 tbsp cream
sea salt and cracked black pepper
2 tbsp chopped flat-leaf parsley

1. Peel and roughly chop your onions, peel and mince your garlic, and wash your mushrooms.
2. Melt the butter in a large saucepan, add the onions and garlic, and cook until they begin to soften but not brown – keep the heat low. It should take 8–10 minutes. Stir occasionally.
3. Add the mushrooms, turn up the heat, and continue to cook until the mushrooms begin to soften, stirring occasionally – approximately 5 minutes.
4. Meanwhile, wash and peel the potatoes and chop into quarters.
5. Add the stock and the potatoes to the saucepan. Bring to the boil and simmer for 10–15 minutes or until the potatoes soften.
6. Remove from the heat – you could cool, blend and freeze at this stage if you want. Otherwise, add the spinach and blend using a hand blender until smooth.
7. Gently reheat the soup, add the cream, taste, add a little seasoning if necessary and sprinkle with chopped parsley.

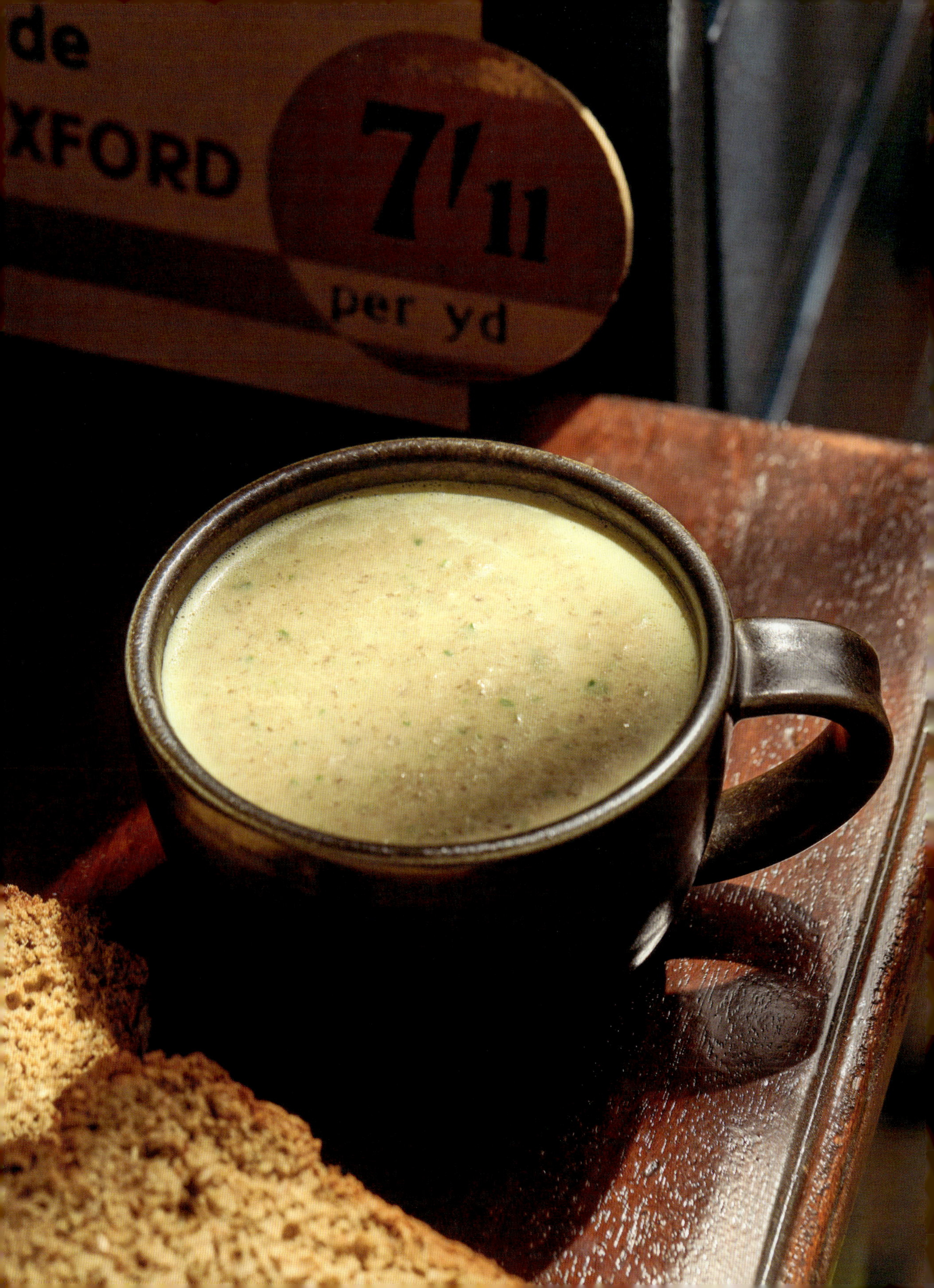
de
XFORD
7/11
per yd

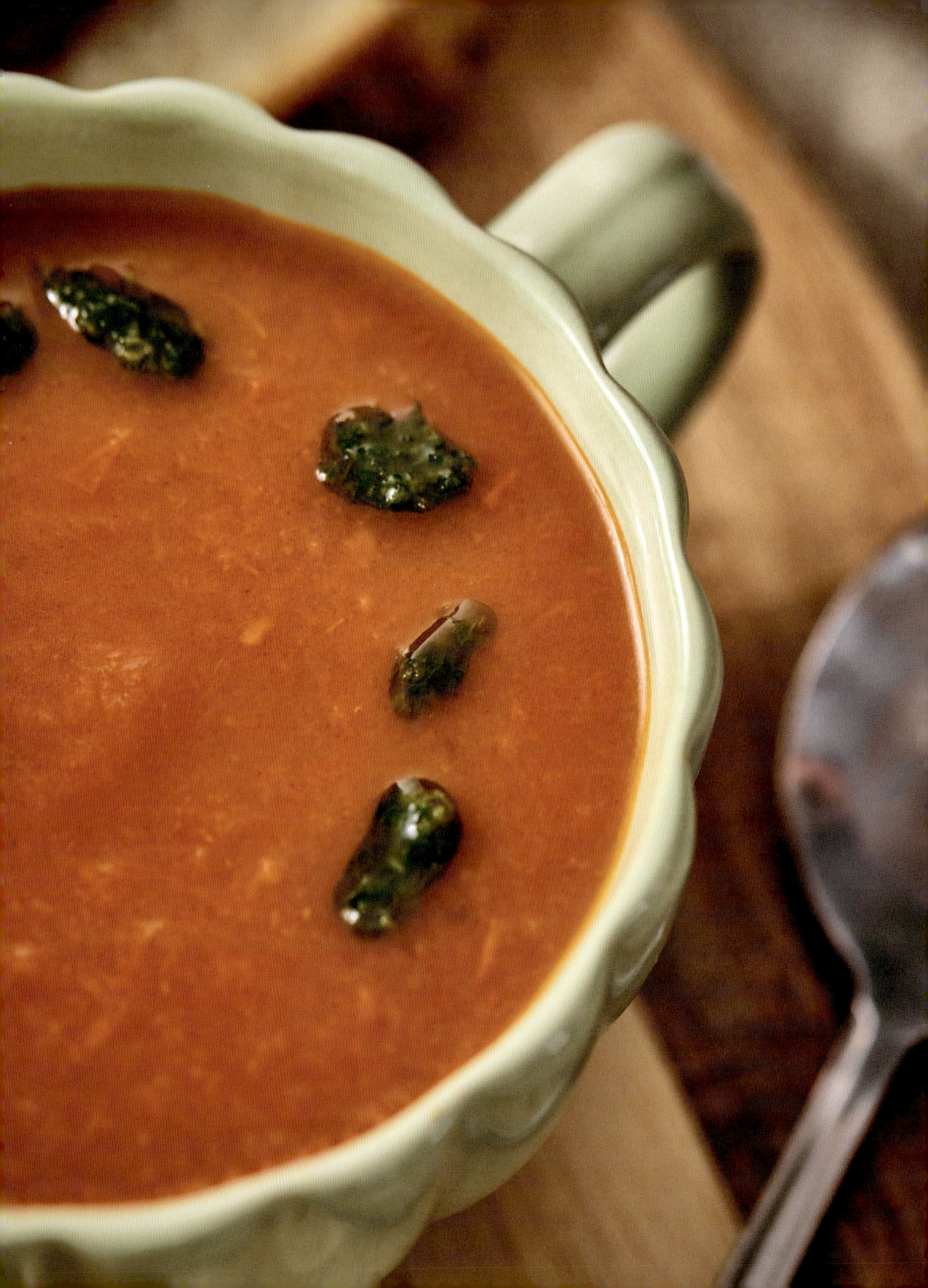

Tomato and Roast Pepper Soup

Roasting your peppers is the key to success with this soup. It sweetens them and highlights their unique flavour. If you don't have fresh basil, a spoon of basil pesto (page 30) would suffice at the end.

SERVES 4

4 large red or orange bell peppers
2 tbsp olive oil
1 medium white onion
3 cloves of garlic
400g chopped tinned or fresh tomatoes
1 litre vegetable stock
25g chopped fresh basil
1 tbsp balsamic vinegar
sea salt and cracked black pepper

1. Preheat your oven to 200°C fan/230°C/gas 8.
2. Using a large chopping knife, halve your peppers, scoop out the seeds and remove the stalks. Place them on a baking tray, cut side down. Drizzle with 1 tablespoon of olive oil and place in the oven. Roast until the skins blister or char. Place in a bowl and cover with cling film or a plate. Set aside.
3. Peel and roughly chop your onion, and peel and mince your garlic.
4. Heat the remaining tablespoon of olive oil in a large saucepan, add the onion and garlic, and cook until they begin to soften but not brown – keep the heat low. It should take 5–6 minutes. Stir occasionally.
5. Add the chopped tomatoes. Cook for a further 5 minutes, stirring occasionally.
6. Peel the peppers. They should be cooler now, and because they were covered while hot, it means the natural steam has lifted the skin so it's an easier task.
7. Add the roasted peppers and the vegetable stock to the saucepan. Bring to the boil and simmer for 15–20 minutes.
8. Remove from the heat and blend using a hand blender until smooth. (You can cool and freeze at this stage if you wish.)
9. Gently reheat the soup. Then remove from the heat and sprinkle with chopped basil. Leave for 1 minute to allow the flavours to infuse. Add 1 tbsp of balsamic for more depth. Season with salt and pepper to taste.

Curried Cauliflower and Coconut Soup

Roasting cauliflower gives this soup a unique flavour, and popping everything on a tray in the oven lessens the workload a little. It's a quick soup to prepare if you're short on time.

SERVES 6

1 medium cauliflower (for about 600g florets)
2 medium white onions
4 cloves of garlic
1 tsp turmeric
2 tbsp olive oil
1 tbsp honey, plus extra to taste
400g tinned coconut milk
600ml vegetable stock
sea salt and cracked black pepper

1. Preheat your oven to 180°C fan/200°C/gas 6.
2. Trim the cauliflower, discarding any of the large green outer leaves, cutting as close to the stalk as possible, and cut into even-sized florets – keep any little white leaves.
3. Peel and roughly chop your onions, and peel and mince the garlic.
4. Place the cauliflower, onion and garlic on a roasting tray. Sprinkle with the turmeric and olive oil and toss together until all the veg are coated. (Beware – turmeric colours everything, including hands!) Drizzle the honey over the veg. Place in the oven and roast for 8–10 minutes until cooked through and browned a little.
5. When the veg are roasted, scrape them from the roasting tray into a large saucepan. Add the coconut milk and stock and slowly bring to the boil.
6. Reduce the heat and simmer for 5 minutes. Remove from the heat. Blend using a stick blender until creamy and smooth – add a little water if it's too thick.
7. Gently reheat the soup. Season with salt and pepper to taste and a little extra honey if you wish.

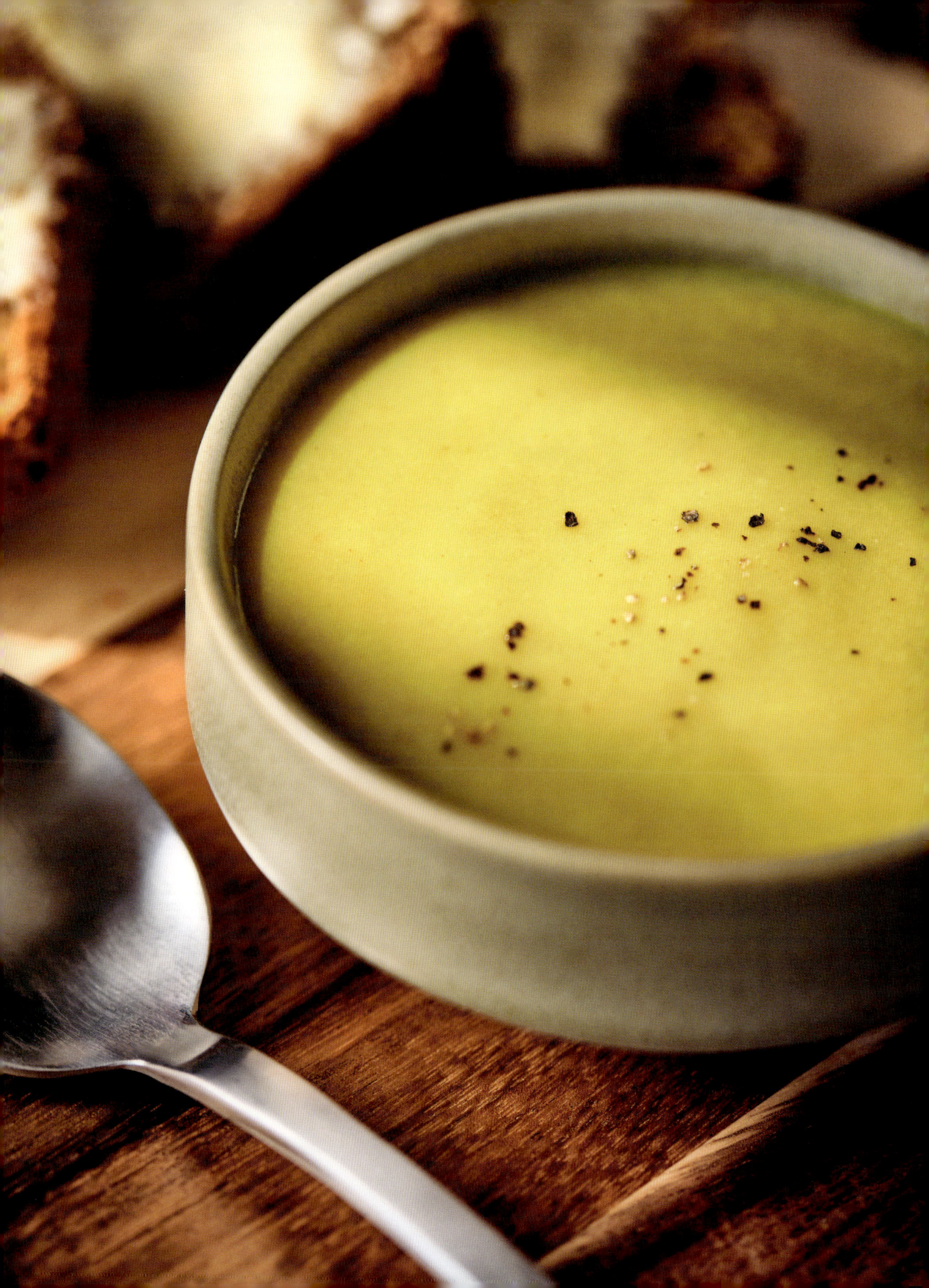

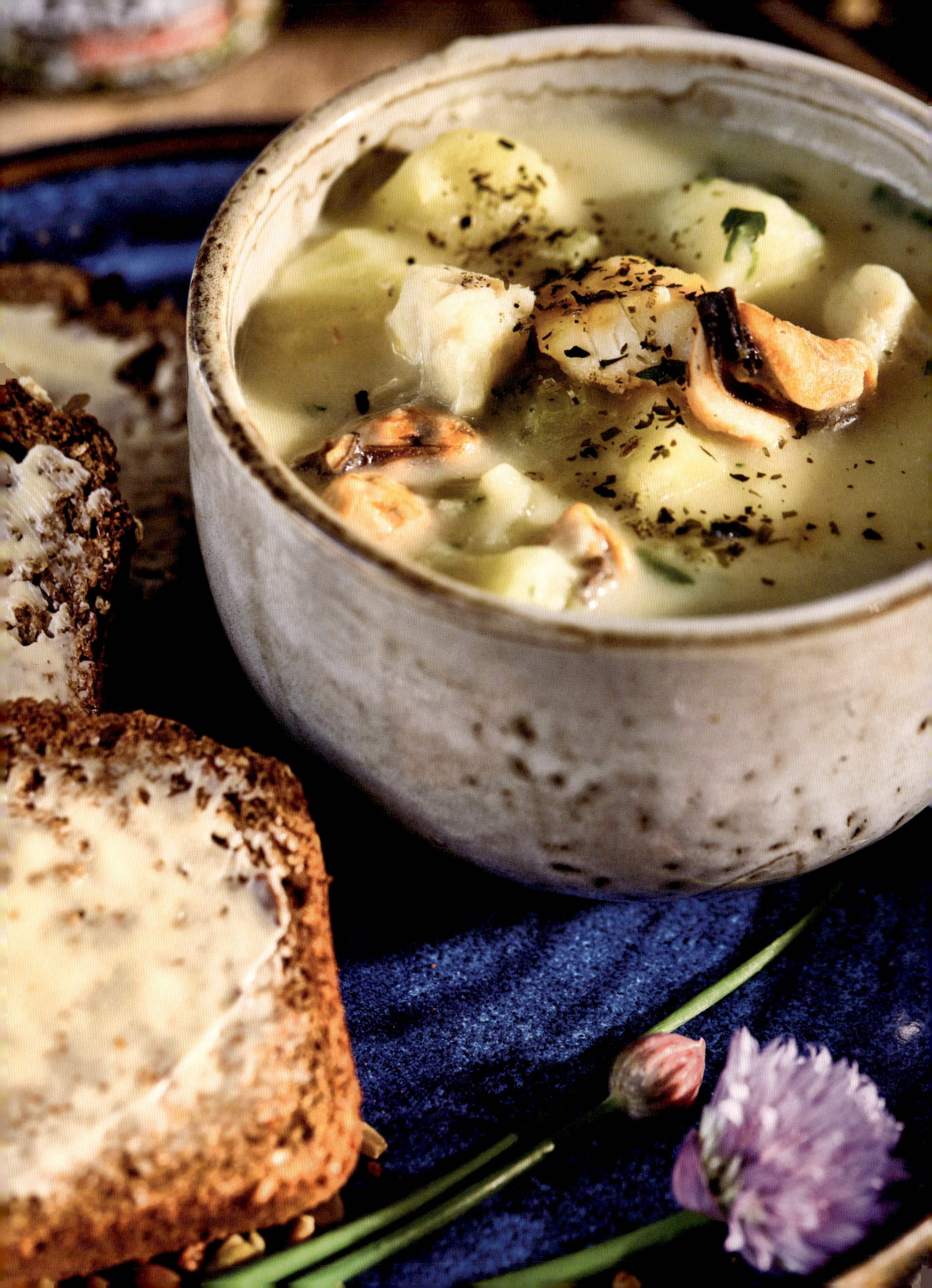

Seafood Chowder

I made my first chowder in Clifden, and I still make it in a similar way. It starts with a good soup base, then some chunks of fish, parsley and cream. I love to finish it with Achill Island Smoked or Seaweed sea salt. They are really special local products! If you can't source them, look out for a version more local to you.

SERVES 4–6

FOR THE BASE

1 small onion
½ clove of garlic
4 sticks of celery
8 medium potatoes
90g butter
4 parsley stalks
1 bay leaf
1 litre vegetable stock

TO FINISH

300g white and smoked fish, diced (I use smoked haddock and any white fish)
10–12 cooked mussels
2 tbsp chopped fresh coriander
2 tbsp chopped fresh flat-leaf parsley
100ml cream
sea salt

1. To make the base, peel and roughly chop your onion, and peel and mince your garlic. Wash and roughly chop 2 sticks of celery and 6 potatoes.
2. Heat the butter in a large saucepan, add the onion and garlic, and cook until they begin to soften but not brown – keep the heat low. It should take 5–6 minutes. Stir occasionally.
3. Add the roughly chopped celery and potato, parsley stalks, bay leaf and stock. Simmer for 20–25 minutes, until the celery is soft.
4. Meanwhile, chop the remaining celery and potato into 1cm dice, and place the celery in a steamer pot. Steam for 5 minutes before adding the potato, then continue to cook for 10–15 minutes, until they are cooked but keep their shape. Carefully remove from the steamer and set aside to cool.
5. Take the pot containing the base from the heat, remove the bay leaf, then blend the base, using a stick blender, until smooth. It should not be too thick – if it is, add a little more vegetable stock.
6. Gently bring the base back to the boil, add your chopped raw fish, stir and simmer for 2 minutes. Then add the cooked diced potato and celery, cooked mussels, chopped herbs and cream. Allow the flavours to combine for a minute or two. Season to taste with the Achill Island Smoked or Seaweed sea salt.

Broccoli, Potato and Spinach Soup

This soup is always a winner on our counter. It's nutrient dense as well as being good for using up any spinach or broccoli that might be near the turn. Cream adds to the texture here, and gives the soup a smooth, satisfying finish.

SERVES 4

2 medium white onions
2 cloves of garlic
2 tbsp olive oil
500g broccoli
2 medium potatoes
1.2 litres vegetable stock
2 handfuls of spinach
200ml cream
sea salt and cracked black pepper, to taste

1. Peel and roughly chop your onions, and peel and mince your garlic.
2. Heat the olive oil in a large saucepan, add the onion and garlic, and cook until they begin to soften but not brown – keep the heat low. It should take 5–6 minutes. Stir occasionally.
3. Meanwhile, trim the broccoli, cutting as close to the stalk as possible, and cut into even-sized florets.
4. Peel and chop your potatoes (you need about 100g).
5. Add the potato and stock to the saucepan, stir and bring back to the boil. Reduce the heat and allow to simmer for about 10 minutes, then add the broccoli and simmer for a further 10 minutes, until the broccoli and potato are soft.
6. Remove from the heat, add the spinach and blend using a hand blender until smooth. Add a little water if it's too thick. (You can cool and freeze at this stage if you wish.)
7. Gently reheat the soup, then remove from the heat and add the cream. Taste and adjust the seasoning, if necessary, with salt and pepper.

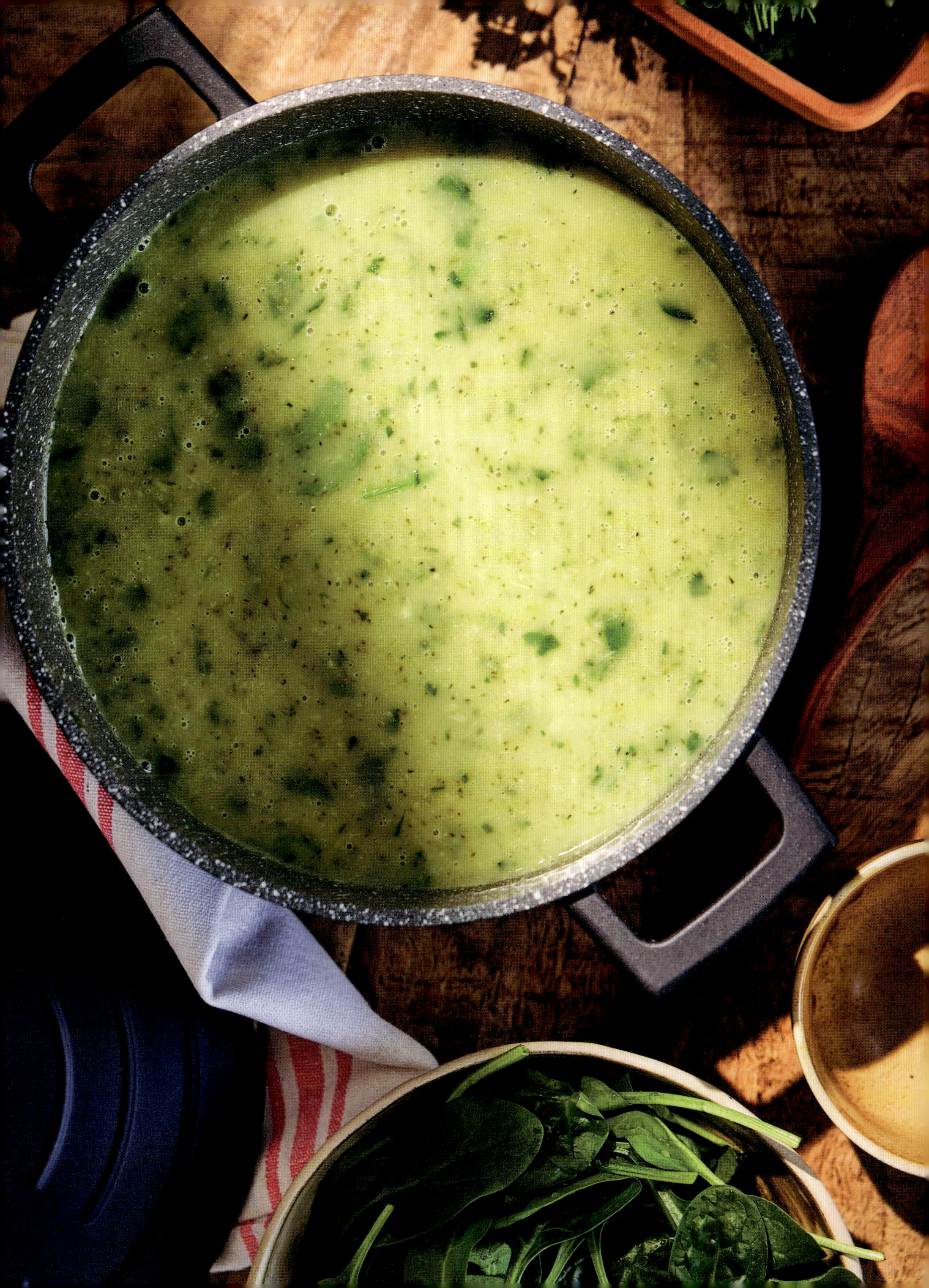

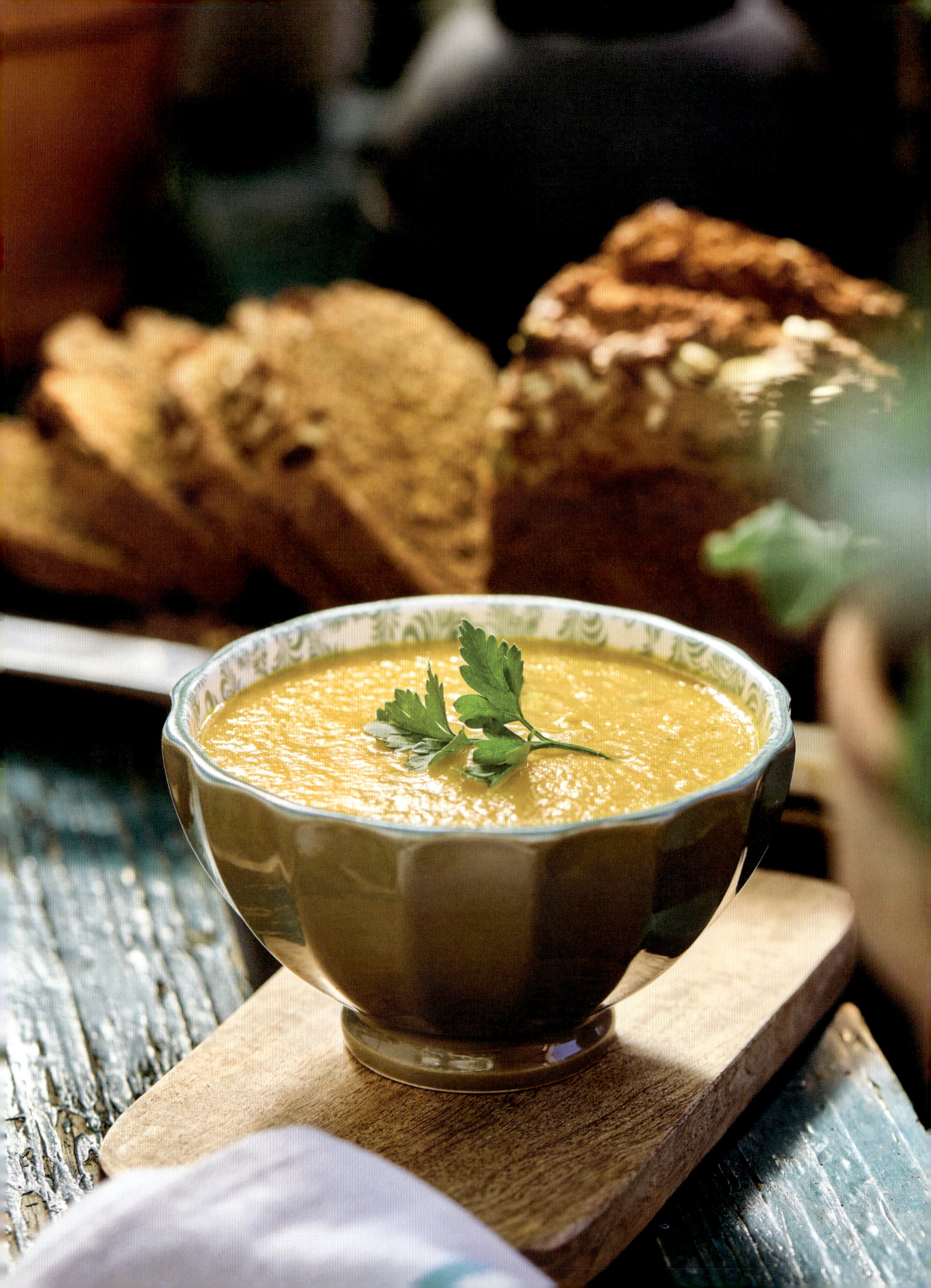

Carrot and Parsnip Soup

Carrots and parsnips are cousins and blend beautifully together. Parsnips are sweeter, and their flavour is more complex, with subtle nutty notes and a light aroma similar to that of fennel (another cousin). Serve with a slice of soda bread (page 60) for a hearty Irish lunch.

SERVES 4

1 medium white onion
1 clove of garlic
1 tbsp olive oil
250g carrots
250g parsnips
1–1.2 litres vegetable stock
200ml cream
sea salt and cracked black pepper
a few sprigs of flat-leaf parsley

1. Peel and roughly chop your onion, and peel and mince your garlic.
2. Heat the olive oil in a large saucepan, add the onion and garlic, and cook until they begin to soften but not brown – keep the heat low. It should take 5–6 minutes. Stir occasionally.
3. Meanwhile, peel and roughly chop your carrots and parsnips.
4. Add the carrots and parsnips to the saucepan, and continue to cook for 5 minutes, stirring occasionally.
5. Add the stock. Bring to the boil and simmer for 20–25 minutes or until the carrots and parsnips soften.
6. Remove from the heat and blend using a hand blender until smooth. (You can cool and freeze at this stage if you wish.)
7. Gently reheat the soup, adding a further 200ml of vegetable stock if the soup is too thick. Remove from the heat, add the cream, and season with salt and pepper to taste. Garnish each bowl with a sprig of parsley.

Cauliflower Cheese Soup

This old-school soup takes me back to my professional cookery course days. It's simple and focuses on really elevating the cauliflower. Cream is often added to soups, but the milk used here adds enough creaminess without dulling the flavour.

SERVES 6

2 medium onions

4 cloves of garlic

90g butter

2 medium cauliflower (for about 900g florets)

1 medium potato

800ml vegetable stock

500ml milk, plus extra to thin (optional)

sea salt and cracked black pepper

100g grated mature Cheddar

1. Peel and roughly chop your onions, and peel and mince your garlic.
2. Heat the butter in a large saucepan. Add the onion and garlic and cook until they begin to soften but not brown – keep the heat low. It should take 5–6 minutes. Stir occasionally.
3. Meanwhile, trim the cauliflower, discarding any of the large green outer leaves, cutting as close to the stalk as possible, and cut into even-sized florets. Keep any little white leaves.
4. Peel and roughly chop your potato.
5. Add the cauliflower, potato, stock and milk to the pot, stir and bring back to the boil. Reduce the heat and allow to simmer for about 30 minutes until the cauliflower and potato are soft.
6. Remove from the heat and blend using a hand blender until smooth. (You can cool and freeze at this stage if you wish.)
7. Gently reheat the soup, adding some more milk if it's too thick. Taste and adjust the seasoning, if necessary, with salt and pepper.
8. Ladle into bowls and sprinkle some grated Cheddar on top of each one.

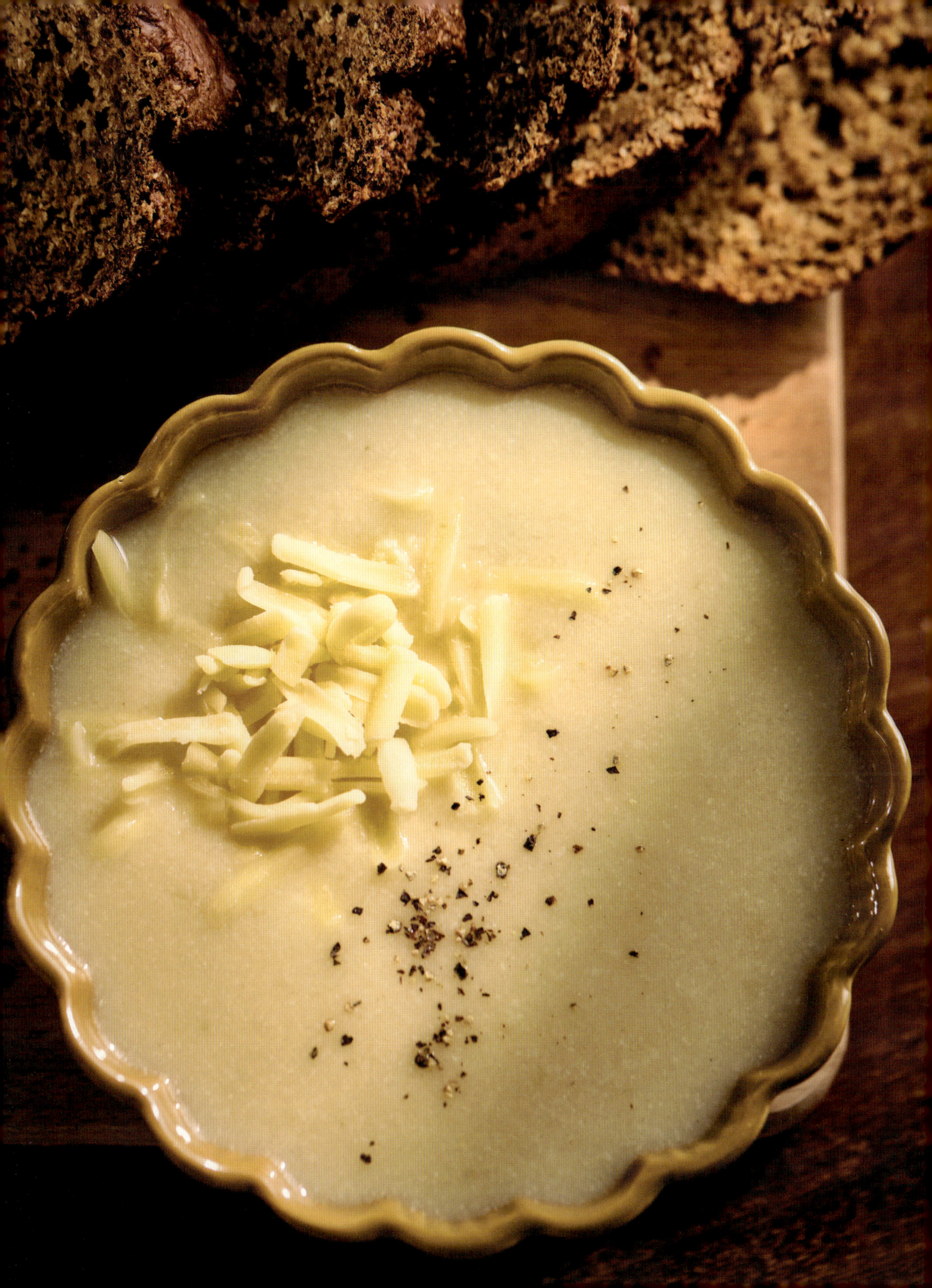

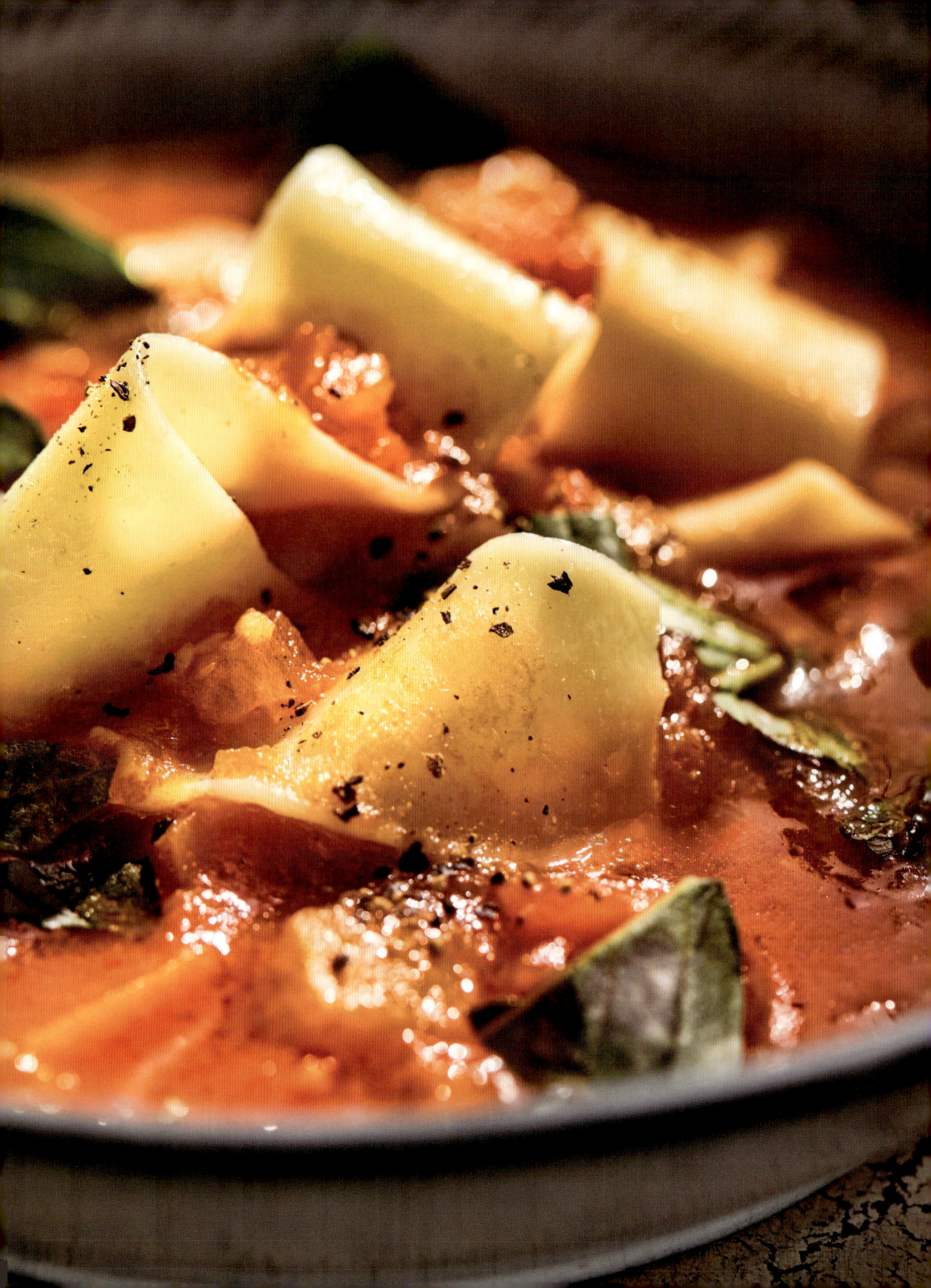

Minestrone Soup

Minestrone is such an aesthetically pleasing soup. I love using pappardelle for texture, but you could use almost any pasta. Just beware that some pastas, like orzo, can thicken the soup too much.

SERVES 4

1 medium white onion
3 cloves of garlic
1 stick of celery
2 carrots
2 tbsp olive oil
400g tinned chopped tomatoes
800–1,000ml vegetable stock
1 large red or orange bell pepper
100g pappardelle pasta (I use De Cecco)
1 tbsp balsamic vinegar
25g chopped fresh basil
sea salt and cracked black pepper, to taste
1 tbsp grated Parmesan

1. Peel and roughly chop your onion, and peel and mince your garlic. Wash and chop the celery into 1cm pieces. Peel and chop the carrots into 1cm dice. Dice the pepper into similar-sized pieces.
2. Heat the olive oil in a large saucepan, add your onion, celery and garlic, and cook until they begin to soften but not brown – keep the heat low. It should take 5–6 minutes. Stir occasionally.
3. Add the chopped tomatoes and cook for a further 5 minutes, stirring occasionally. Add the carrots and 800ml of the vegetable stock. Bring back to the boil, then simmer for 15–20 minutes or until the vegetables are cooked.
4. Add your diced pepper and pasta, cover and leave to simmer for about 6 minutes, depending on the pasta – some dried versions will need longer so continue until the pasta is cooked. Add some extra stock if it has thickened too much.
5. Remove from the heat, stir through the balsamic vinegar and sprinkle with chopped basil. Leave for 1 minute to allow the flavours to infuse, then season to taste with salt and pepper.
6. Spoon into bowls, sprinkle with some grated Parmesan and serve.

Brown Soda Bread

This is a basic brown soda bread with no sugar or treacle to sweeten it. It keeps for 2–3 days and freezes well also. It's a wet mix but don't be alarmed by that. This recipe makes two loaves, so you can freeze one for later (I don't like using half an egg or having the oven on for just one loaf). Always choose a good-quality buttermilk for soda bread – I use Connacht Gold, as it's thick and creamy.

MAKES 2 X 450G (1 LB) LOAVES

280g wholemeal flour
280g plain flour
1 tbsp pinhead oatmeal
½ tsp salt
1½ tsp bicarbonate of soda
35g butter
1 egg
500ml cultured buttermilk
sunflower and pumpkin seeds, for sprinkling (optional)

1. Preheat the oven to 170°C fan/190°C/gas 5.
2. Place the flours, pinhead oatmeal and salt in a large bowl. Sieve in the bicarbonate of soda and mix well using a rubber spatula.
3. Melt your butter over a low heat or in the microwave. Use a little of it to grease two 450g (1 lb) loaf tins.
4. Crack your egg into the buttermilk and whisk to combine.
5. Make a well in the centre of your dry ingredients, add the buttermilk and egg mix and then the melted butter. Mix immediately using a rubber spatula or your hand until all the ingredients have combined. Do not over-mix or beat with a mixer, as this will make the bread tough and chewy.
6. Scoop into the tins, and lightly push the mix into the corners – don't smooth it completely on top.
7. Sprinkle with some sunflower and pumpkin seeds, if you wish, and bake for 1 hour. Turn the loaves out of the tins then place them back in the oven for a further 10 minutes. They should sound hollow when you knock on the bottom of them.
8. Place on a wire rack to cool before slicing.

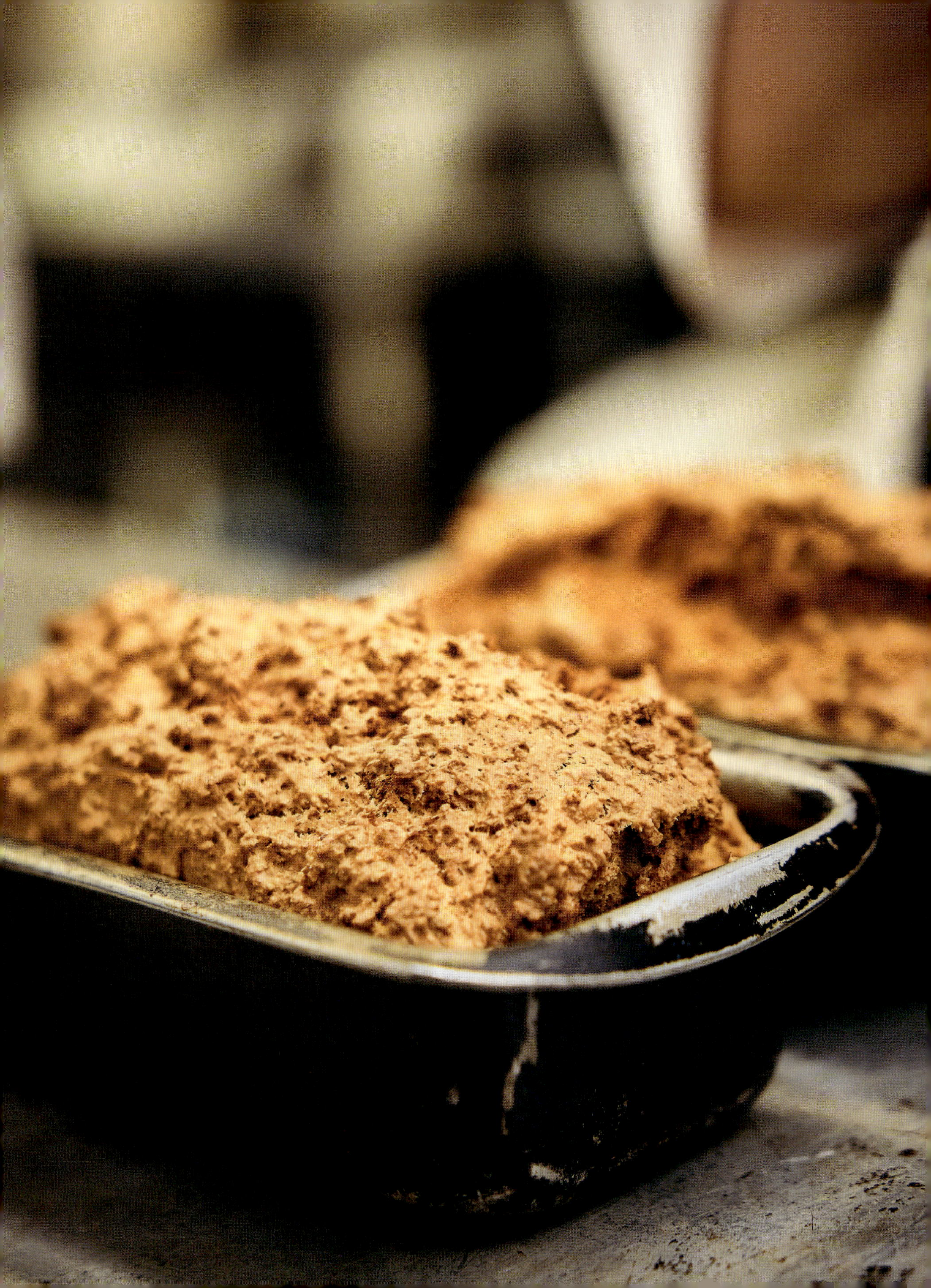

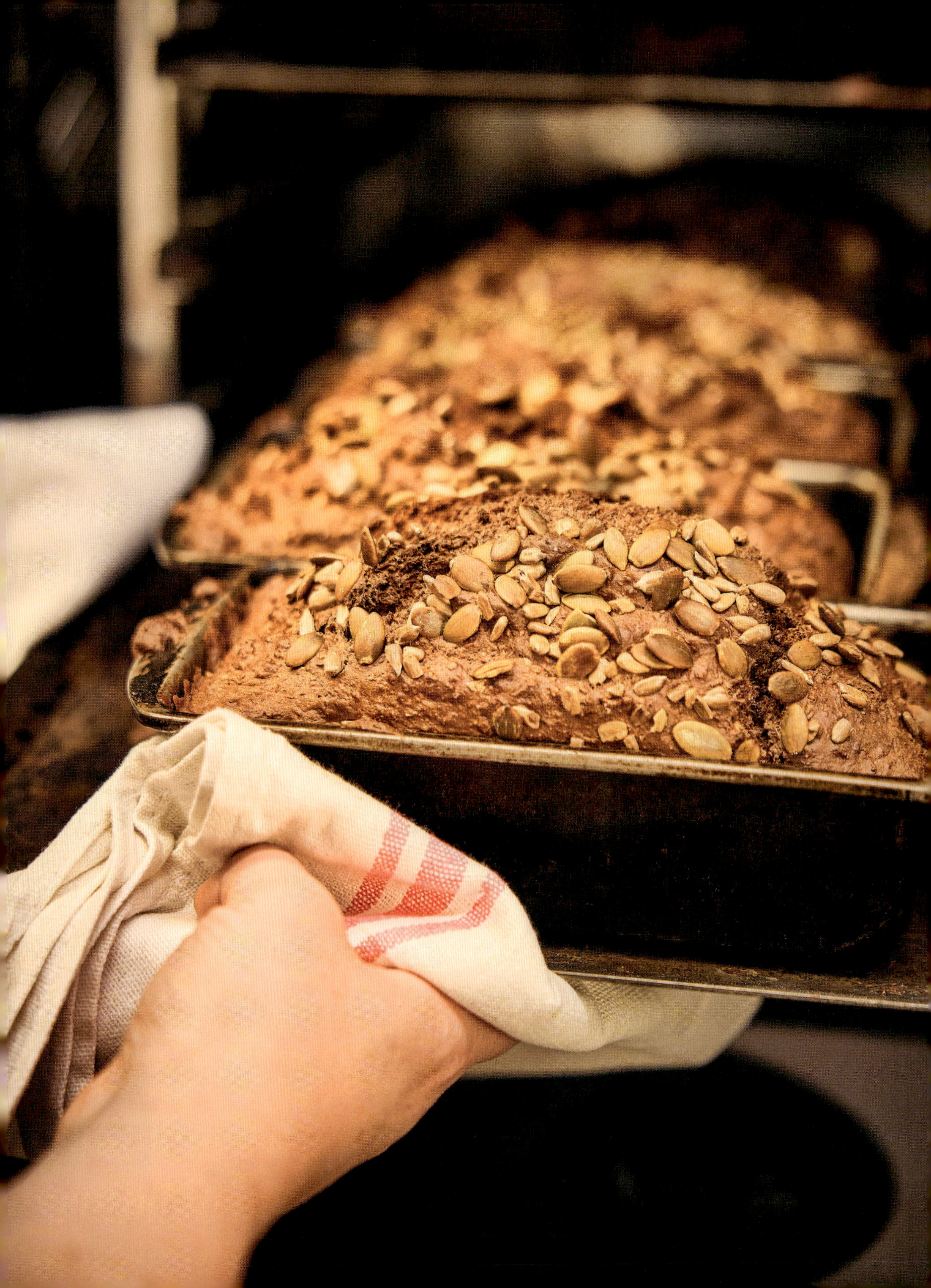

Brown Treacle Soda Bread

This is another version of our basic brown soda, with the sweetness of treacle to add to the appeal. There is also a lot more wholemeal flour in this version, and I use vegetable oil instead of butter, as it gives a softer and more tender crumb.

MAKES 2 X 450G (1LB) LOAVES

2 tbsp vegetable oil, plus extra for greasing
500g wholemeal flour
140g plain flour
1 tbsp pinhead oatmeal
½ tsp salt
1½ tsp bicarbonate of soda
60g treacle
600ml cultured buttermilk
1 egg
sunflower and pumpkin seeds, for sprinkling (optional)

1. Preheat the oven to 170°C fan/190°C/gas 5. Grease two 450g (1 lb) loaf tins with a little vegetable oil.
2. Place the flours, pinhead oatmeal and salt in a large bowl. Sieve in the bicarbonate of soda and mix well using a rubber spatula.
3. Weigh your treacle directly into a microwave-suitable bowl or small saucepan. Place on a low heat and warm a little, then remove and whisk in your oil and buttermilk. Crack in your egg and whisk again.
4. Make a well in the centre of your dry ingredients and add the liquid mixture. Mix using a rubber spatula or your hand until all the ingredients have combined. Do not over-mix or beat with a mixer, as this will make the bread tough and chewy.
5. Scoop into the tins, and lightly push the mix into the corners – don't smooth it completely on top.
6. Sprinkle with sunflower and pumpkin seeds, if you wish, and bake for 1 hour. Turn the loaves out of the tins and place them back in the oven for a further 10 minutes. They should sound hollow when you knock on the bottom of them.
7. Place on a wire rack to cool before slicing.

Fruity Soda Bread

This is one of my favourite breads to make – it's simple and always a crowd-pleaser. It is best eaten on the day it's made with lots of butter. I love it toasted with butter on day two.

MAKES 1 ROUND

1 egg
330ml cultured buttermilk
450g plain flour
½ tsp salt
½ tsp bicarbonate of soda
1 tbsp granulated sugar
100g sultanas

1. Preheat your oven to 250°C fan, or the next highest setting, and flour a heavy baking sheet.
2. Whisk the egg and buttermilk together.
3. Sieve the flour, salt and bicarbonate of soda into a bowl. Add the sugar and sultanas and mix by hand into the dry ingredients.
4. Pour in all the liquid to the dry ingredients at once. Using your spatula or hand, stir in a full circular movement from the centre to the outside of the bowl. The dough should be softish, not too wet and sticky. When it all comes together, turn it out onto a floured work surface. Wash and dry your hands. Gently shape the dough into a round, about 4cm deep, and turn it over gently onto the well-floured baking sheet.
5. Using a sharp knife, mark with a deep cross.
6. Place in the oven for 10 minutes, then reduce the temperature to 190°C fan/220°C/gas 7 for a further 30 minutes, until cooked. It should sound hollow when the base is tapped. Cool on a wire rack.

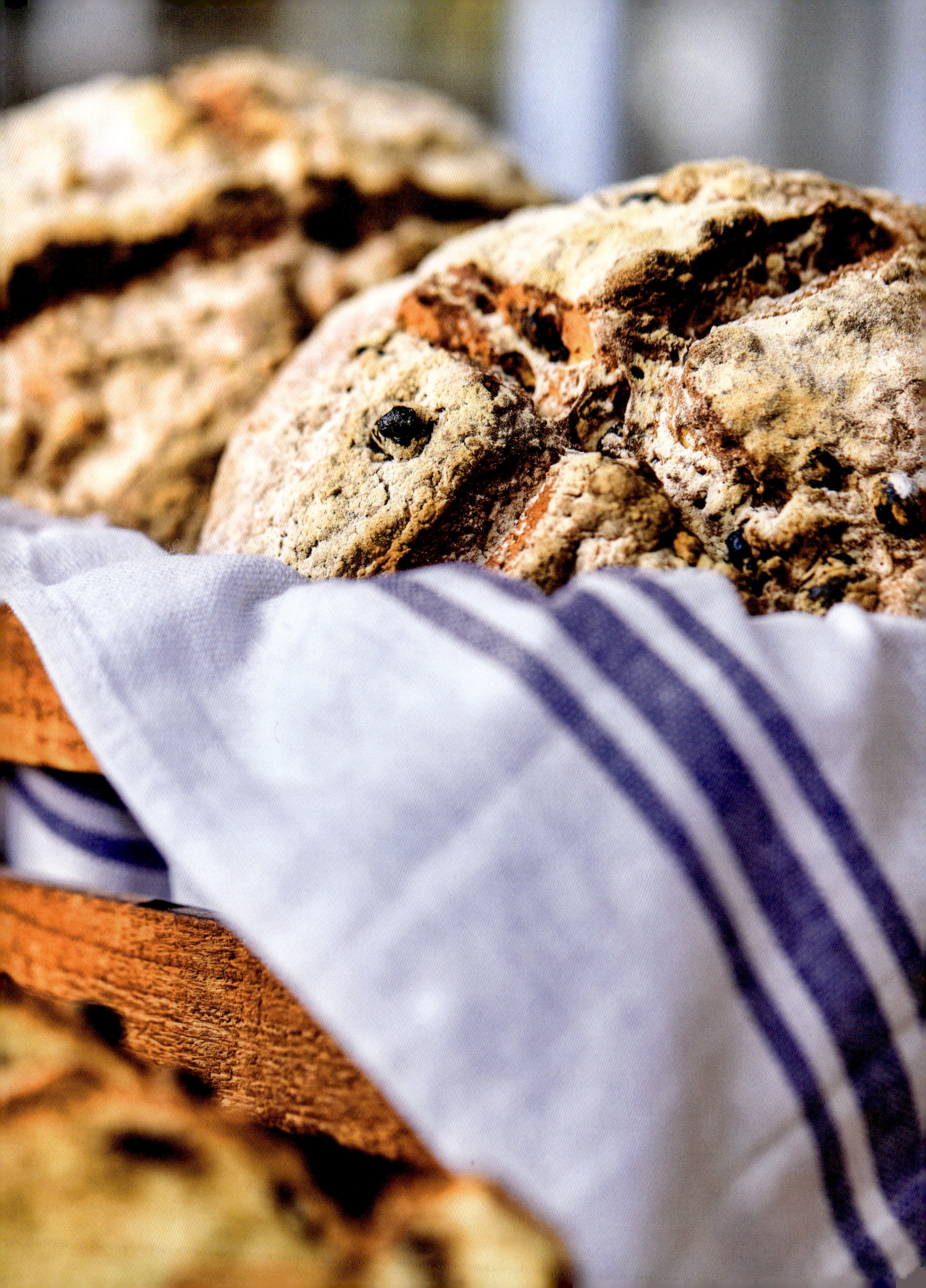

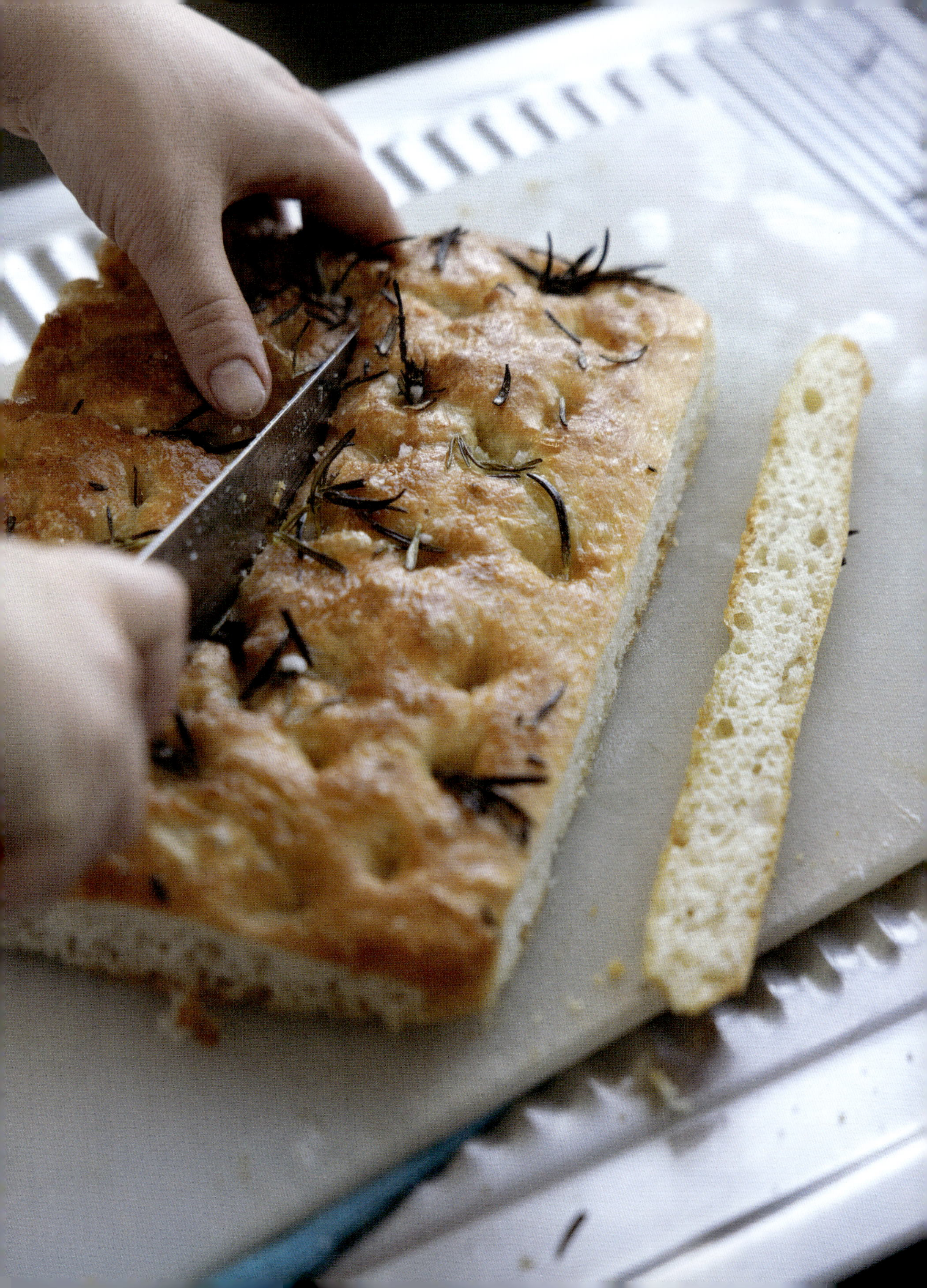

Focaccia

Anyone can make this simple focaccia, with no special equipment required, just your hands and some time! It is perfect for a Sicilian-style pizza base also, which is thick-crusted and rectangular. After baking, just add some tomato sauce, mozzarella and your favourite toppings, then return to the oven for 5–7 minutes, and there you have your pizza.

MAKES A 37 X 26CM
FOCACCIA

500g 00 flour or pizza flour
7g dried yeast (1 sachet)
350ml warm water
10g salt
1 tsp honey
30ml olive, plus extra for oiling and drizzling

FOR TOPPING

3 tbsp grated Parmesan
or
1½ tbsp olive oil
1 tbsp sea salt (I use Achill Island)
sprigs of fresh rosemary

1. Place the flour and dried yeast in a bowl and mix. Add the warm water, and mix by hand until it just comes together as a dough.
2. Add the salt, honey and oil to the bowl, and continue mixing until it forms a ball.
3. Oil a clean large bowl, place the dough ball inside, cover with a clean tea towel and leave in a warm place until it doubles in size. (Use a glass bowl and mark it if you are afraid you won't be able to tell.)
4. Knock back the dough by pushing your hand into it until it flattens. Cover it again with the tea towel, and leave it until it triples in size.
5. Oil a 37 x 26 x 4cm baking tray. Preheat your oven to 200°C fan/220°C/gas 8.
6. When the dough has tripled (the time will vary according to the warmth of your kitchen), tip it onto the oiled tray. Oil your hands and, using the tips of your fingers, push it into the corners. Then make dimples in the dough with your fingers.
7. Allow it to proof for 30–35 minutes. It should have puffed up and doubled in size. I usually just sprinkle grated Parmesan over the dough, but you can also mix the olive oil, a tablespoon of water and the sea salt together and drizzle over the dough, then gently push a few sprigs of rosemary into the dimples, being careful not to knock the air out of the dough.
8. Place in the oven and bake for 15–20 minutes until golden brown.
9. While the bread is still warm, drizzle a few tablespoons of olive oil over the top. Cut into squares and serve hot or cold.

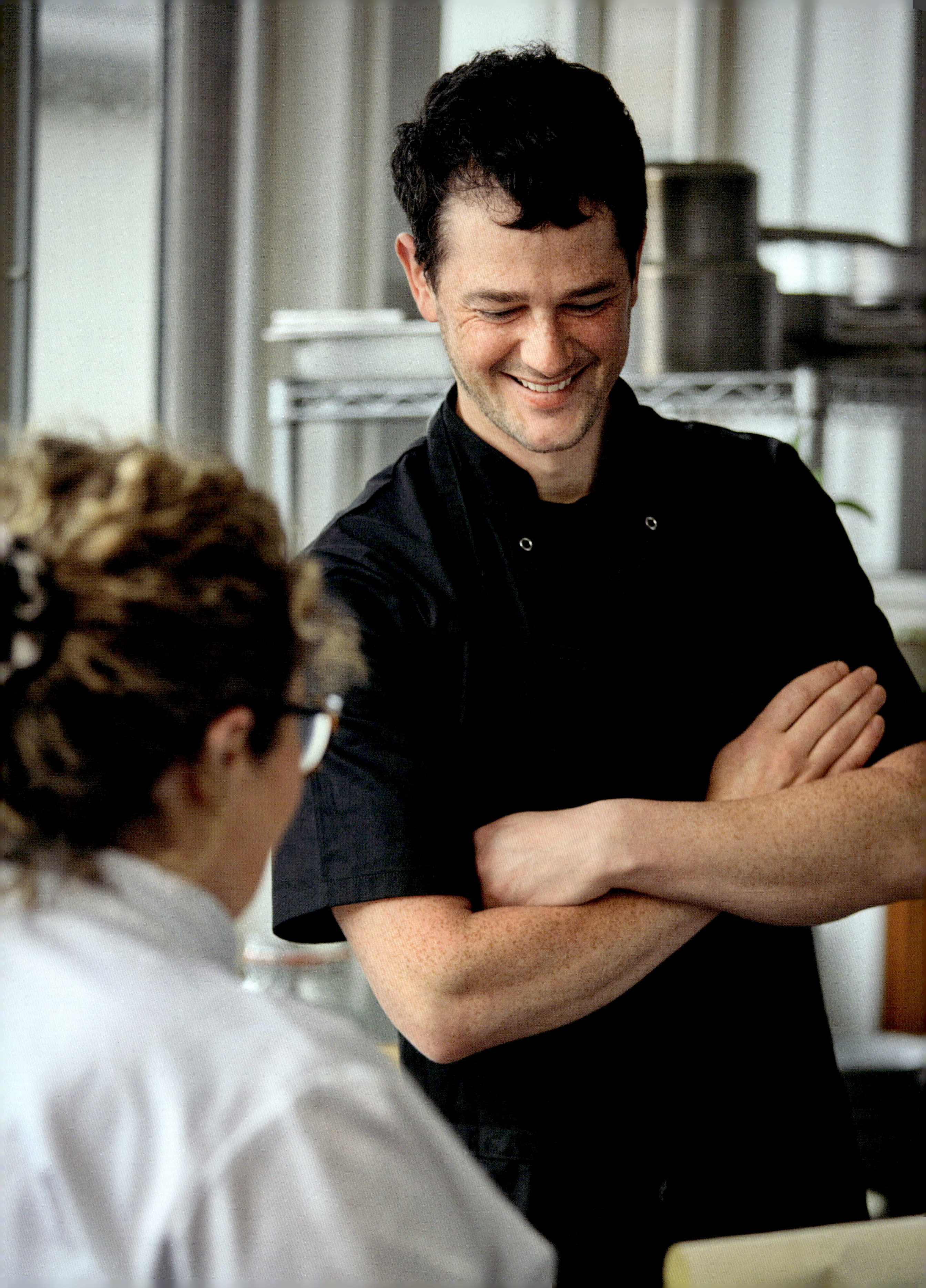

CAFE FAVOURITES

This is a selection of favourite dishes from the cafe, inspired by seasonal produce, local producers and suppliers.

I love to use lamb on our menus when I can, as it's an ingredient that was a huge part of my childhood. My parents, like many others, had their lambs slaughtered for our own use – a great example of the sustainable practices that were once common. This would provide chops and stews on a weekday and roasts for Sunday lunch for many a week throughout the year. This, alongside homegrown vegetables, salads and potatoes, was our norm and where my love of great simple food started.

There are lots of vegetable-based dishes in this section, which change throughout the year in the cafe. While I appreciate the exotic fruits and vegetables that can be found now on our supermarket shelves, there are many wonderful homegrown vegetables available to us here in Ireland. Simple carrot, cauliflower and beetroot dishes stand alone next to our meat and fish options.

For you to truly be able to replicate our dishes at home, I have included recipes for sauces or accompaniments and tips on how to use some dishes in different ways for different occasions. Versatility is key in preventing food waste.

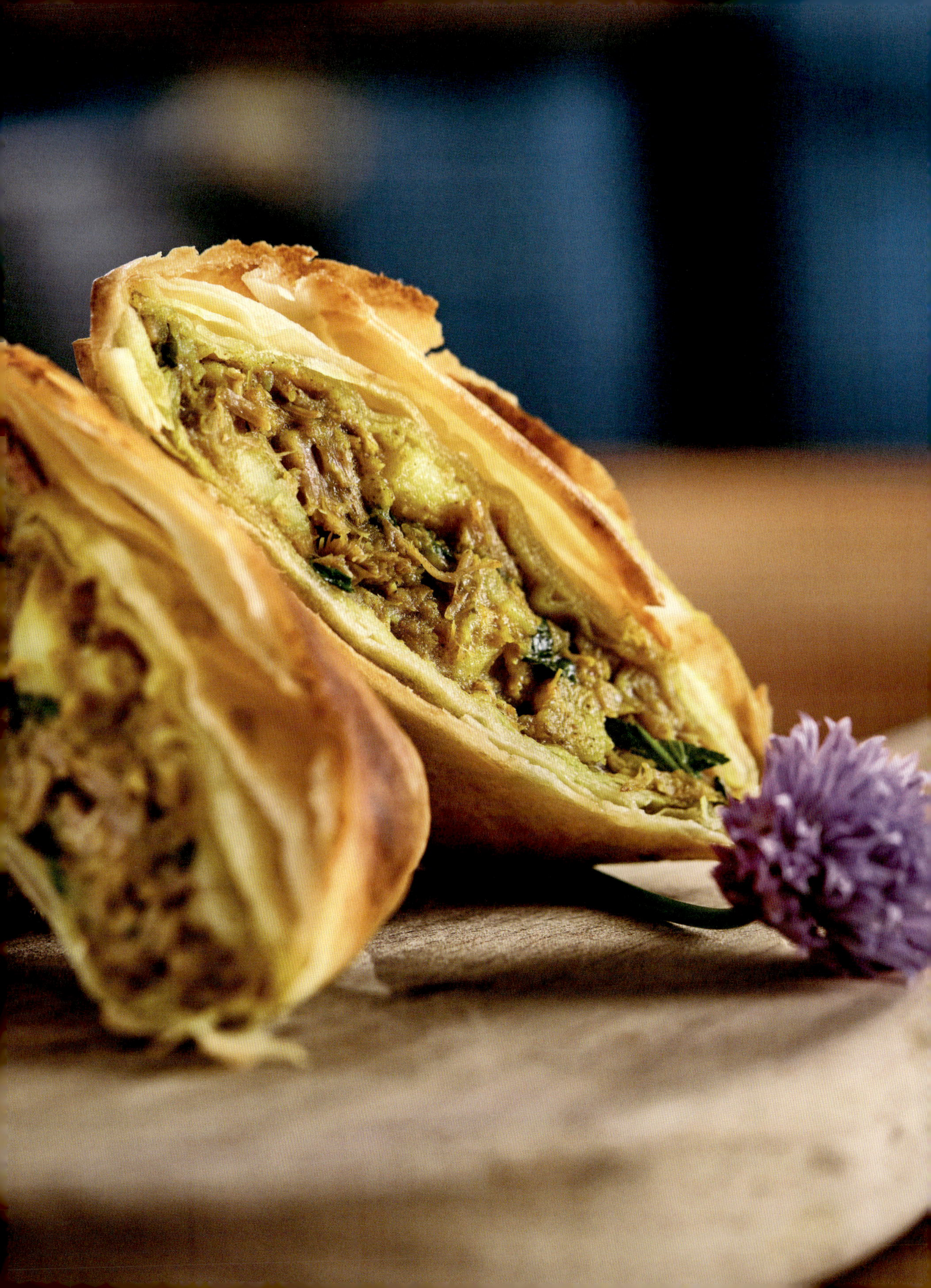

Spiced Lamb and Potato Parcels

This is a great recipe for using up leftovers, as well as making from scratch. If you have roast lamb on Sunday and have some left over, simply trim any fatty bits, dice it up and substitute it for the lamb in the recipe below, saving time and waste. I also like to use raw cauliflower pieces instead of the lamb for a great veggie version, which is equally tasty and nutritious.

MAKES 8 PARCELS

500g stewing lamb
1 large carrot
1 large Rooster potato
1 small red onion
1 tbsp rapeseed or cooking oil
½ tbsp Madras curry powder
½ tbsp cumin
250ml vegetable stock
sea salt and cracked black pepper to taste
handful of chopped fresh coriander
spring roll pastry sheets, 25cm x 25cm
100g melted butter

1. Place the stewing lamb in a saucepan with a pinch of salt and cover with cold water. Bring to the boil and simmer until tender – 35–40 minutes. Drain and allow to cool. Trim any fat away. Chop into 1cm pieces.
2. Meanwhile, wash and peel your vegetables. Dice the carrot and potato into 1cm cubes. Finely dice the red onion.
3. Heat the oil in a heavy-based saucepan. Sauté the red onion on a low heat till soft – do not allow it to brown. When the onion has softened, add the spices and allow them to toast for a few minutes.
4. Add the diced veg and the vegetable stock. Allow the mix to simmer, stirring occasionally, until the veg is soft but still has its shape. Taste and season. Remove from the heat.
5. Add the lamb and allow the mix to cool. Roughly chop the coriander leaves and add to the mix.
6. Preheat your oven to 170°C fan/190°C/gas 5.
7. Take a sheet of spring roll pastry, brush with melted butter, then place 2–3 generous tablespoons of the mix in the middle. Fold 3 corners into the centre and fold into a pillow shape. Butter another slice of pastry and double wrap the parcel. This prevents it from bursting during cooking.
8. Repeat this until all the mix is gone, then brush the parcels with butter. Place on a tray lined with parchment paper and bake until crispy and golden brown – 20–30 minutes.
9. Serve with a chutney of your choice or Foxford piccalilli.

Frittata Three Ways

Irish people tend to love frittata – I think it's our natural affinity with the potato. My top tip here is to season the layers lightly to get the balance right, depending on your choice of the three toppings.

SERVES 8

1kg potatoes

10 medium eggs

100g baby spinach

1 red onion

½ tbsp olive oil

sea salt and cracked black pepper

GOAT'S CHEESE AND PEPPER TOPPING

200g goat's cheese, crumbled

½ red pepper, sliced

SMOKED SALMON AND PARMESAN TOPPING

200g BBQ smoked salmon, skin removed and flaked

2 tbsp grated Parmesan

CASHEL BLUE AND SPINACH TOPPING

200g Cashel Blue cheese, crumbled

extra handful of baby spinach

1. Preheat your oven to 140°C fan/160°C/gas 3. Butter and line the base of a 20cm cake tin with a closed base with parchment paper. (You can also use an ovenproof frying pan.)
2. Peel and cut the potatoes into approximately 0.5cm slices. Steam for about 10 minutes. They should be cooked but still have some bite. Set aside to cool slightly.
3. Crack and whisk your eggs and season lightly with salt and pepper.
4. Wash and drain the spinach, then pat dry using a clean tea towel.
5. Peel the red onion and slice thinly.
6. Heat the oil in a frying pan over a medium heat. Add the onion and season with a little salt and pepper. Cook for 5 minutes, or until the onions begin to soften, stirring occasionally. Do not allow the onions to brown – turn down the heat if they start to take colour.
7. Layer the cooked potatoes, the spinach and the warm onions in the cake tin.
8. Sprinkle your choice of toppings on top, pushing some inside the layers of potato.
9. Pour the egg mix into the tin slowly, then bake for 40–50 minutes, until the egg is set and no liquid appears when you insert a clean knife.
10. Allow to cool for an hour at least.
11. Run a palette knife around the edge of the tin to ensure the frittata is not sticking. Place a serving plate face down on the tin and flip over quickly. Remove the tin and parchment paper, then place a second plate face down on the frittata and flip both plates over, so your frittata is right side up.
12. Slice and serve. Leftovers will keep in sealed containers in the fridge for 2–3 days.

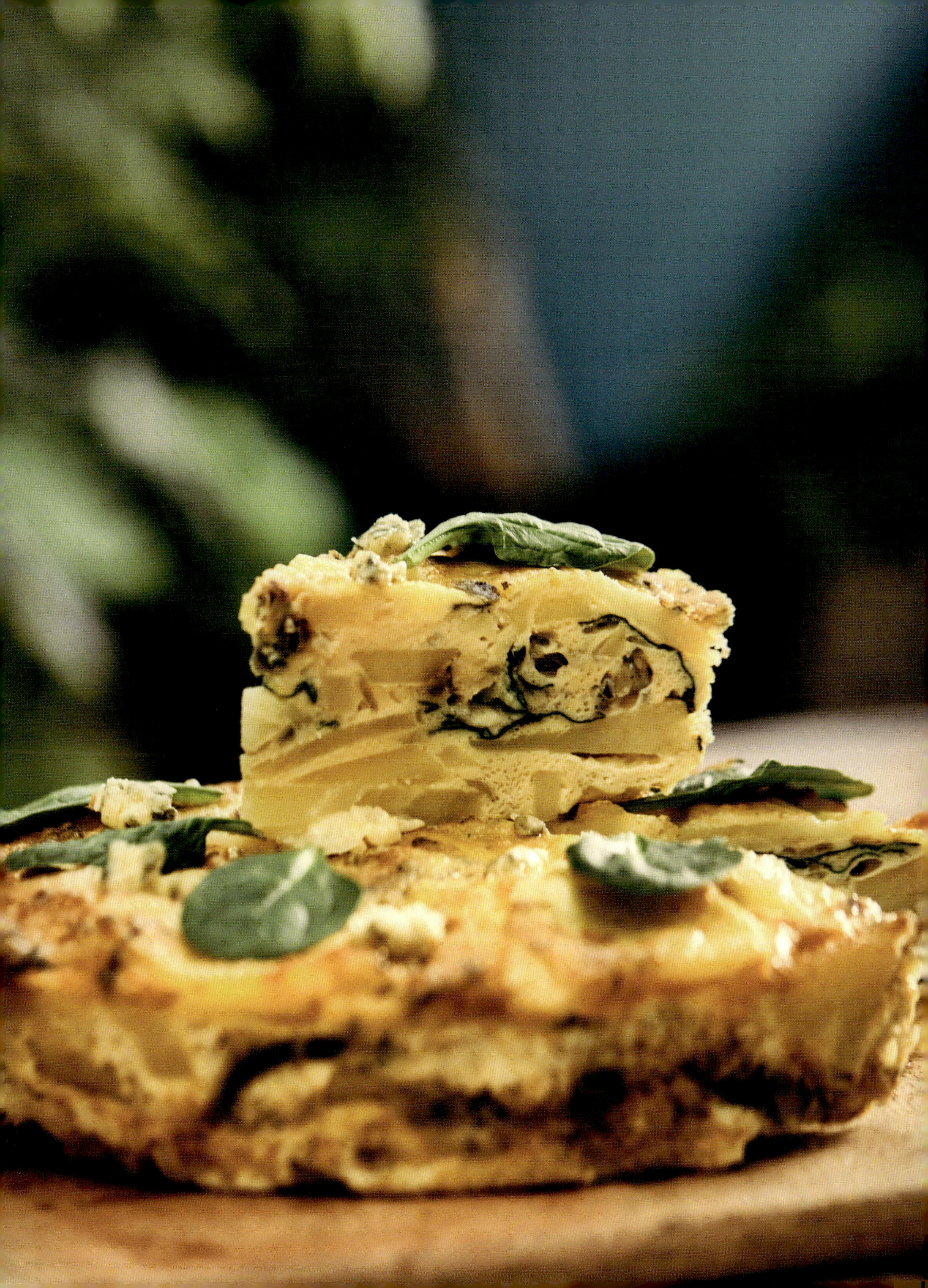

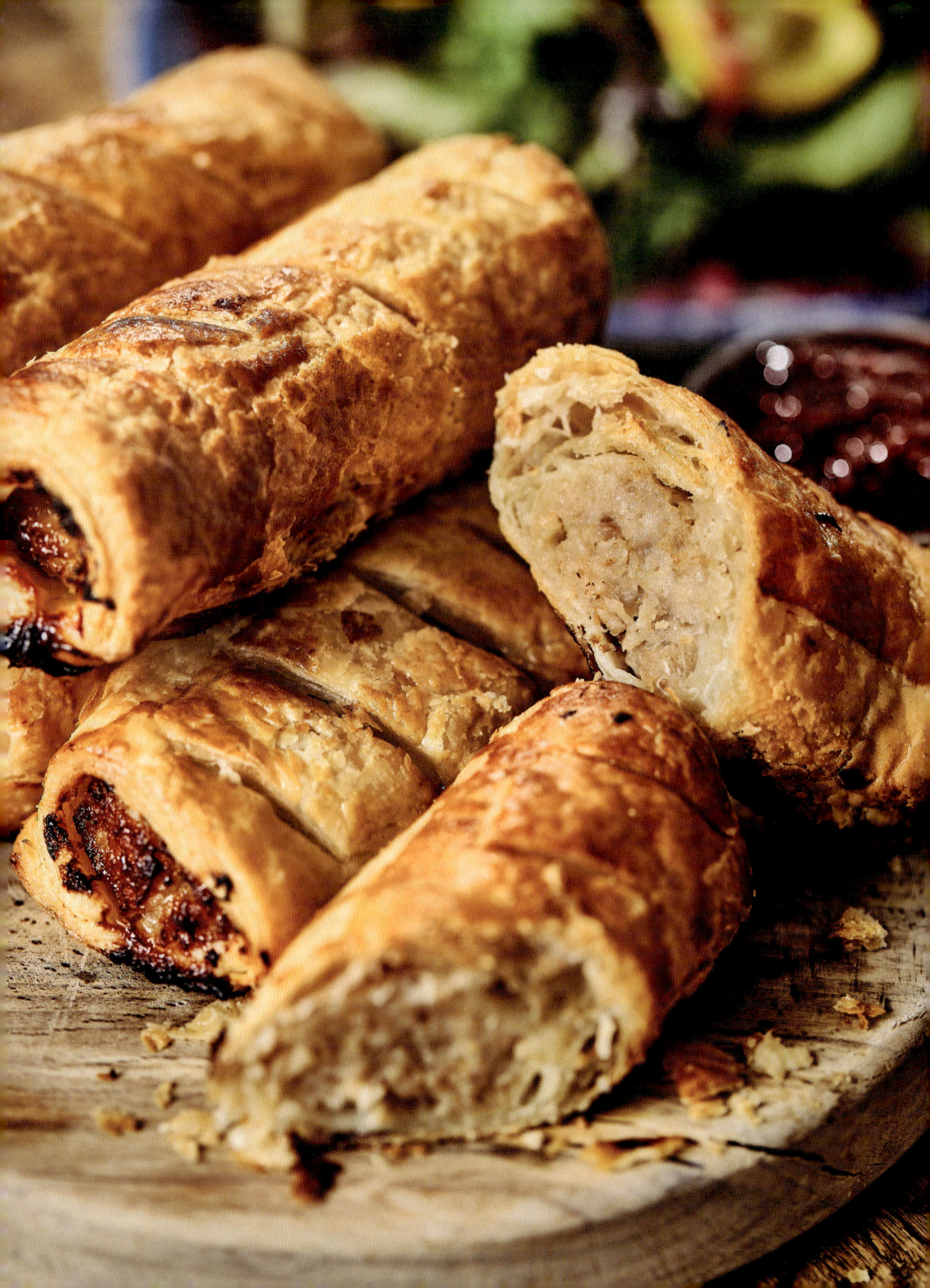

Pork and Apple Sausage Rolls

I use pork and apple sausage meat here, supplied by our local butcher Clive. If you can't find it in your usual shopping spot, ask your butcher for some advice. Most good butchers will have their own version or something similar. These sausage rolls are a firm favourite among staff and customers.

MAKES 6 FULL SIZE OR 12 MINI

1 sheet of pre-rolled puff pastry, 35cm x 23cm

400g pork and apple sausage meat

2 eggs

2 tbsp sesame seeds (optional)

1. Cut the puff pastry in half across lengthways. Place half of the sausage meat in a line, about 4cm in, across the longest side of each piece.
2. Whisk your eggs in a small bowl. Brush the ends of the pastry with the egg wash.
3. Tightly roll up each piece, ending up with the open side on the bottom. Cut each log in 3 or 6, depending on your size preference.
4. Brush with egg wash. Sprinkle with sesame seeds if using. Place on a parchment-lined baking tray and then place in the freezer for 30 minutes to really chill them.
5. Preheat your oven to 180°C fan/200°C/gas 6.
6. Place the rolls in the oven and bake for 20–25 minutes, until the puff pastry is crispy and golden. If you turn them over carefully, the pastry should be cooked on the base too – if not, return them to the oven for a few minutes.
7. Serve with our beetroot orange chutney (page 169).

Beetroot Patties with Roast Carrot Hummus

These patties are filling and versatile in terms of size – you could make them as a canapé, lunch or dinner. They chill well, so you can make them and reheat later, or have them cold in a lunchbox with some salad.

SERVES 6

FOR THE PATTIES

4 raw beetroot

1 small red onion

1 carrot

340g tinned chickpeas

3 cloves of garlic

1½ tsp salt

generous pinch of black pepper

1½ tbsp tahini paste

2 tbsp olive oil

70g plain flour (regular or GF)

50g sesame seeds, for coating

FOR THE ROAST CARROT HUMMUS

3 carrots

2 tbsp olive oil

sea salt

200g tinned chickpeas

1 clove of garlic

4 tbsp olive oil

pinch each of sea salt and cracked black pepper

juice of 1 lemon

2 tbsp tahini

1. Peel and then grate the raw beetroot, red onion and carrot for the patties using a food processor. Remove and set aside.
2. Add the chickpeas, garlic, salt, pepper and tahini to the food processor and blend. Place in a large bowl.
3. Heat 1 tablespoon of oil in a large non-stick frying pan. Add the grated vegetables, stir and cook for about 5 minutes – the veg should still have some bite.
4. Add the flour, stir and cook for 2–3 minutes till thickened and sticky.
5. Add to the chickpea mix, combine thoroughly, then allow to cool for about 30 minutes.
6. Line a baking tray with parchment paper.
7. Divide the mix into 8–12 pieces using a spoon – I usually serve 2 per portion. Place the sesame seeds on a plate, roll each piece of chickpea mix in them, then shape into little patties. Place on the lined tray, then chill in the fridge while you make your hummus.
8. Preheat your oven to 170°C fan/190°C/gas 5.
9. For the hummus, first peel and chop the carrots. Place on a roasting tray, drizzle with the olive oil, sprinkle with sea salt and roast for 15–20 mins, until well cooked. Set aside to cool.
10. Blend the cooled carrots in a food processor with the remaining ingredients. Add a little cold water if it's too thick. Check the seasoning and adjust to taste.
11. Preheat your oven again to 170°C fan/190°C/gas 5.
12. Heat 1 tablespoon of oil in a non-stick pan and turn it to a medium heat. Fry your patties, allowing them to take colour – about 1 minute each side. Place on a roasting tray and finish in the oven for 8–10 minutes, until hot throughout.
13. Serve with the roast carrot hummus and some salads.

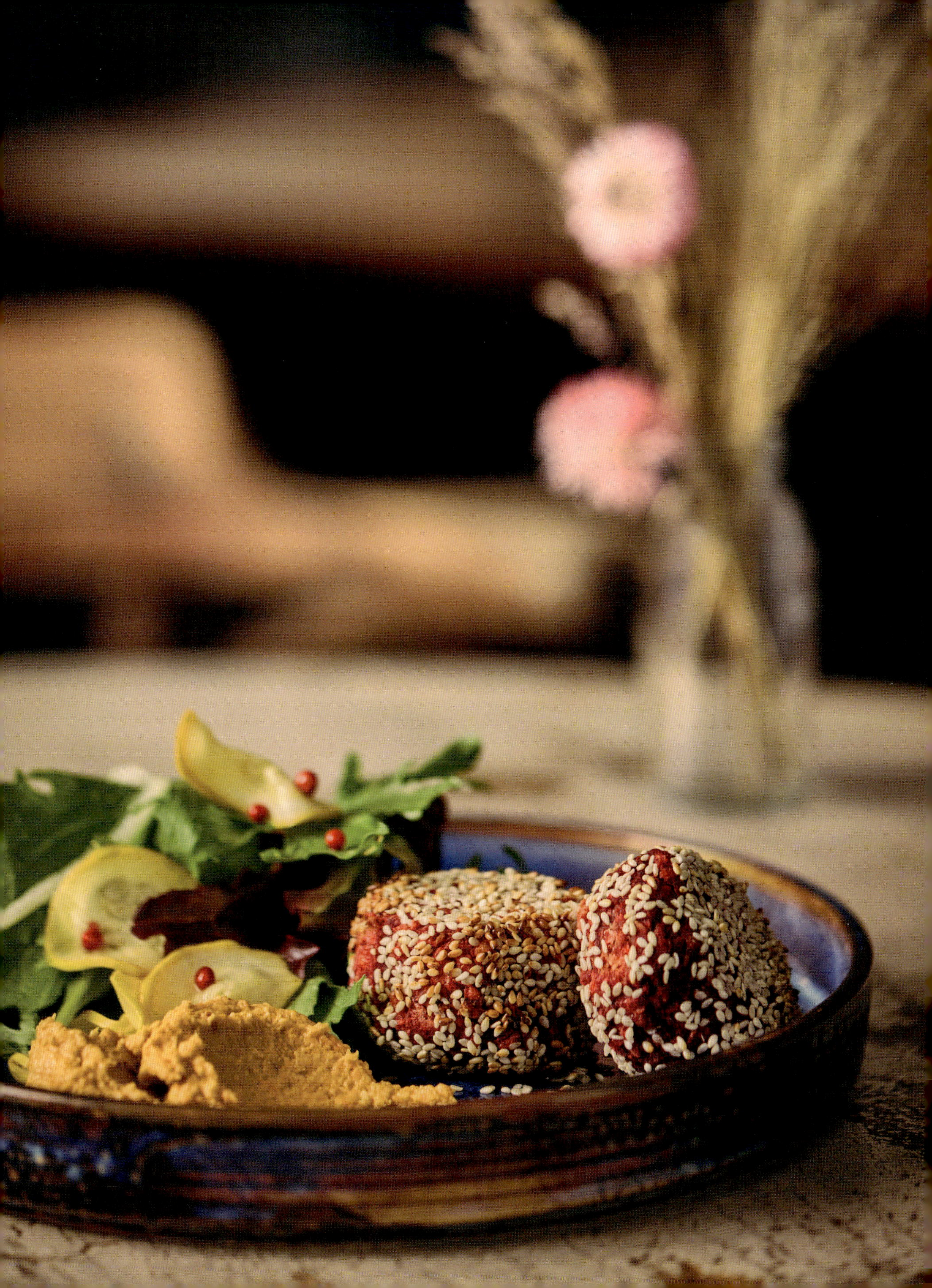

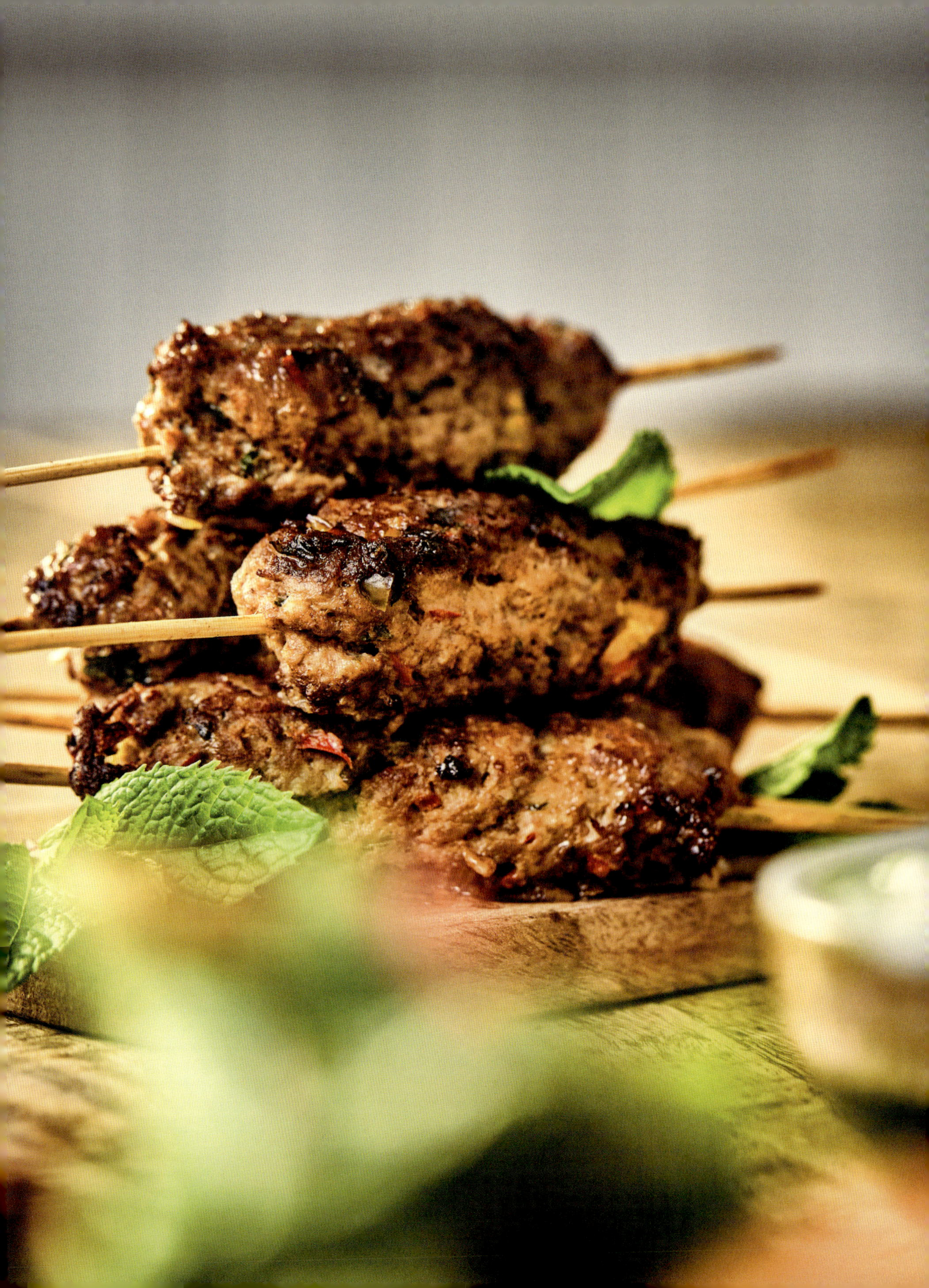

Lamb Koftas with Tzatziki

You can use good-quality beef mince for this recipe, but I prefer lamb. Tzatziki is a perfect accompaniment, as it cools the palate after the hot chillies. Koftas are best prepared in advance and chilled well before being cooked. This gives the flavours time to infuse and helps them to keep their shape when frying.

MAKES 8 PIECES (SERVES 4)

1 small chilli
1 red pepper
2 cloves of garlic
1 handful of chives
1 handful of coriander
500g lamb mince
2 tsp paprika
2 tsp cumin
¾ tsp salt
¾ tsp black pepper
1 tsp lemon juice
1 tbsp oil, for searing

FOR THE TZATZIKI

½ cucumber
4 cloves of garlic
150g full fat Greek yoghurt
1½ tbsp olive oil
1½ tsp lemon juice
2 tsp chopped mint leaves
¾ tsp salt
pepper to taste

1. Dice your chilli and pepper as small as you can, or blitz them in a blender.
2. Mince the garlic. Finely chop the chives. Roughly chop the coriander leaves.
3. Place the lamb mince in a large bowl, and add the spices, seasoning, chilli, pepper, lemon juice and all the herbs.
4. Wearing disposable gloves, mix well by hand so the vegetables and spices are evenly distributed. Divide the mix into 8.
5. Take your wooden or metal skewers, and place a portion of the mix onto each one, squeezing it into a sausage shape along the skewer about 10cm in length.
6. Place on a clean plate, cover with cling film or a plate and chill in the fridge for at least half an hour.
7. Meanwhile, make your tzatziki. First wash and peel the cucumber, then grate using the larger side of your grater. Squeeze excess water out of the cucumber. Mince the garlic.
8. Mix all the tzatziki ingredients together and place in a bowl in the fridge until your koftas are ready.
9. Preheat your oven to 160°C fan/180°C/gas 4.
10. Heat 1 tablespoon of oil in a non-stick pan and turn it to a medium heat. Fry your koftas, allowing them to take colour – about 1 minute each side. Place on a roasting tray and finish in the oven for 8–10 minutes until piping hot throughout.
11. Serve with the tzatziki and a mixed leaf salad (page 25), watermelon salad with honey and pink peppercorn dressing and feta (page 21) or roast cauliflower salad with pearl couscous and zhoug (page 37) for a super summery dish.

Falafels

Falafels can seem a little daunting at first, but with a little practice you will be making these nutritious delicacies in no time. They are great served with a simple green salad and a dollop of chutney – here in the cafe, we use our beetroot orange chutney (page 169). They will keep for three days so are ideal for busy folks who like to prepare in advance.

SERVES 4-6

- 1 large white onion
- 680g tinned chickpeas, drained and washed
- 2 handfuls of flat-leaf parsley
- 4 handfuls of fresh coriander
- ½ tsp cayenne pepper
- 1 tsp ground cumin
- 1 tsp ground coriander
- 1 tsp baking powder
- 2 level tsp salt
- 60ml water
- 60g plain flour (regular or GF)
- 50g sesame seeds, for coating
- 1 tbsp oil, for frying

1. Peel and chop your white onion as small as possible.
2. Using a food processor, pulse the chickpeas until they are almost smooth. It doesn't need to be a complete purée.
3. Roughly chop the parsley and coriander.
4. Place all the ingredients, except the sesame seeds and oil, in a large bowl and mix using a rubber spatula. Make sure it's evenly combined.
5. Divide the mix into 8 or 12 pieces, depending on your preference. I usually keep them about the size of a scoop of mash.
6. Place the sesame seeds on a plate. Roll each piece of falafel mix in the seeds, then shape like little patties. Chill in the fridge for 20–30 minutes.
7. Preheat your oven to 170°C fan/190°C/gas 5.
8. Heat the oil in a non-stick pan and turn it to a medium heat. Begin to fry your falafels, allowing them to take colour – about 1 minute on each side. Place on a roasting tray and finish in the oven for 8–10 minutes until piping hot throughout.

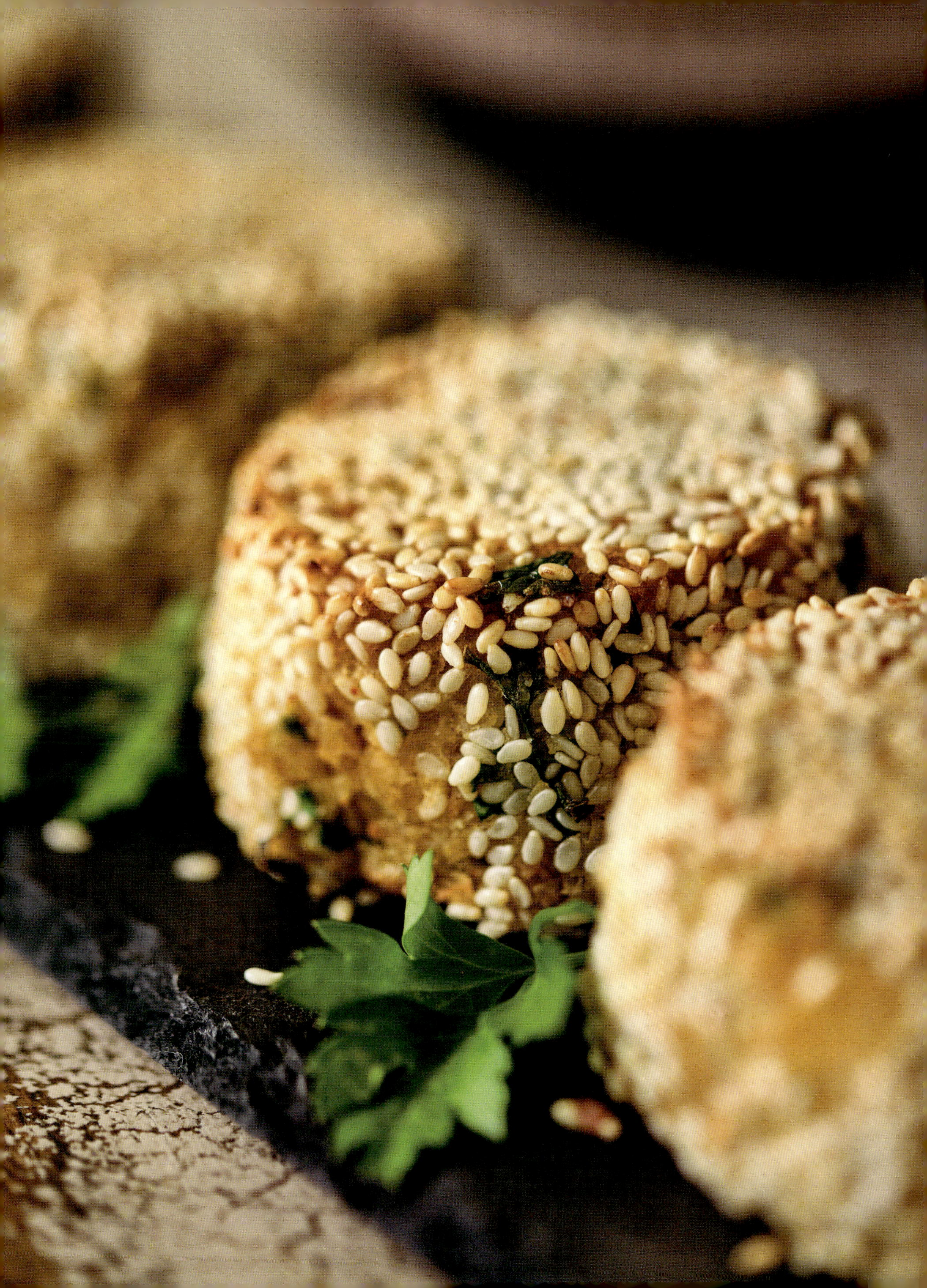

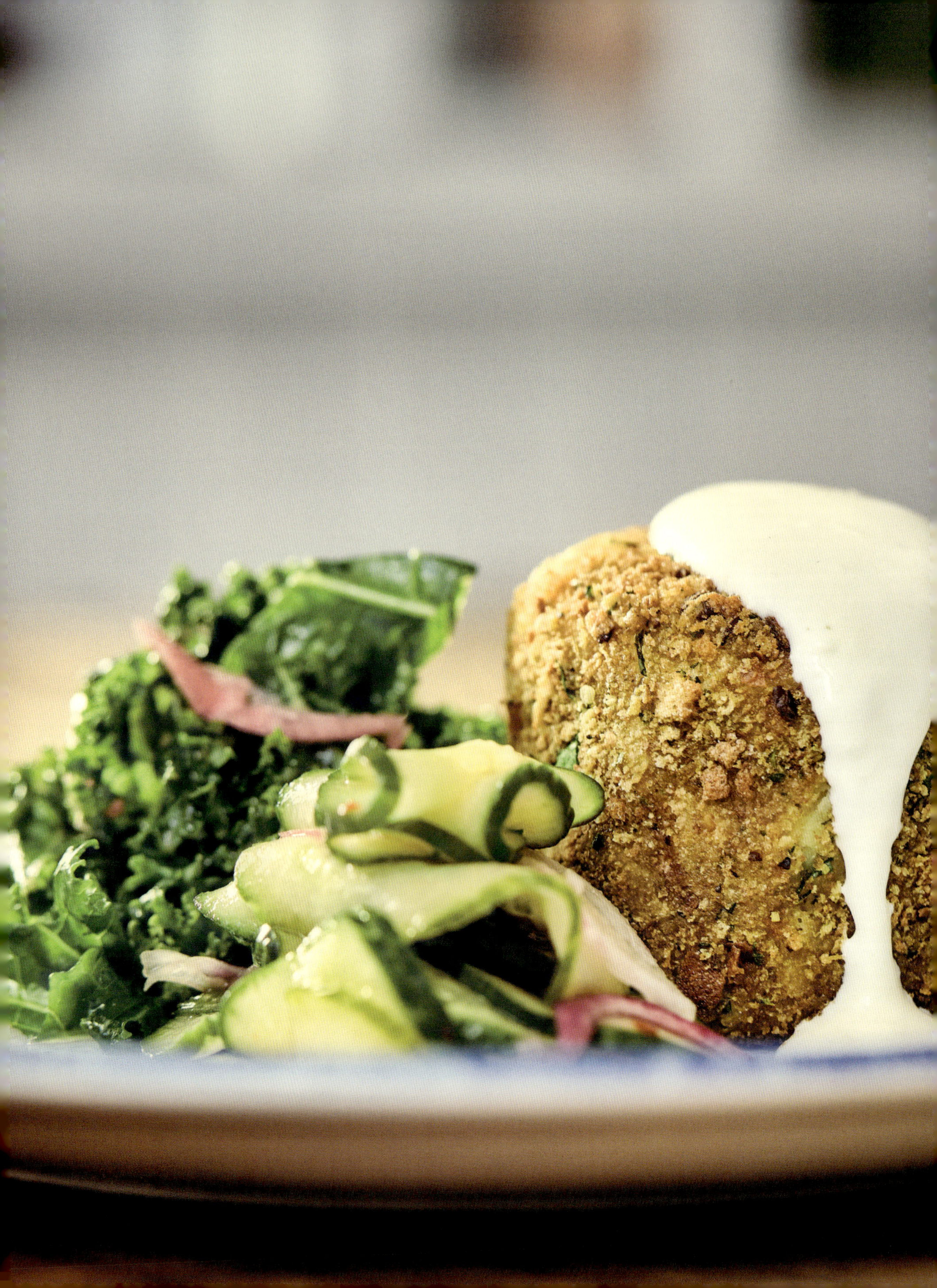

BBQ Smoked Salmon Fishcakes

These beauties are one of the signature dishes on our menu. We use Clare Island organic salmon smoked by Clarkes Salmon Smokery in Ballina and serve with our famous buttermilk dressing (see page 185). You can also use leftover mash – just check the seasoning and follow the quantities below.

MAKES 6 LARGE

FOR THE MASH

750g peeled potatoes
25g butter
70ml cream
½ tsp salt
pinch of pepper

FOR THE CAKES

250g BBQ or hot smoked salmon
½ red onion
small bunch of chives
1 handful of fresh coriander
2 handfuls of fresh parsley
zest of ½ lemon
sea salt and cracked black pepper, to taste
100g bread (regular or GF)
1 egg
100g flour (regular or GF)
1 tbsp oil, for frying

TO SERVE

cucumber pickle (page 14)
buttermilk dressing (page 185)

1. Steam the potatoes until soft – 15–25 minutes depending on their size. Allow to sit for 2–3 minutes.
2. Place the cooked potatoes in a bowl and, using a masher or mixer, mash or beat until smooth. Add the butter, cream, salt and pepper. Mix until completely combined. Allow to cool fully.
3. Remove any skin from your salmon, and make sure there are no bones. Flake it into the mash.
4. Chop your red onion and chives finely. Roughly chop the coriander and parsley, and set 2 tablespoons of parsley aside for the coating. Add all these and the lemon zest into the bowl with the salmon. Mix well. Taste and add some seasoning if you wish.
5. Divide into 6 pieces. Roll into balls and pat lightly to flatten on top and bottom.
6. Place in the fridge to chill while you prepare the coating.
7. For the coating, first toast your bread and cool it, then blend into breadcrumbs. Add the reserved parsley to the blender and pulse.
8. Whisk the egg in a bowl. Place your flour in another bowl with a pinch of salt and pepper, and place your breadcrumbs in a third bowl.
9. Preheat your oven to 170°C fan/190°C/gas 5.
10. For each fishcake, dredge it in the flour, shake off the excess, then dip in the egg, let the excess drip off, then finally coat in the breadcrumbs.
11. Heat 1 tablespoon of oil in a non-stick pan and turn it to a medium heat. Fry your fishcakes, allowing them to take colour – about 1 minute each side. Place on a roasting tray and finish in the oven for 10–15 minutes until piping hot throughout.
12. Serve with a green leaf salad, some cucumber pickle and a drizzle of buttermilk dressing.

Cauliflower Tacos

I love versatility in recipes – substituting lemon caper aioli (page 26) for the buttermilk dressing below and adding some spinach are simple changes that will give you a different, equally delicious version of this dish. The battered cauliflower is relatively simple to do, so it's worth taking the time to make the sides. I also make canapés with this recipe and use the romesco sauce or aioli as dips.

SERVES 4-6

½ head of cauliflower
1 tsp harissa paste
100g flour (regular or GF)
pinch of salt
vegetable oil, for deep frying

FOR THE BATTER

125g self-raising flour (regular or GF) – if you only have plain, add 1 tsp of baking powder (regular or GF)
125ml chilled sparkling water
½ tsp salt
½ tsp paprika

TO SERVE

8-12 corn tortillas
romesco sauce (page 17)
pickled red onion (page 34)
buttermilk dressing (page 185)
1 lime, cut into wedges

1. Preheat your oven to 170°C fan/190°C/gas 5. Line a baking tray with parchment paper.
2. Using a sharp knife, cut the cauliflower florets as close as possible to the stalk, then cut them into 3-4cm pieces. Toss in the harissa paste. Mix until the cauliflower is coated lightly.
3. Sieve the flour and salt into a large bowl. Add the cauliflower, and mix again until completely coated in flour. Shake off any excess and place on a clean tray.
4. Whisk all the ingredients for the batter together until smooth. Do not mix it until you are ready to use it.
5. To use a deep fryer, add oil to the manufacturer's recommended fill line, and heat to 190°C. To use a large wok, add 2.5-3.5cm oil, and heat to 190°C – use a thermometer to measure this and do not leave it unattended.
6. Coat some of the cauliflower in the batter, then use a slotted spoon to carefully lift it into the hot oil. Deep-fry the cauliflower for 2-3 mins until golden and puffy. Drain on kitchen paper and continue with the rest in batches. Place on the lined tray and put in the oven for 4-6 minutes until cooked through.
7. Place your non-stick pan or cast-iron skillet over a medium heat. After a few minutes place a corn tortilla on it and turn after 15-30 seconds. Repeat until you've heated all the tortillas you require.
8. To serve, spread some romesco sauce on each tortilla, add a few pieces of cauliflower, some pickled red onions, a drizzle of the buttermilk dressing and a squeeze of lime.

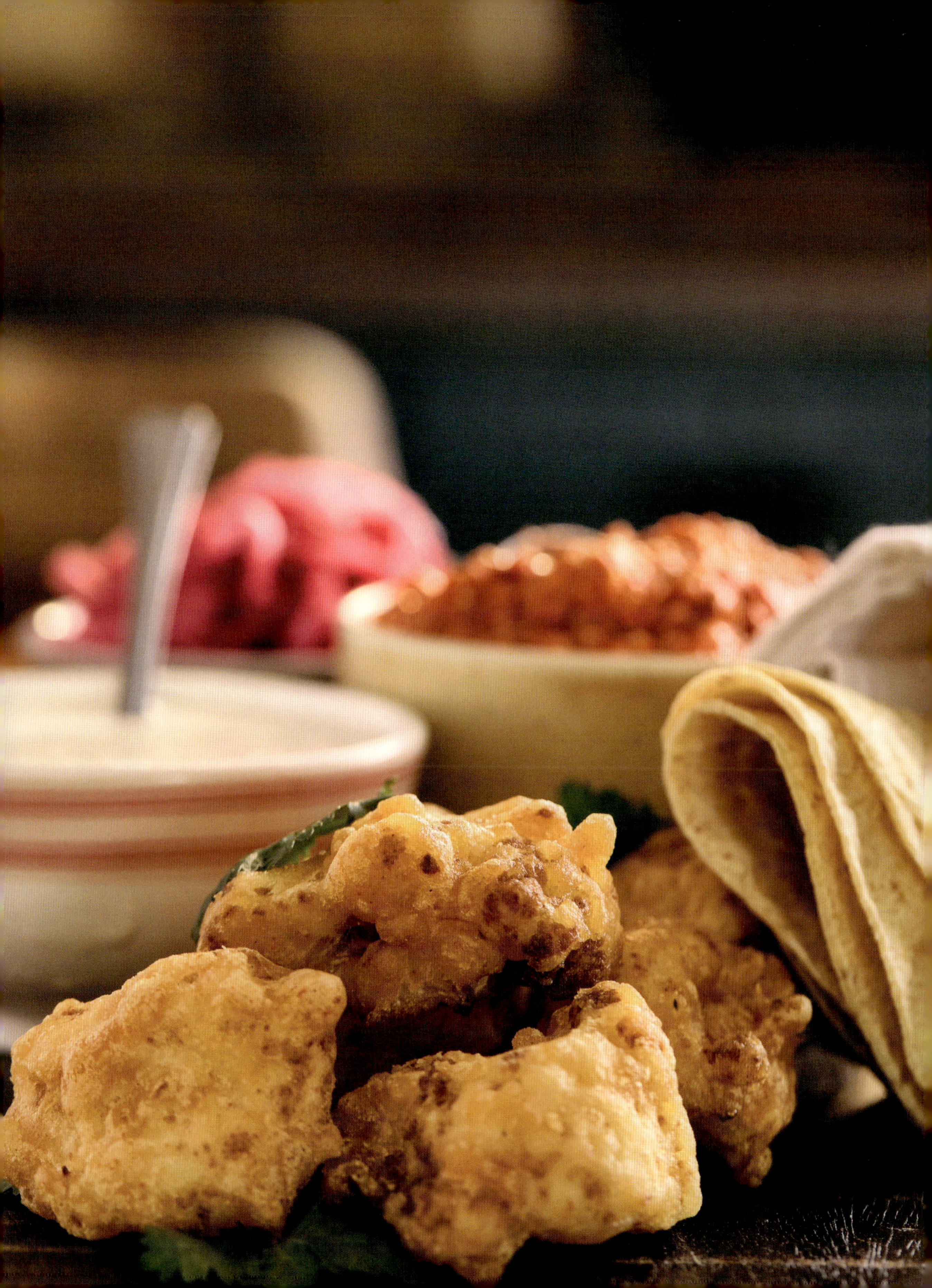

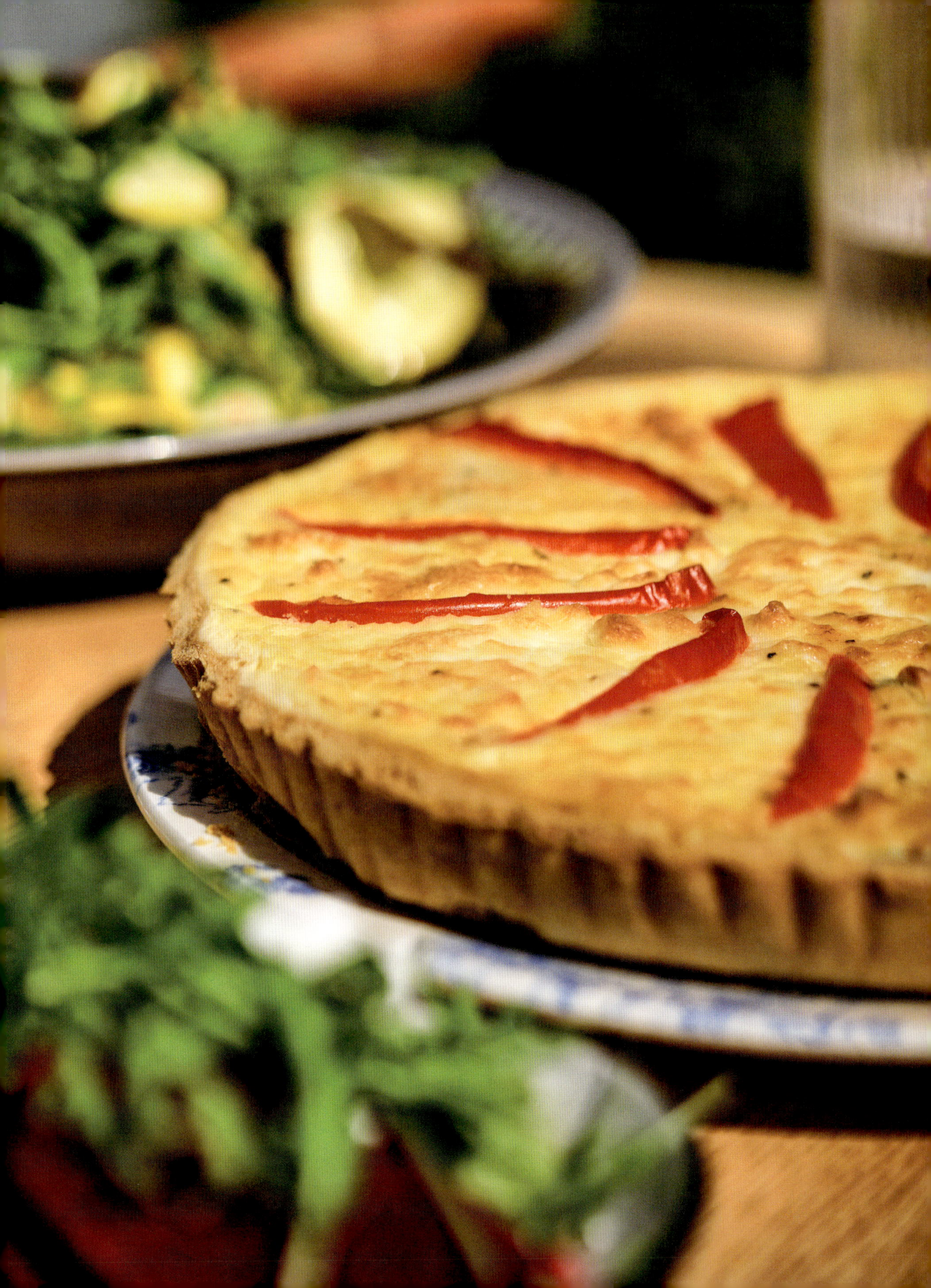

Free-Range Egg Quiche Three Ways

We have to mention quiche when we talk about bestsellers on the menu. I would suggest making two bases and freezing one to bake at a later date. This way you will have a quick lunch at any time. The three filling options here are easy – just lightly season the layers. I love to add Irish cheeses as they're a simple way to really elevate your quiche.

SERVES 8

FOR THE PASTRY

330g butter
530g plain flour, plus extra for rolling
2 eggs
80ml cold water

FOR THE QUICHE MIX

6 medium free-range eggs
250ml cream
250ml milk
pinch of salt
pinch of pepper

HAM AND CHEDDAR FILLING

200g cooked home-baked ham
2 tbsp chopped chives
100g grated Irish Cheddar

VEGGIE QUICHE FILLING

2 tbsp red onion marmalade
½ pepper sliced
handful of baby spinach
200g Irish soft goat's cheese

SMOKED SALMON FILLING

handful of baby spinach
½ red onion, sliced
200g BBQ smoked salmon
1 tbsp grated Parmesan

1. Grease a 28cm loose-bottomed fluted tart tin well and line the base with a disc of parchment paper.
2. To make the pastry, use a hand-held or stand mixer to mix the butter and flour until they resemble crumbs.
3. Add the eggs and water and mix on the lowest speed until it comes together.
4. Remove the pastry from the bowl and knead gently on a very lightly floured surface until it's smooth and forms a ball. Keep the mixing and kneading to the bare minimum, as it can make the pastry tough and elastic, which will cause it to shrink when rolling and baking. Wrap in clingfilm or place in a sealed container (a glass or plastic lunchbox) and pop in the fridge for half an hour.
5. Lightly flour your rolling surface and rolling pin. Roll out your pastry until the disc is slightly bigger than the tin. Only roll in one direction, back and forward, never side to side (this prevents the pastry from stretching and contracting) – turn the pastry rather than the rolling pin.
6. Roll the pastry back over the rolling pin to help lift it over the tart tin. Gently sit the pastry into the tin; then, using your thumbs, press it all the way round into the sides of the tin. The pastry should be falling over the sides and will be rough around the edges, which is fine. Place in the freezer for an hour.
7. Preheat your oven to 160°C fan/180°C/gas 4.
8. Pop a disc of parchment 5cm bigger than the tin on top of the pastry, and fill with beans for baking blind (I use dried chickpeas or rice).
9. Place in the oven and bake for 30 minutes until the pastry is golden brown at the edges.

CONTINUED OVERLEAF

10. Place on a wire rack and carefully lift off the disc of parchment with the beans inside. Store the beans for next use, and allow the tart to cool completely.
11. When you're ready to bake the quiche, preheat your oven to 140°C fan/160°C/gas 3.
12. Whisk all of the quiche mix ingredients together in a large jug. Place the tin with the prebaked case on a flat baking tray.
13. In general, I do a light layer of each filling ingredient and then pour over the mix.
14. **For the ham and Cheddar filling:** dice the ham into 1cm cubes. Sprinkle the chives on the base, then the grated cheese and then the diced ham.
15. **For the veggie filling:** spread the onion marmalade on the base, then add the spinach, peppers and, finally, the goat's cheese broken into smaller pieces.
16. **For the smoked salmon filling:** sprinkle the spinach on the base, then the sliced red onion, then the smoked salmon and, finally, the Parmesan on top.
17. Whisk the quiche mix one more time before pouring it on top of the filling. Do this carefully and slowly.
18. Place in the oven on the tray and bake for 35–40 minutes – the veggie quiche will take longer, as it has more liquid from the veg. To check if it's done, give the tin a wobble: the egg should be set like custard.
19. Cool the quiche for a couple of hours. Use a sharp knife to trim the rough pastry edges, then lift the quiche out of the tin using the loose base.
20. Using a palette knife or large chopping knife, slide the quiche off the base onto a flat plate or cake stand. Slice and serve.

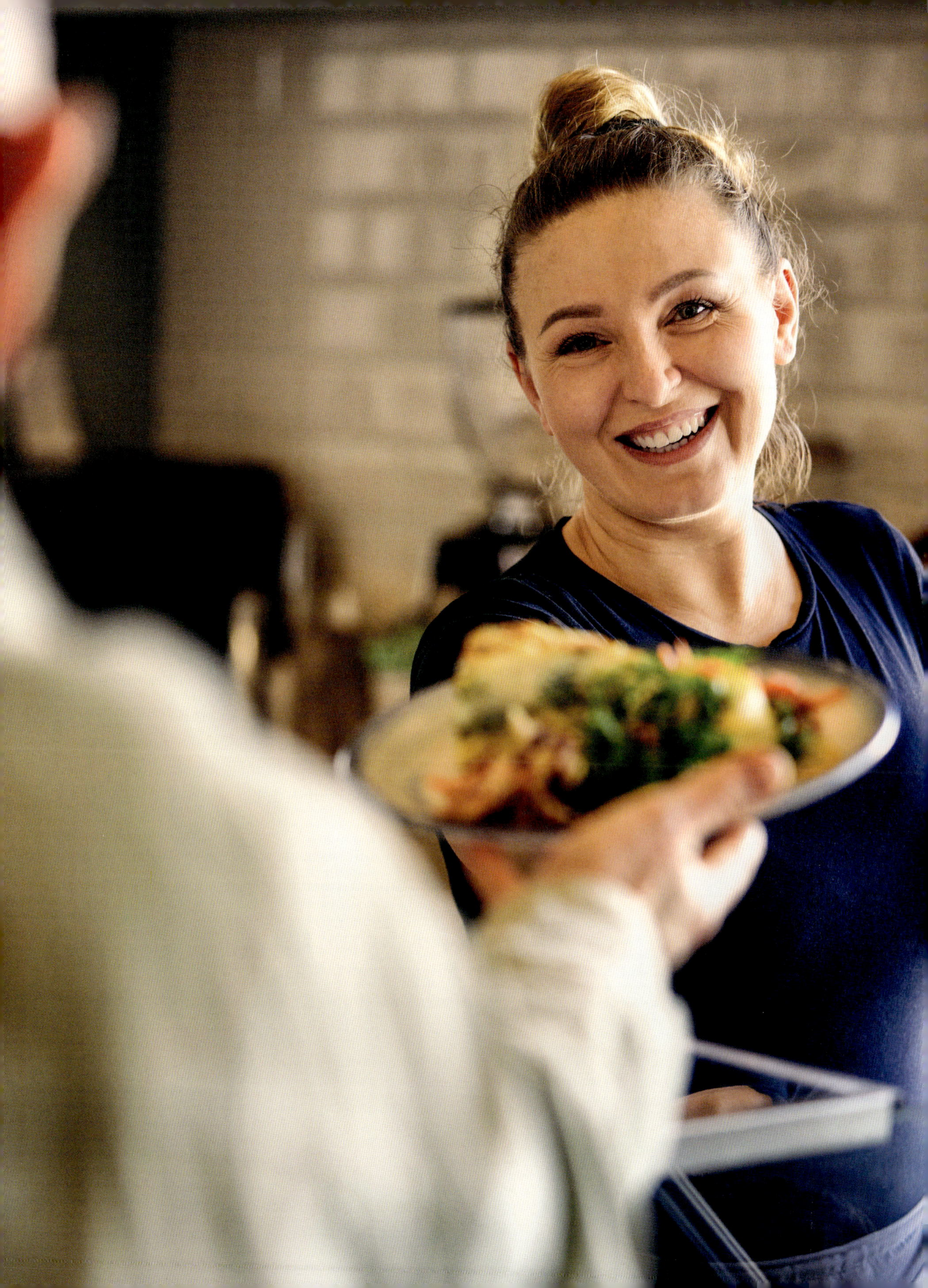

Roast Carrot and Chickpea Rolls

These chickpea rolls are immensely popular with our customers and staff. We tried a few versions until we hit the jackpot with this one. The carrot is key, as it gives moisture and a little sweetness. They are best served warm with a good dollop of homemade chutney.

MAKES 6 FULL SIZE OR 12 MINI

3–4 large carrots
2 tbsp olive oil
1 heaped tsp ground cumin
2 cloves of garlic
340g tinned chickpeas, drained and washed
1 heaped tsp harissa paste
generous handful of coriander leaves
2 level tsp salt
1 sheet of pre-rolled puff pastry, 35cm x 23cm, at room temperature
50ml plant-based milk or 1 beaten egg, for glazing
2 tbsp poppy seeds

1. Preheat your oven to 170°C fan/190°C/gas 5.
2. Peel and grate the carrots on the largest side of your grater until you have 250g.
3. Place the carrot on a roasting tray, sprinkle with the olive oil and cumin, toss and roast for 10 minutes. Toss, then place back in the oven for a further 5 minutes. Remove and allow to cool.
4. Mince your garlic, then blend the chickpeas, harissa and garlic in a food processor using the pulse button so it doesn't blend to a complete purée – it's better with a little texture.
5. Scoop the mix into a bowl. Roughly chop the coriander leaves, then add them to the chickpea mix with the salt and the roasted carrot. Mix well with a rubber spatula and taste to check the seasoning.
6. Cut the puff pastry in half longways. Place half of the mix in a line, about 4cm in, across the longest side of each piece. Brush the ends of the pastry with the plant-based milk or beaten egg.
7. Tightly roll up each piece, long side to long side, ending up with the open side on the bottom. Cut each log into 3 or 6, depending on your size preference.
8. Brush with plant-based milk or beaten egg. Sprinkle with poppy seeds. Place on a parchment-lined baking tray and then into the freezer for 30 minutes to chill.
9. Preheat your oven to 180°C fan/200°C/gas 6.
10. Bake the rolls for 20–25 minutes, until the pastry is crisp and golden. If the bases aren't fully cooked, return to the oven for a few minutes.
11. Serve with our beetroot orange chutney (page 169).

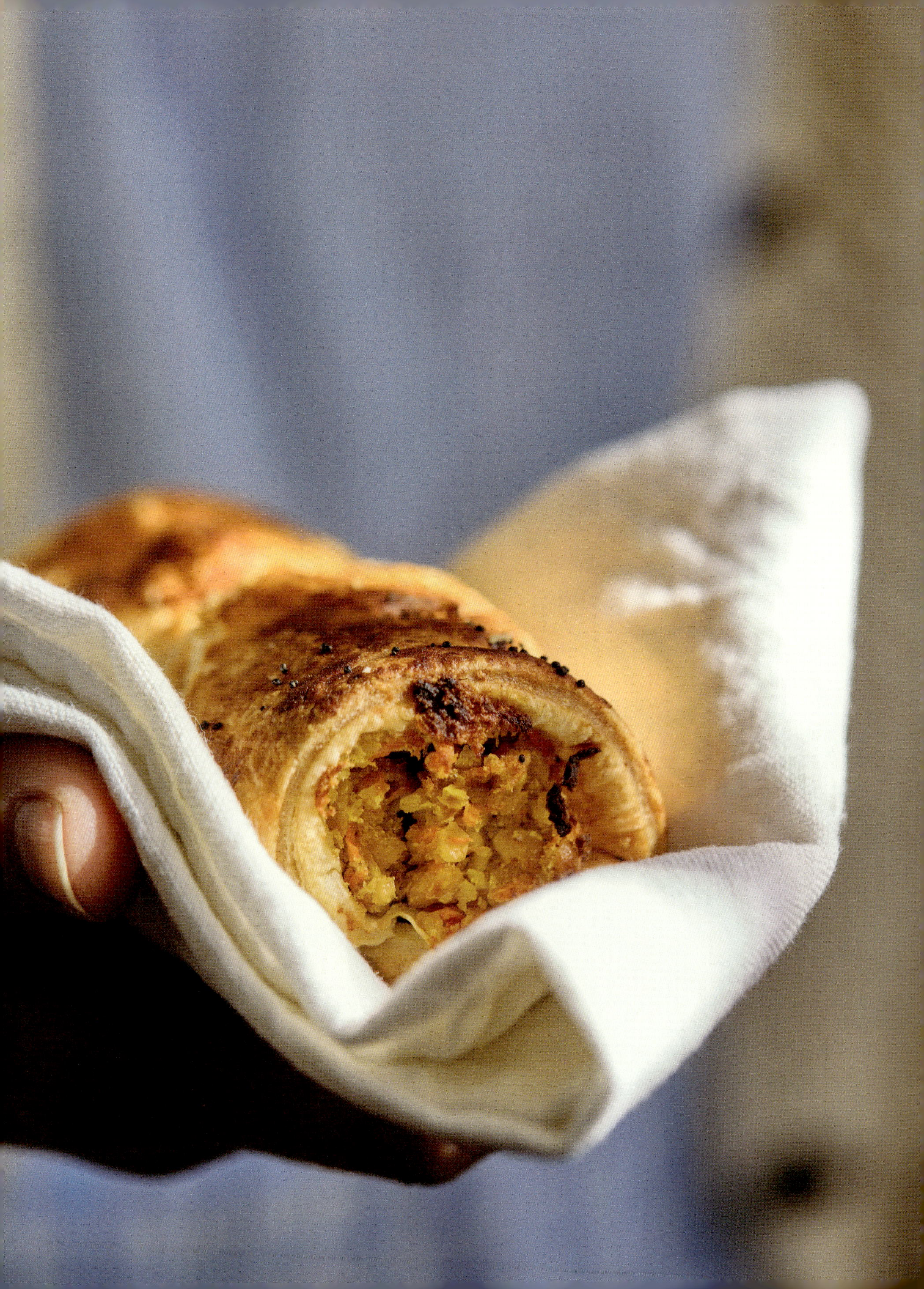

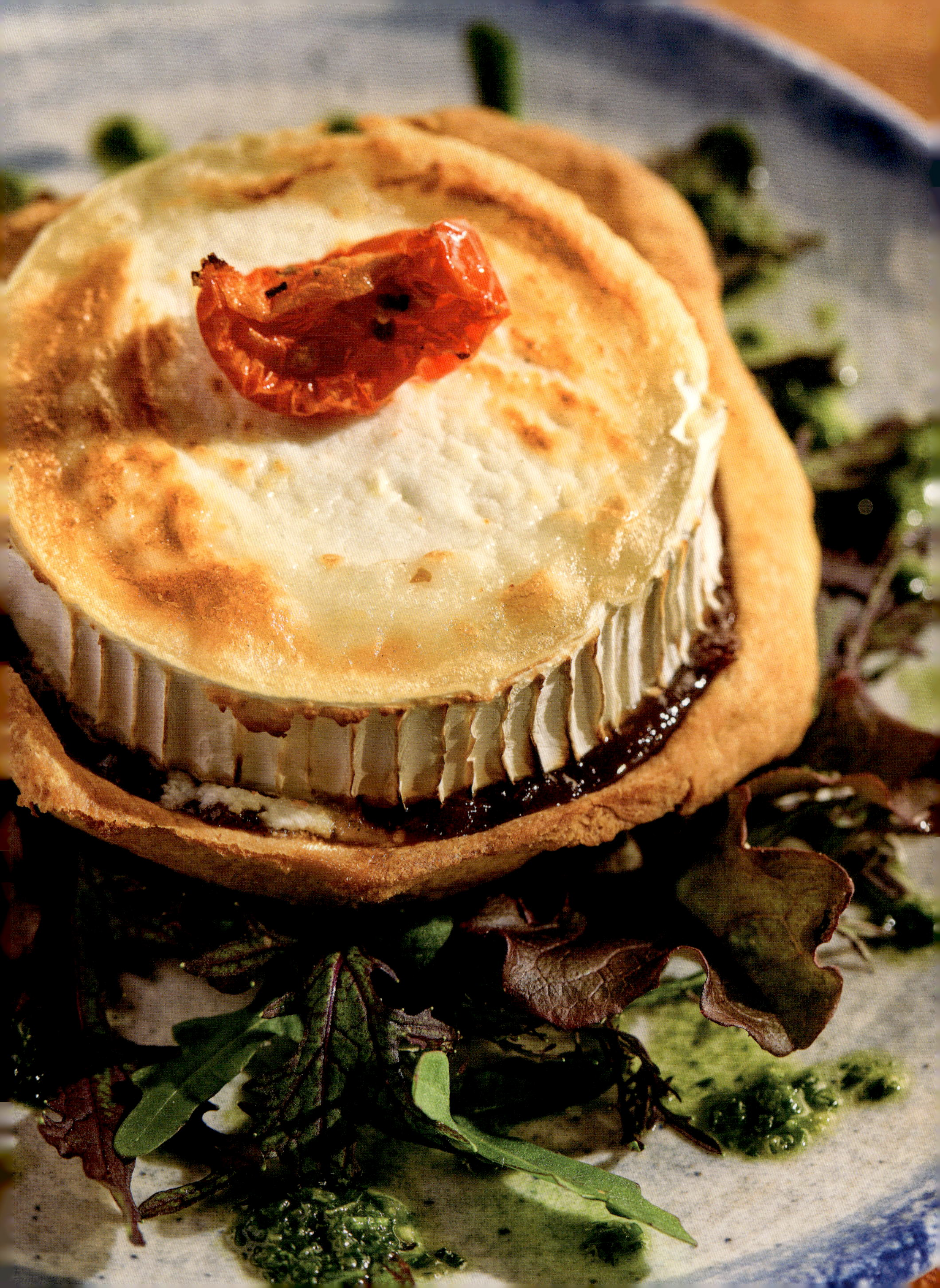

Goat's Cheese Tartlets with Red Onion Marmalade

This was one of the first items I put on the menu, and soon afterwards we began selling jars of the Foxford Red Onion Marmalade. It is now one of our top-selling retail items. While the filling below is for four tartlets, the pastry makes eight cases – it's worth making a few extra to keep on hand. Once cooked and cooled, the cases will keep in an airtight container for two weeks.

MAKES 8 CASES AND 4 TARTLETS

FOR THE PASTRY

330g butter
530g plain flour
2 eggs
80ml cold water

FOR THE TARTLETS

200g red onion marmalade (we use Foxford Red Onion Marmalade)
400g goat's cheese
4 pieces of semi-dried tomatoes
basil pesto (optional), for drizzling
balsamic vinegar, for drizzling

FOR THE PASTRY CASES

1. Use a hand-held or stand mixer to mix the butter and flour, until they resemble crumbs.
2. Add the eggs and water and mix on the lowest speed until it comes together.
3. Remove the pastry from the bowl and knead gently on a very lightly floured surface until it's smooth and forms a ball. Keep the mixing and kneading to the bare minimum, as it makes the pastry tough and elastic, which will cause it to shrink when rolling and baking. Wrap in cling film or put in a sealed container (a glass or plastic lunchbox) and pop in the fridge for half an hour.
4. Preheat your oven to 160°C fan/180°C/gas 4. Grease eight 10cm tartlet tins well.
5. Divide the pastry into 8 pieces. Lightly flour your rolling surface and rolling pin. For each piece of pastry, roll out in one direction, back and forward, never side to side (this prevents the pastry from stretching and contracting) – turn the pastry rather than the rolling pin. Keep doing this until the disc is slightly bigger than the tin.
6. Roll the pastry back over the rolling pin to help you lift it over the tart tin. Gently sit the pastry into the tin; then, using your thumbs, press it all the way round into the sides. The pastry should be falling over the sides of the tin and will be rough around the edges, which is fine. Place the cases in the freezer for an hour.

CONTINUED OVERLEAF

7. Pop a disc of parchment 5cm bigger than the tins on top of each pastry case and fill with beans for baking blind (I use dried chickpeas or rice).
8. Place the cases in the oven and bake for 30 minutes until the pastry is golden brown at the edges. Remove and cool. Remove the baking beans and store for use again.
9. Once the pastry has completely cooled, trim the rough edges (I prefer to keep them!) and pop the cases out of the tins. Store in an airtight container until you are ready to use.

FOR THE TARTLETS

10. Place 4 tart cases on a plate and keep 4 for later in the airtight container.
11. Preheat your oven to 170°C fan/190°C/gas 5, or use an air fryer at 170°C.
12. Place 2 heaped tablespoons of red onion marmalade in the base of each tartlet and top with a slice of goat's cheese (about 90–100g). Place the tartlets in the oven for 8–10 minutes until the cheese has softened and begins to take colour – an air fryer will be much quicker, so be careful it does not burn.
13. Garnish with a piece of semi-dried tomato and a drizzle of basil pesto if you wish. Serve with a green leaf salad and a drizzle of balsamic vinegar.

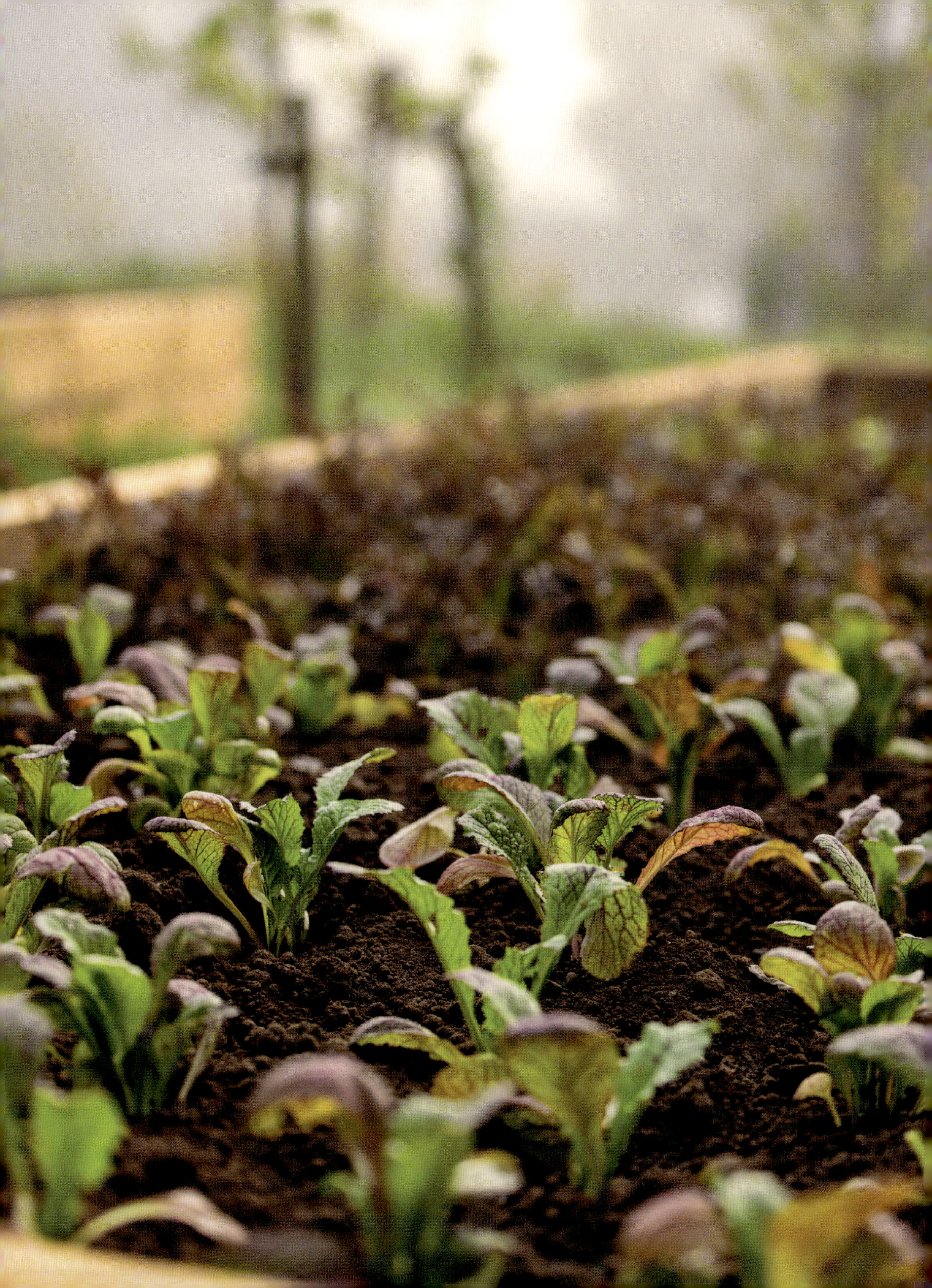

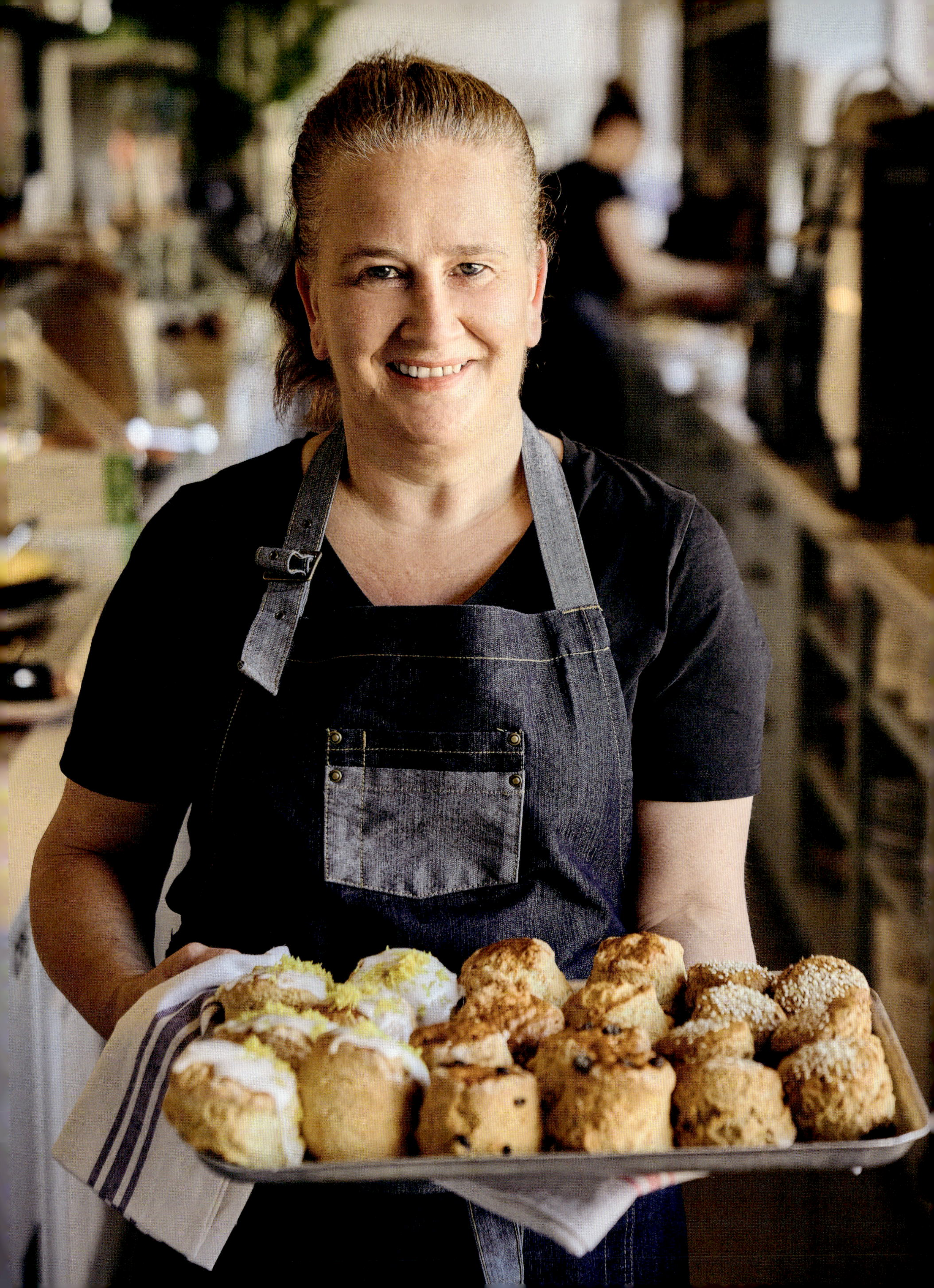

SOMETHING SWEET

This section includes a variety of small bites, bakes, cookies and loaf cake recipes that all feature on our cafe counter throughout the year. These bakes are suited to ambient temperatures (don't require refrigeration). You can pop them in a tin or even freeze and enjoy them later. They are great to bake and share with friends.

I believe in keeping it real when baking. I love using natural flavours and have a few must-haves when choosing ingredients. Always use real butter – we are so fortunate in Ireland with the quality of our dairy products. Use free-range or organic eggs. Use fresh cream. Invest in a little digital scale, as they are more accurate for smaller quantities, and weighing your ingredients correctly is so important – baking is a science. If your budget doesn't stretch to a stand mixer, buy a little hand mixer. They are cheap and cheerful and will get you through most jobs, albeit a little slower, but good things come to those who wait.

If you're new to baking, don't be intimidated: start with scones or loaf cakes and work your way up to the fancier bakes in the Cakes and Tarts section. The taste is what's important – the look will come!

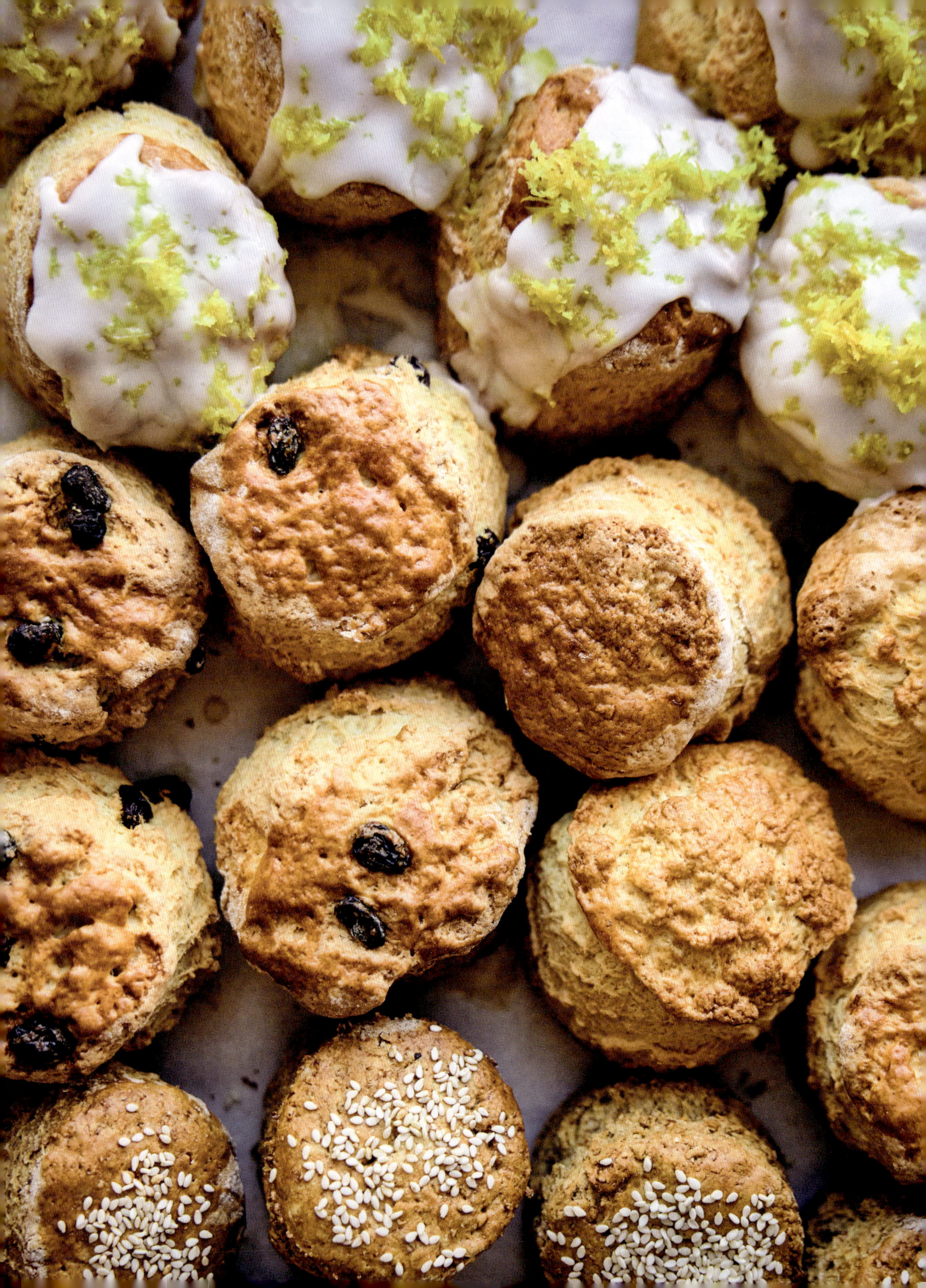

Scones Three Ways

I have included a few scone recipes here: plain or fruit, treacle and iced lemon. I prefer them not to be too big, as they bake faster and the crust is more delicate, and I use buttermilk as it keeps them nice and moist. The best tips I can give you are to work the dough as little as possible, always let them rest and flour your cutter.

MAKES 8

375g plain flour, plus extra for dipping

1 tbsp baking powder

60g caster sugar

90g butter

2 medium eggs (1½ for the scones – mix the other ½ with a drop of milk for the egg wash)

100ml buttermilk

50g raisins or sultanas (optional)

Fruit or Plain Scones

1. Preheat your oven to 160°C fan/180°C/gas 4. Line a baking tray with parchment paper.
2. Sieve your flour and baking powder into a mixing bowl. Add the sugar.
3. Cut the butter into cubes. Rub it into the flour mix between your fingers and thumbs until the mixture resembles crumbs.
4. Whisk 1½ eggs and the buttermilk together. Make a well in the centre of your flour mix, pour in the buttermilk, and, using one hand, stir in a full circular movement from the centre to the outside of the bowl with your fingers. The dough should be softish, not too wet and sticky. Add the dried fruit if using. When it all comes together, turn it out onto a floured work surface. Wash and dry your hands.
5. Knead the dough very lightly, then flour your rolling pin and roll the dough out to the height of your cutter or slightly lower.
6. Dip your 5cm cutter in flour, then push it straight down on the dough, no twisting. Remove, turn over and place the scone on the tray. Repeat, dipping the cutter in flour every time.
7. Brush the tops of the scones with the egg wash. Place in the freezer for 15 minutes to rest.
8. Bake for 18–20 minutes, until the scones are well risen and a pale golden-brown colour. Lift onto a wire rack to cool.
9. Serve with jam and cream – they are best eaten as fresh as possible.

CONTINUED OVERLEAF

MAKES 10

2 lemons

375g plain flour

1 tbsp baking powder

60g caster sugar

90g butter

2 medium eggs (1½ for the scones – mix the other ½ with a drop of milk for the egg wash)

75ml buttermilk

200g icing sugar

Iced Lemon Scones

1. Preheat your oven to 160°C fan/180°C/gas 4. Line a baking tray with parchment paper.
2. Zest and juice your lemons, reserving ¼ each of the juice (for the icing) and zest (for garnish).
3. Sieve your flour and baking powder into a mixing bowl. Add the caster sugar.
4. Cut the butter into cubes. Rub it into the flour mix between your fingers and thumbs until the mixture resembles crumbs.
5. Whisk together 1½ eggs, 25ml lemon juice, the zest and buttermilk. Make a well in the centre of your flour mix, pour in the buttermilk mix and, using one hand, stir in a full circular movement from the centre to the outside of the bowl with your fingers. The dough should be softish, not too wet and sticky. When it all comes together, turn it out onto a floured work surface. Wash and dry your hands.
6. Knead the dough very lightly into a ball, flour your rolling pin, and roll the dough out to the height of your cutter or slightly lower.
7. Dip your 5cm cutter in flour, then push it straight down on the dough, no twisting. Remove, turn over and place the scone on the tray. Repeat, dipping the cutter in flour every time.
8. Brush the tops of the scones with the egg wash. Place in the freezer for 15 minutes to rest.
9. Bake for 18–20 minutes until the scones are well risen and are a pale golden-brown colour. Lift onto a wire rack to cool.
10. For the icing, place the icing sugar in a bowl and add in the reserved lemon juice little by little, stirring until all the icing sugar has dissolved but it's still thick and white. Drizzle it over the scones and sprinkle them with a little of the reserved zest to garnish.
11. Serve with whipped cream and lemon curd.

MAKES 8

190g wholemeal flour

190g plain flour

1 tbsp baking powder

90g butter

20g treacle

2 medium eggs (1½ for the scones – mix the other ½ with a drop of milk for the egg wash)

75ml buttermilk

2 tbsp sesame seeds, for topping

Brown Treacle Scones

1. Preheat your oven to 160°C fan/180°C/gas 4. Line a baking tray with parchment paper.
2. Sieve your flours and baking powder into a mixing bowl.
3. Cut the butter into cubes. Rub it into the flour mix between your fingers and thumbs until the mixture resembles crumbs.
4. Weigh your treacle into a bowl. Whisk 1½ eggs and the buttermilk together. Add them to the treacle and whisk until all of the treacle has mixed in.
5. Make a well in the centre of your flour mix, pour in the buttermilk mix and, using one hand, stir in a full circular movement from the centre to the outside of the bowl with your fingers. The dough should be softish, not too wet and sticky. When it all comes together, turn it out onto a floured work surface. Wash and dry your hands.
6. Knead the dough very lightly into a ball, flour your rolling pin and roll the dough out to the height of your cutter or slightly lower.
7. Dip your 5cm cutter in flour, then push it straight down on the dough, no twisting. Remove, turn over and place the scone on the tray. Repeat, dipping the cutter in flour every time.
8. Brush the tops of the scones with the egg wash. Sprinkle with the sesame seeds. Place in the freezer for 15 minutes to rest.
9. Bake for 18–20 minutes until the scones are well risen and are a pale golden-brown colour. Lift onto a wire rack to cool.
10. Serve with real butter.

Date, Coconut and Dark Chocolate Powerballs

Our powerballs were a huge hit with regular customers when we introduced them, particularly for those on the go. They are a great small bite to enjoy with a takeaway coffee. They're best prepared in advance – a great Sunday afternoon task. Rope your family into helping – they will thank you later in the week when they are enjoying a satisfying sweet treat in their lunchbox or with a cuppa in the evening.

MAKES ABOUT 20

FOR THE POWERBALLS

60ml water
180g dates
125ml maple syrup or honey
60ml olive oil
200g desiccated coconut
1 tbsp cocoa
120g ground almonds
125g crunchy peanut butter

FOR THE COATING

125g good-quality dark chocolate
100–140g desiccated coconut
10g chopped pistachios (optional)

1. Warm the water and soak the dates in it for 30 minutes to soften them slightly.
2. Blend the dates and water with the syrup or honey and olive oil, using a food processor. It doesn't need to be very smooth.
3. Scrape the mix into a large bowl and stir in the remaining powerball ingredients.
4. Divide the mix into about 20 pieces, depending on your size preference. Roll into balls and chill in the fridge while you're melting the chocolate. (You could just chill and eat them like this but I find the next step elevates them!)
5. To make the coating, first break the dark chocolate into pieces. Place in a microwave-safe bowl and melt on a low setting, stirring frequently. Or to use the water-bath method instead, place the chocolate in a glass bowl over a saucepan of warm water on a low heat – the water should not touch the bowl. Stir frequently using a dry, clean spatula. Use a dry tea towel to lift off the bowl once the chocolate has melted, being careful of the escaping steam.
6. Place the coconut – and chopped pistachios if using – on a flat tray.
7. Roll the balls in the melted chocolate using the tips of your fingers – disposable gloves are essential here!
8. Pop each ball onto the tray with the coconut coating. Roll gently till well covered, then place on a clean platter. Refrigerate until set (at least 30 minutes) and enjoy!

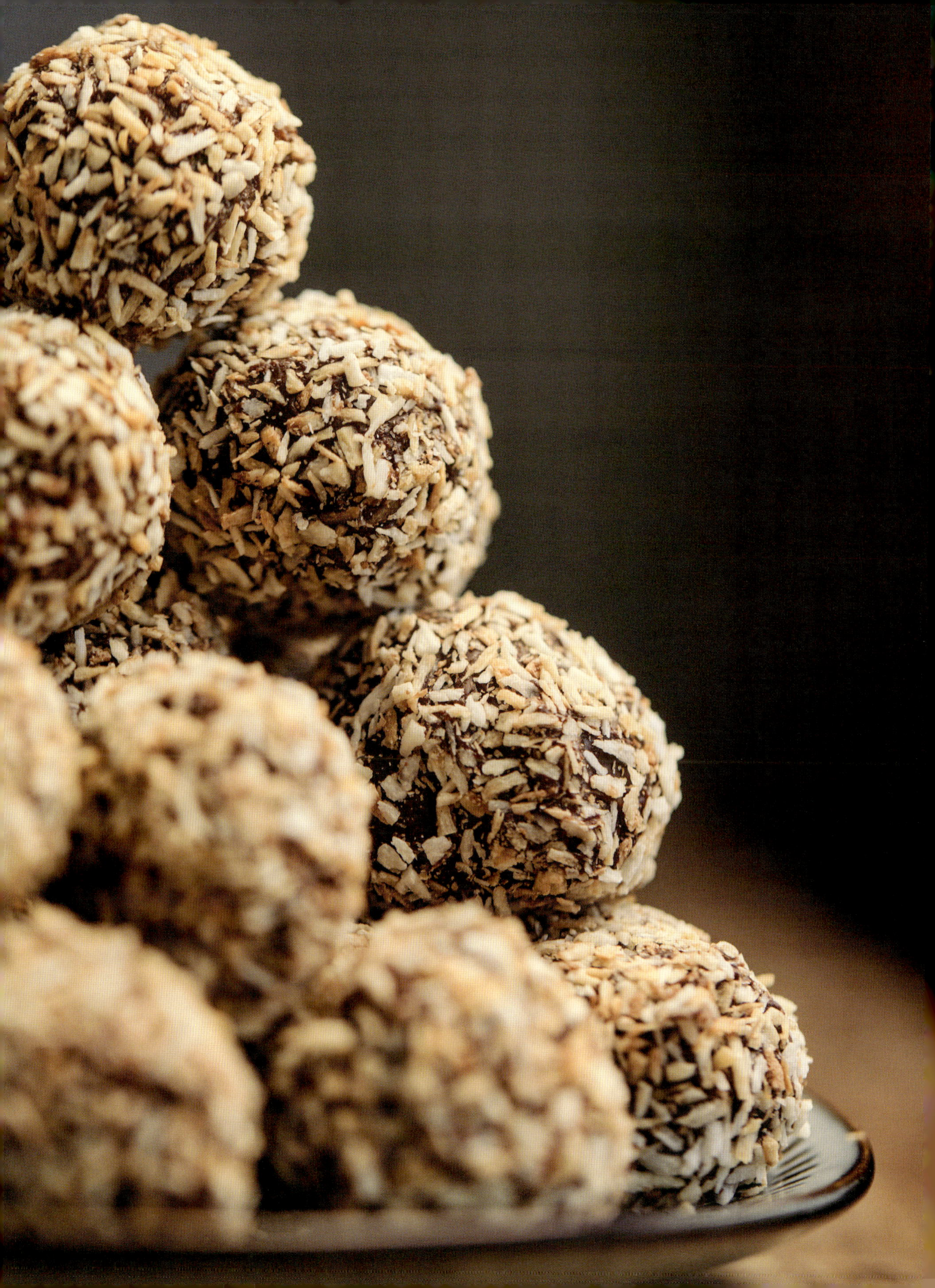

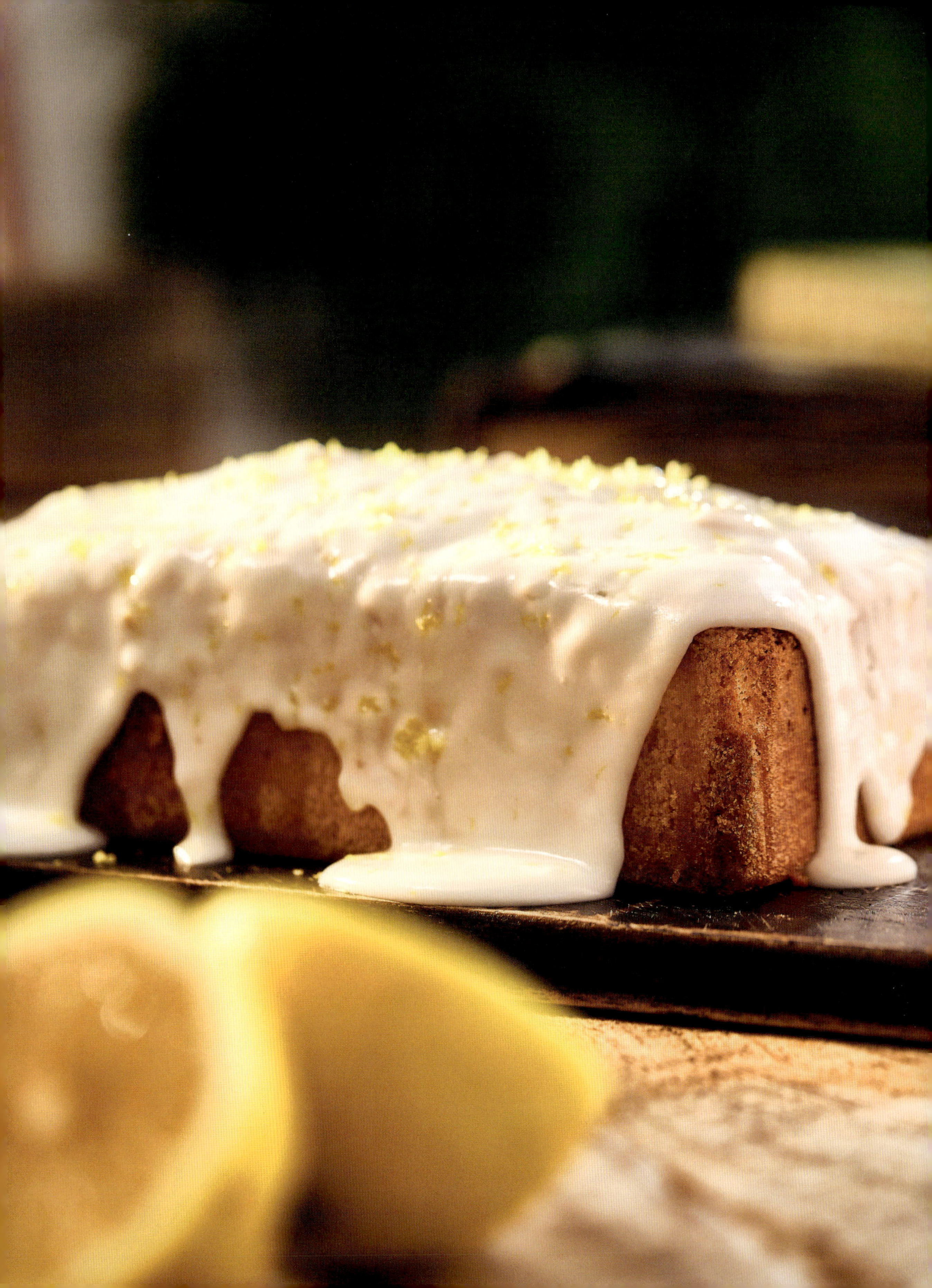

Iced Lemon Loaf

I've used this recipe for well over twenty years – it was a childhood recipe a French student called Cedric used to make, and it's one I've used umpteen times with my own children! It also works perfectly with gluten-free flour and a pinch of xanthan gum. It's best served with a giant mug of tea and a dollop of whipped cream, if you're so inclined.

MAKES 1 x 900G (2 LB) LOAF

340g plain flour
1½ tsp baking powder
125g butter, plus extra for greasing
300g caster sugar
5 medium eggs
zest of 1 lemon
125ml cream

FOR THE SYRUP

150g caster sugar
150ml water
juice of 1 lemon

FOR THE ICING

250g icing sugar
juice of 1 lemon

TO GARNISH

zest of 1 lemon

1. Preheat your oven to 160°C fan/180°C/gas 4. Grease a 900g (2 lb) loaf tin, and line as on page 112.
2. Sieve your flour and baking powder and set aside.
3. Using a hand-held or stand mixer, cream the butter and sugar until light, white and fluffy. Scrape down the bowl regularly.
4. While continuing to beat, add the eggs one by one, ensuring the mix returns to its light, fluffy consistency after each addition. This will take some time.
5. Using a spatula, gently fold in the sieved flour mix by hand, then follow this with the lemon zest and cream.
6. Scrape into the lined tin and bake for 50 minutes to 1 hour. Use a clean skewer to ensure the cake is fully baked through to the centre.
7. Meanwhile, to make the syrup, place all the ingredients in a small saucepan and bring to the boil, stirring occasionally. Remove from the heat and set aside.
8. When the cake is done, remove it from the oven, and while it is still in the tin, pierce it 8–10 times with a knife so the syrup soaks into the cake evenly. Pour the syrup over the surface, then leave to cool for an hour or so.
9. Run a palette knife around the sides of the cake to ensure it's not stuck. Turn the cake out of the tin, remove the parchment and place on a platter.
10. To make the icing, sieve the icing sugar into a bowl, and gradually add the lemon juice, stirring continuously until thick and creamy.
11. When the cake is completely cool, drizzle the icing over it, allowing it to flow down the sides. Sprinkle with the lemon zest to garnish.

Chocolate Chip Cookies

Who doesn't love a homemade chocolate chip cookie? They are a permanent fixture on our cafe counter – we bake them fresh daily. The smell of chocolate, brown sugar and vanilla is guaranteed to make your mouth water if you enter a kitchen where they are being baked. Prepare in advance, and wow your next batch of visitors!

MAKES 12 LARGE OR 24 SMALL

180g butter, at room temperature
190g demerara sugar
½ tsp vanilla extract
1 egg
270g plain flour, plus extra for rolling
½ tsp bicarbonate of soda, sieved
pinch of salt
180g dark chocolate chips
60g white chocolate chips

1. Using a hand-held or stand mixer, mix the butter and sugar on the lowest speed until smooth, scraping the bowl down regularly. Do not speed up! You just need to mix the butter and sugar evenly – you are not aerating it.
2. Add the vanilla, egg, flour, bicarbonate of soda, salt and chocolate chips, and mix on speed 1 until thoroughly mixed through.
3. Divide into 12 pieces for giant cookies, 7cm in diameter, or 24 pieces, depending on your preferred size. Roll into balls – you may need to use a little flour so they don't stick to your hands – then chill for at least an hour in the fridge. (The dough balls can be kept in the fridge for 2–3 days before baking if in a sealed container.)
4. Preheat the oven to 170°C fan/190°C/gas 5. Line two baking trays with parchment paper.
5. Place the chilled dough balls on the lined trays. The giant cookies need to be 5cm apart. The smaller ones need less space.
6. Place in the oven for 18 minutes, check, and rotate the tray if your oven bakes unevenly. The smaller size will take slightly less cooking time. The cookies should be a pale golden colour and lighter in the centre. This will give you a gooey/chewy centre.
7. Allow to cool on the trays. Once completely cooled, they will keep in a tin lined with parchment for a couple of days, if they last that long.

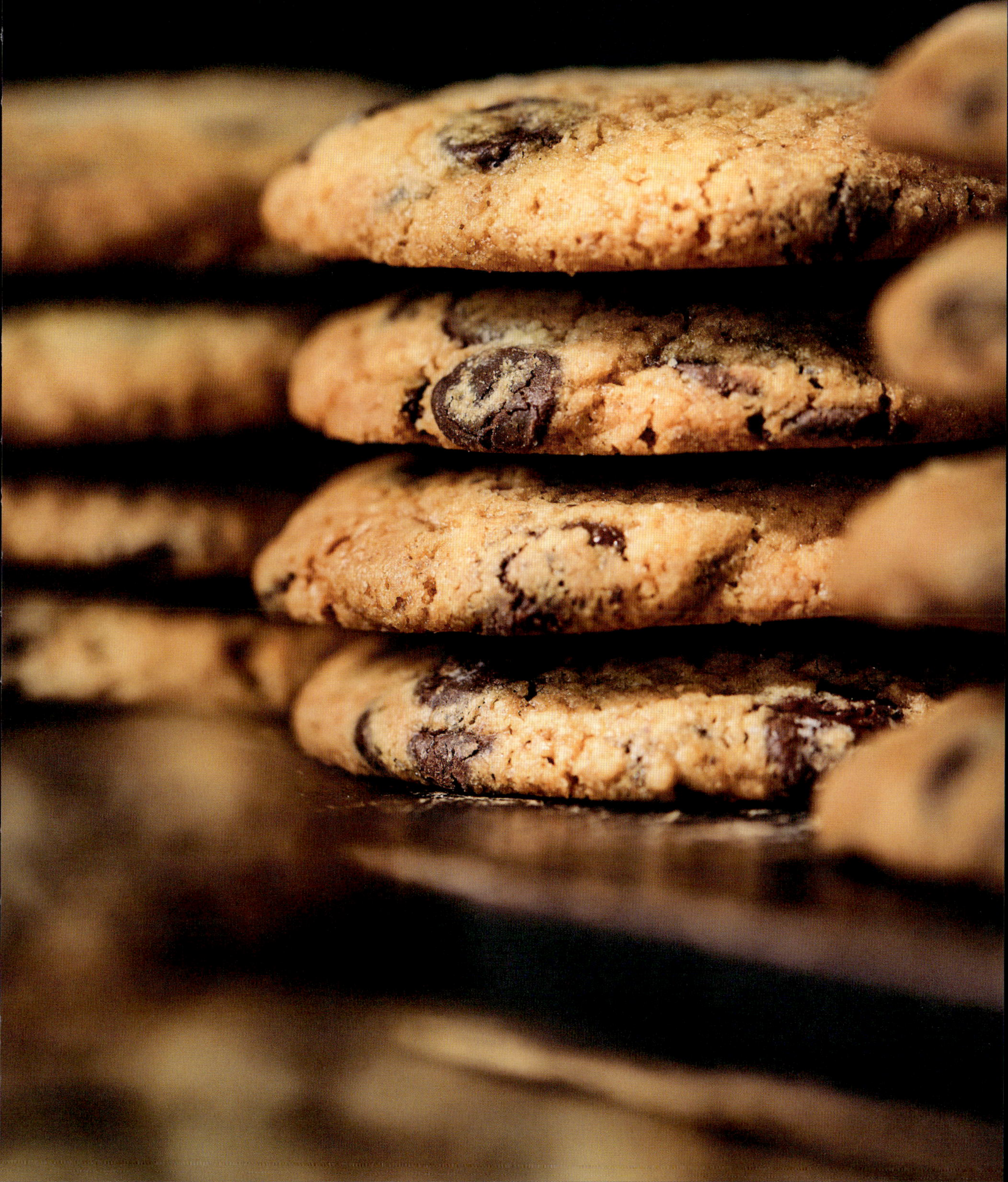

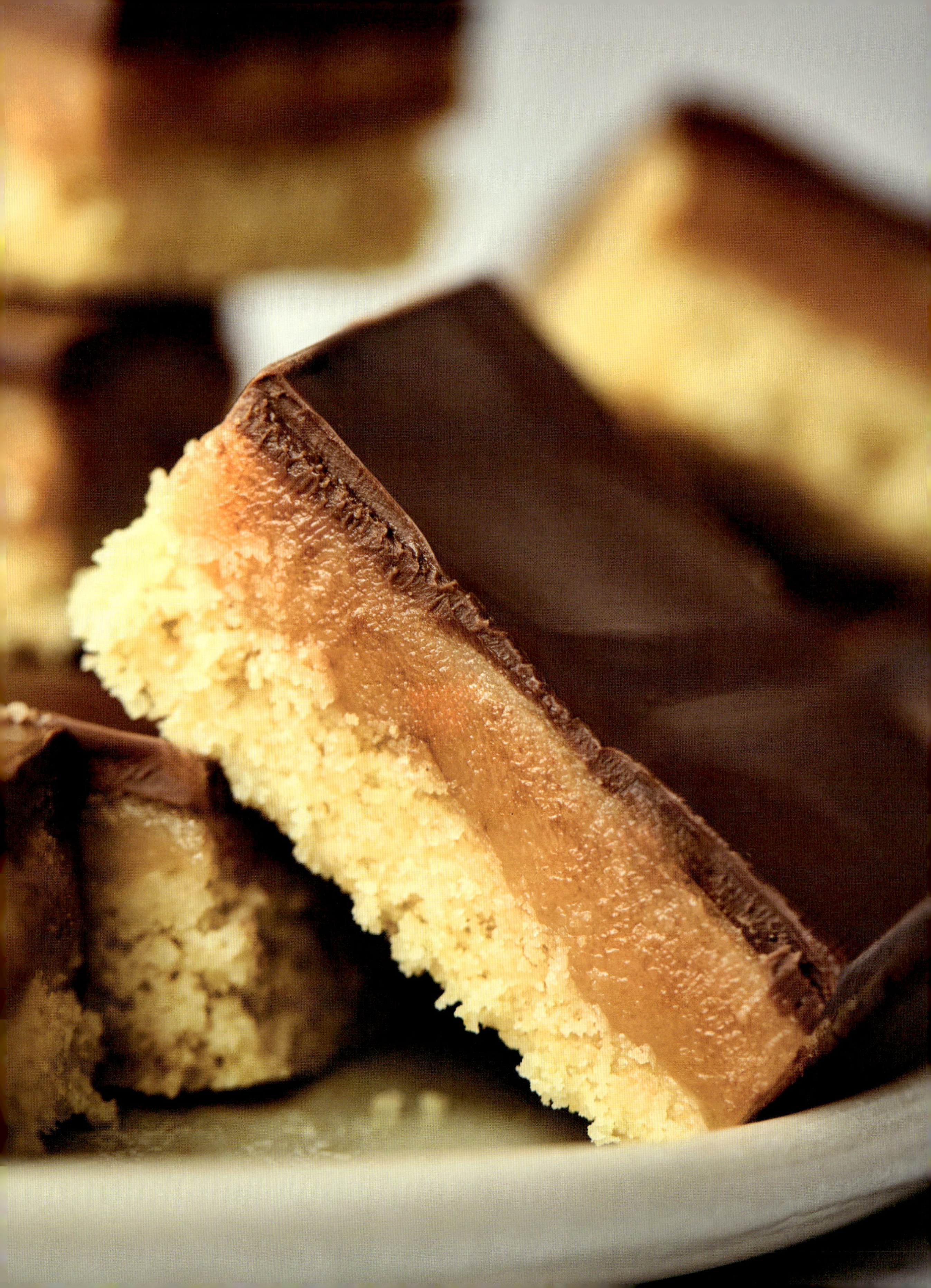

Gluten-Free Millionaire's Shortbread

These decadent slices are, as their name suggests, the definition of luxury. We make a gluten-free version in the cafe, but you can do either – just swap the GF flour for plain and drop the xanthan gum. This is a large batch, but it uses a full tin of condensed milk so you're not wasting or trying to find another use for the remainder. You can always gift or freeze half the batch!

MAKES 10 SLICES OR 20 SMALLER BITES

FOR THE BASE

225g butter
350g gluten-free flour
1 tsp xanthan gum
3 level tsp baking powder
110g caster sugar

FOR THE FILLING

225g caster sugar
225g butter
75g golden syrup
1 x 397g tin condensed milk

FOR THE TOPPING

135g milk chocolate
260g dark chocolate, around 55%

1. Preheat your oven to 160°C fan/180°C/gas 4. Grease and line a shallow rectangular baking tray, about 32 x 21cm. Cut a piece of parchment slightly larger than the tin. Using your scissors, cut a 6cm slit towards the centre from each corner. Place the paper in the tin, and it will sit perfectly.

2. To make the base, dice your butter into small pieces, then place all of the ingredients in a bowl for mixing. To do this by hand, rub the butter into the flour using the tips of your fingers until the mix resembles crumbs. You can also use a hand-held or stand mixer.

3. Press the crumb mix into the tray, using your hand or the back of a spoon. Ensure the mix is evenly distributed. Place in the oven and bake for 12 minutes only – do not overbake. It should not take too much colour and will have the appearance of shortbread. Place the tray on a rack to cool.

4. To make the filling, place all the ingredients in a heavy-based saucepan over a medium heat and stir continuously using a rubber heatproof spatula. The butter will melt, and the sugar will dissolve. Turn down the heat if it starts to catch, or take it off and return to the heat. Continue like this, stirring all the time, until the mix takes a light caramel colour.

5. Pour over the base immediately, scraping all the caramel mixture from the pot. Spread using a palette knife. Do not be tempted to dip a finger in – it is extremely hot! Allow to cool for 30 minutes at least.

CONTINUED OVERLEAF

SOMETHING SWEET

6. To make the topping, first chop the chocolate. Place in a microwave-safe bowl and melt on a low setting, stirring frequently. Or to use the water bath method instead, place the chocolate in a glass bowl over a saucepan of warm water on a low heat – the water should not touch the bowl. Stir frequently using a dry, clean spatula. Use a dry tea towel to lift off the bowl once the chocolate has melted, being careful of the escaping steam.
7. Pour your chocolate on top of the caramel layer, scraping the bowl clean. Using a palette knife, spread the chocolate evenly over the whole tray. Refrigerate for 3 hours at least or overnight.
8. Lift the shortbread out of the tray and onto a chopping board. For clean cuts, heat the blade of your chopping knife under a hot tap, quickly wipe it dry with kitchen paper, then slice your shortbread, first lengthways and then across. Repeat the heating of the blade between each cut.
9. These freeze well or will keep in the fridge in an airtight container for up to 2 weeks between layers of parchment.

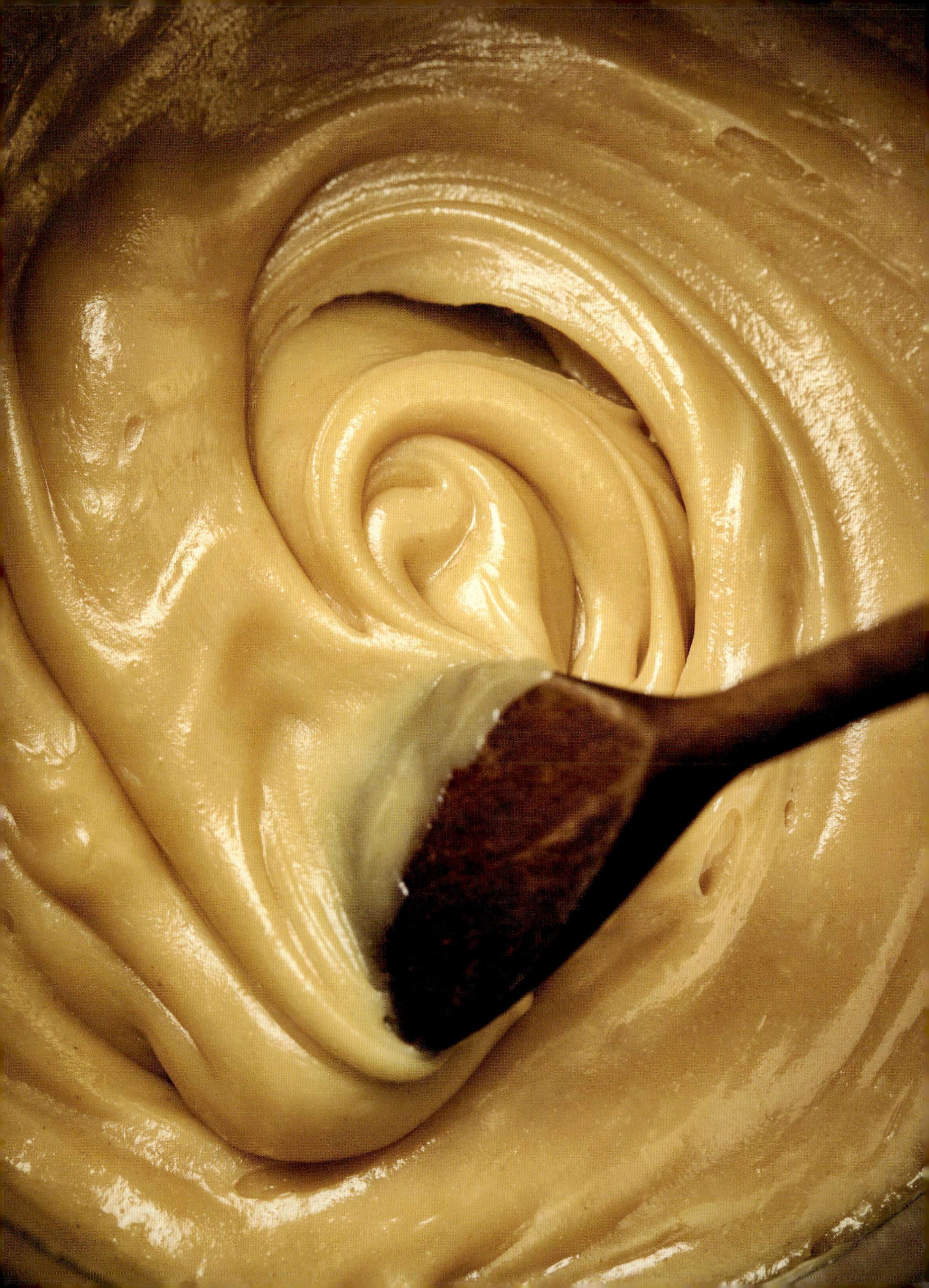

Rich Fruit Loaf Cake

A good fruit cake is not just for Christmas. This is the type you would keep for a month, rather than ageing it like a Christmas cake before icing or eating. I like to leave it five days or so before slicing, but it can be eaten once cooled. It's a lovely gift and pretty simple to make!

MAKES 1 X 900G (2 LB) LOAF

FOR THE FRUIT MIX

65g dates
15g glacé cherries
115g butter, plus extra for greasing
115g dark soft brown sugar
100g raisins
100g sultanas
15g mixed peel
110ml orange juice
zest of 1 orange
25g treacle

FOR THE CAKE

140g plain flour
1 tsp baking powder
1 tsp ground cinnamon
½ tsp mixed spice
30ml vegetable oil
2 eggs
30g flaked almonds

FOR THE GLAZE

50ml water
50g sugar

TO DECORATE (OPTIONAL)

Dehydrated orange slices (see page 174)

1. Chop the dates into small pieces the size of the raisins. Cut the cherries in quarters.
2. Add all the ingredients for the fruit mix into a saucepan, and place on a medium heat. Using a heatproof spatula, stir continuously until the butter has melted and the sugar has dissolved. If the mix is starting to catch, lower the heat.
3. Continue to stir over the heat until the fruit has softened – another minute or so.
4. Remove from the heat, scrape into a mixing bowl and allow to cool.
5. Preheat your oven to 140°C fan/160°C/gas 3. Thoroughly grease a 900g (2 lb) loaf tin, using a pastry brush and soft butter. Cut 2 strips of parchment paper – one narrow, to run lengthways, and another to go side to side. The paper must reach all the way up the sides of the tin. (Alternatively, use a loaf tin liner.)
6. Sieve the flour, baking powder and spices together. Then whisk the oil and eggs together.
7. Take your bowl of cooled fruit mix and, using a rubber spatula, stir in the egg and oil mix. Gently fold in the dry ingredients and the almonds, making sure the spatula scrapes the bottom of the bowl each time. Once everything is combined, scoop the mix into the loaf tin, scraping the bowl fully with the spatula. Completely cover the tin, over and under, using 2 sheets of tin foil.

CONTINUED OVERLEAF

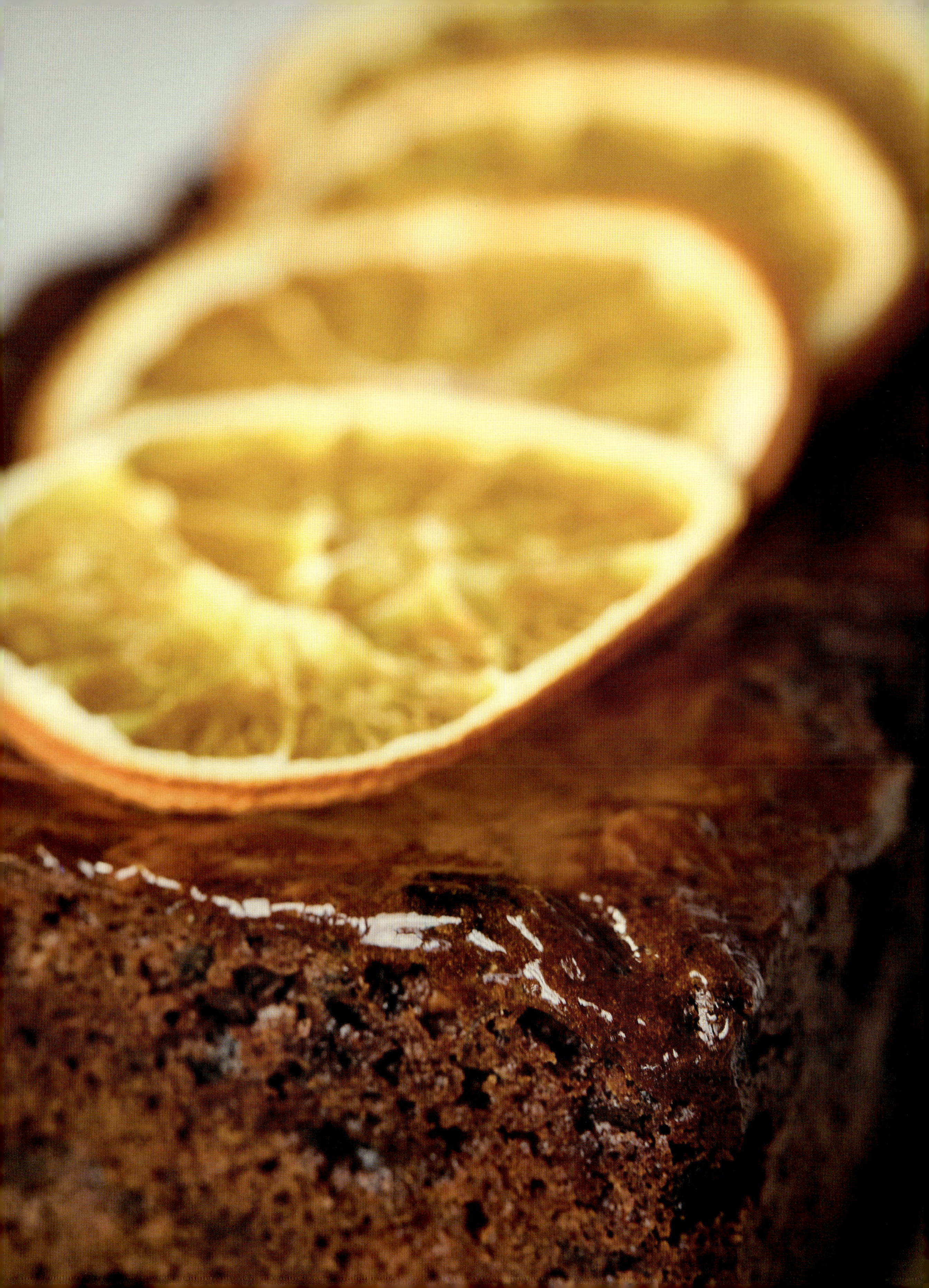

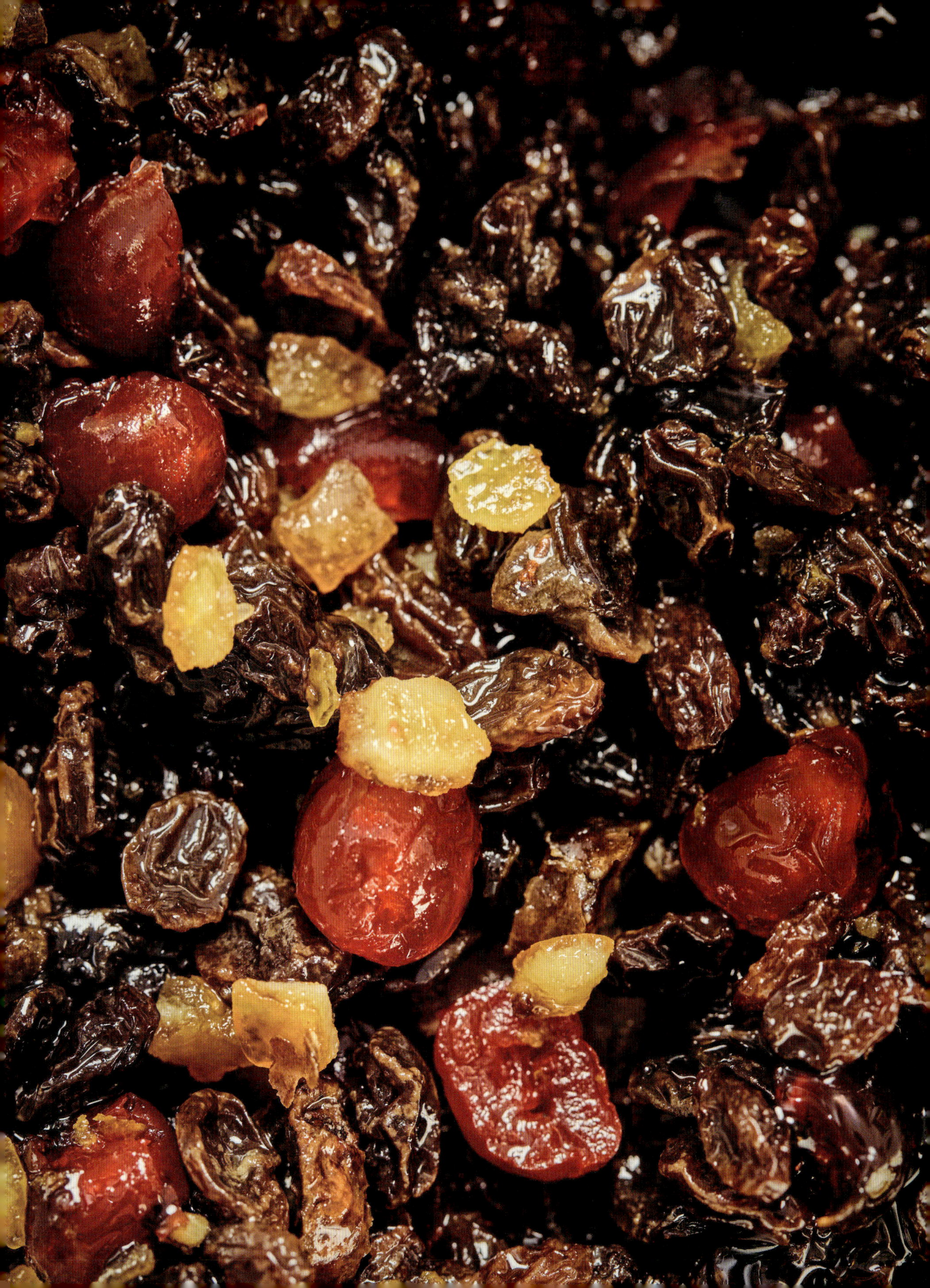

8. Place in the oven and bake for 1 hour and 10 minutes before removing the foil and placing back in the oven for a further 15–20 minutes. Check the loaf is baked through by piercing with a skewer – if it comes out clean, it's done. Otherwise return it to the oven for a further 5 minutes, then repeat the check.

9. While the cake is finishing baking, make the glaze. Put the water and sugar in a small saucepan and bring to the boil – the sugar will dissolve and form a syrup. Turn off the heat.

10. When the cake is fully baked, place it on a wire rack and brush with the glaze while both are hot. Do not re-brush any area – just quickly brush the whole cake once. Decorate with some dehydrated orange slices, if using, then leave for at least 6 hours to cool.

11. Once the cake is fully cooled, run a palette knife around the edges, right down to the bottom of the tin. Turn the tin over, tap it on the counter and the cake should pop out. Wrap in parchment paper and store in a cake tin. I prefer to leave fruit cakes for at least 4 days before slicing.

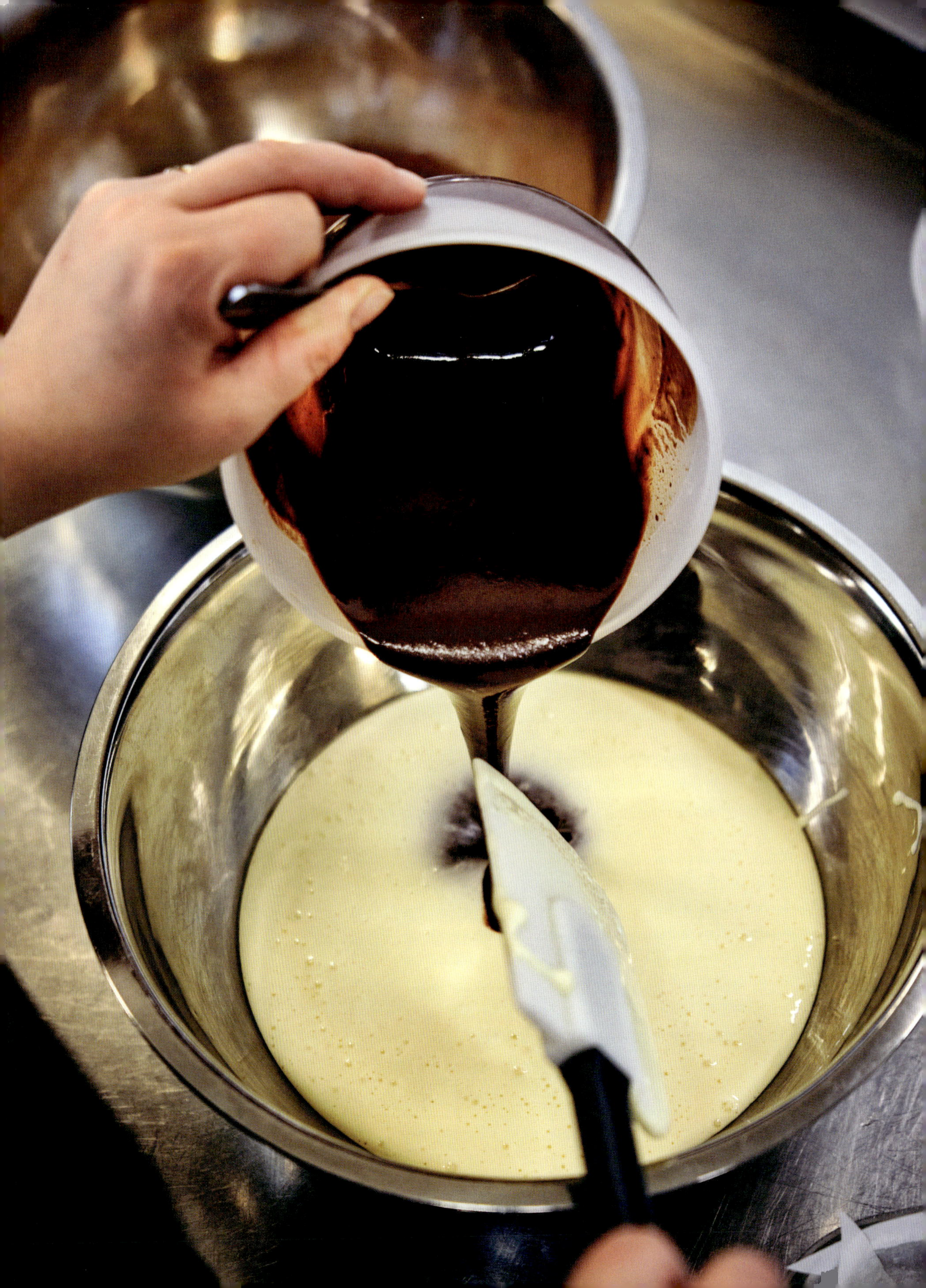

Chocolate Brownies

I've made both gluten-free and regular versions of these many times: they are divine. If you're bringing something to a party where there is already a cake, this is your recipe.

MAKES 9 OR 18

180g butter
180g dark chocolate, 54–70%
50g white chocolate
50g milk chocolate
270g caster sugar
3 eggs
80g plain flour (GF or regular)
40g cocoa powder

1. Dice the butter and chop the dark chocolate. Place in a microwave-safe bowl and melt on a low setting, stirring frequently. Or to use the water-bath method instead, place the chocolate in a glass bowl over a saucepan of warm water on a low heat – the water should not touch the bowl. Stir frequently using a dry, clean spatula. Use a dry tea towel to lift off the bowl once the chocolate and butter have melted, being careful of the escaping steam. Leave to cool to room temperature.
2. Preheat your oven to 160°C fan/180°C/gas 4. Grease a shallow 20cm square tin. Then line it by cutting a piece of parchment slightly larger than the tin. Next cut a 6cm slit towards the centre from each corner. Place the paper in your tin, and it will sit perfectly.
3. Chop your white and milk chocolate into small bite-sized pieces.
4. Place the caster sugar and eggs in a mixing bowl and whisk on top speed. The mix should double in size and be thick and a pale creamy colour. If you lift the whisk, the mix which runs off should leave a ribbon trail on the surface for a second or two.
5. Pour in the cooled chocolate mix and gently fold together with a rubber spatula, scraping the bottom of the bowl each time, going under and over the mix in a figure-of-eight motion.
6. When it's mostly blended, sieve the flour and cocoa powder directly into it. Fold again as above. When it's almost completely mixed in, add the chocolate pieces, give it one or two more folds, then scrape into the lined tin.
7. Bake for 25 minutes. If it's wobbly in the middle, bake for a further 5 and recheck. The sides should be just pulling away from the tin and the top should be shiny and crunchy.
8. Leave to cool completely, then slide out of the tin and cut into 9 squares or 18 triangles.
9. Keeps in an airtight tin for a week and also freezes well.

Apple Bakewell Slices

Bakewell tart is a classic, and this is our take on it. We change the fruit with the season but mostly keep it to apples, which are a delicious, sharp contrast to the sweet frangipane. Raspberries also work well.

MAKES 10 SLICES

FOR THE SWEET PASTRY

100g butter

50g caster sugar

1 egg

20ml cold water

210g plain flour

FOR THE FRANGIPANE

285g butter

285g sugar

4 eggs

30g plain flour

285g ground almonds

FOR THE FILLING

2 heaped tbsp strawberry jam

3-4 Bramley cooking apples

2 tsp ground cinnamon

4 tbsp caster sugar

FOR THE GLAZE (OPTIONAL)

2 heaped tbsp apricot jam

few drops of water

FOR THE SWEET PASTRY

1. Using a hand-held or stand mixer, beat the butter and sugar until well mixed and creamy.
2. Add the remaining ingredients and mix on the lowest speed until it comes together.
3. Remove the pastry from the bowl and knead gently on a very lightly floured surface until it's smooth and forms a ball. Wrap in cling film or place in a sealed container (a plastic or glass lunchbox) and pop in the fridge for half an hour.
4. Preheat your oven to 160°C fan/180°C/gas 4. Grease a 32 x 21cm tin, then line by cutting 2 strips of parchment paper – one to run lengthways, and another to go side to side. The paper must reach all the way up the sides of the tin.
5. Lightly flour your rolling surface and rolling pin. Roll out your pastry to a rectangular shape slightly bigger than the tin and about 3mm thick. Only roll in one direction, back and forward, never side to side – turn the pastry rather than the rolling pin.
6. Roll the pastry back over the rolling pin to help lift it over the tart tin. Gently sit the pastry into the tin; then, using your thumbs, press it all the way round into the sides of the tin. The pastry should be falling over the edge of the tin and will be rough around the edges, which is fine. Place in the freezer for an hour.

FOR THE FRANGIPANE AND FILLING

7. Meanwhile, to make the frangipane, cream the butter and sugar together using a hand-held or stand mixer until it becomes light and fluffy and paler in colour – this could take 5 minutes. Scrape the bowl down several times during this process.

CONTINUED OVERLEAF

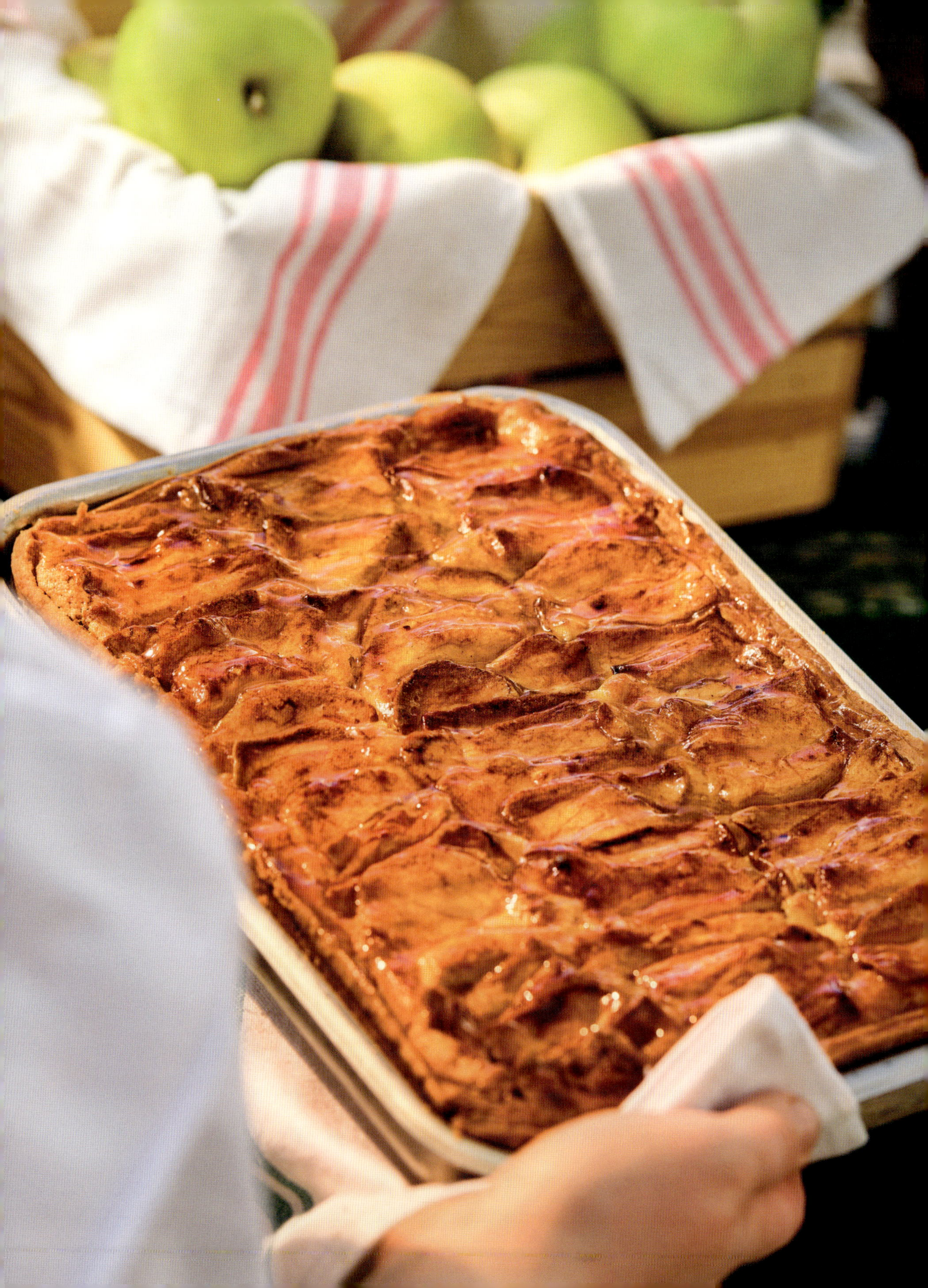

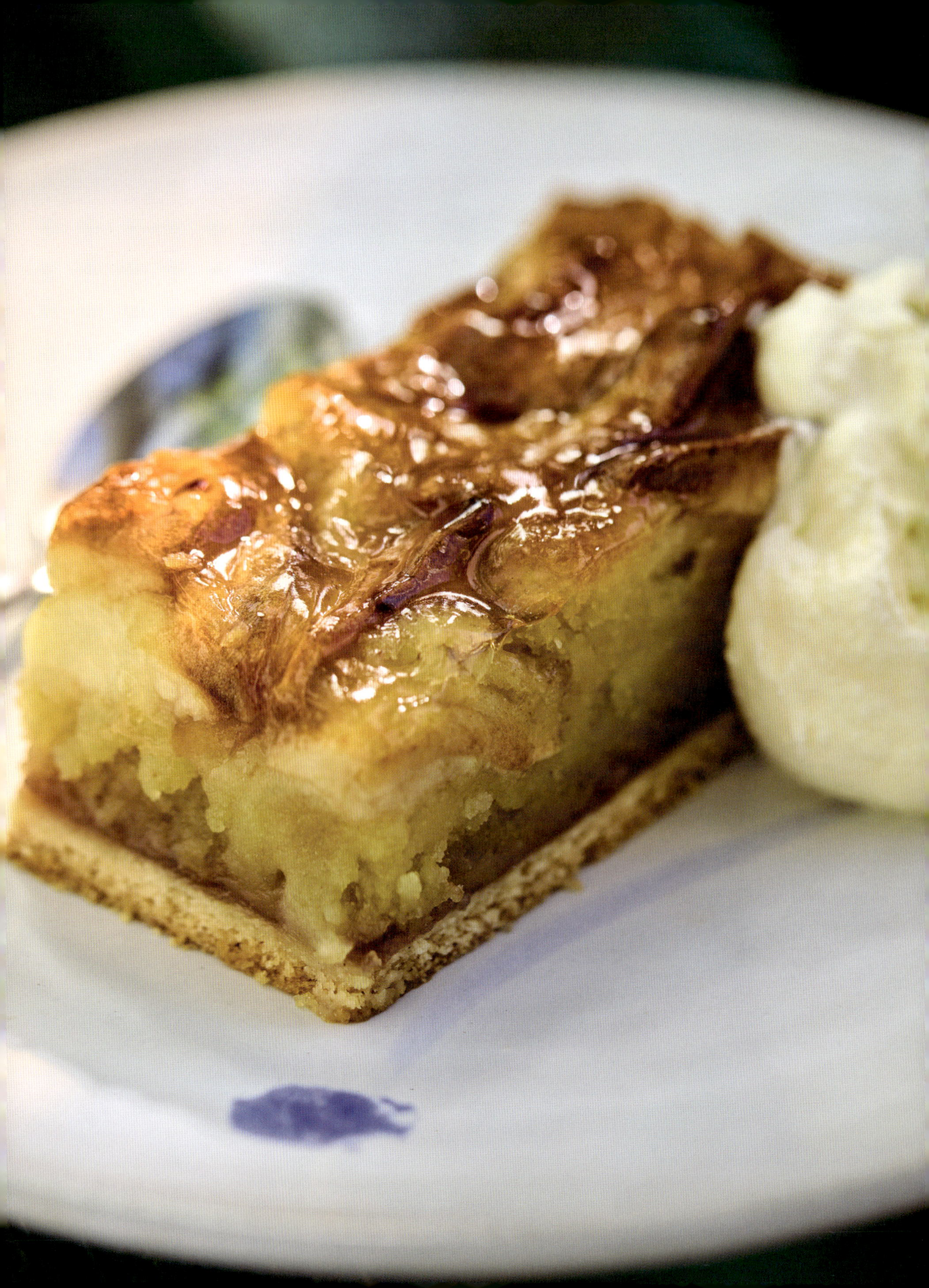

8. Add the eggs one by one, mixing up to that fluffy texture after each addition – don't rush this process. Once they are all in, add the flour and almonds and slowly mix until they are incorporated.
9. Take out your tart base and spread the strawberry jam over it, leaving 1cm free all around the bottom. Scoop your frangipane into the base and spread evenly with a palette knife. Trim the excess pastry from the edges. Pop in the fridge while you do the next part.
10. Preheat the oven to 150°C fan/170°C/gas 3.
11. Wash, peel and core the apples, then cut in half and slice lengthways, about 3mm thick. Toss the slices in the cinnamon and sugar, then arrange on top of the frangipane in a fan style, overlapping each slice.
12. Pop the tart in the oven and bake for 45 minutes. To check, wobble the tin: the centre should be set and firm to touch and the apples golden brown.
13. When the bake has cooled, run a knife around the sides of the tart to ensure it's not sticking anywhere. Using the edge of the parchment paper, slide the Bakewell out onto a chopping board.
14. To glaze the tart, place your apricot jam and a couple of teaspoons of water in a saucepan over a medium heat, and allow to dissolve – the mix should be syrup-like. Strain to remove any bits. Using a pastry brush, lightly brush the syrup over the tart – do not re-brush any area, as the glaze will just become sticky and lose its shine.
15. Using a clean, sharp knife, slice your Bakewell lengthways down the centre. Clean your blade and slice each half into 5 or more pieces.
16. Serve with whipped cream or ice cream. Store in a cool, dry place in a lined sealed tin or plastic container. It will keep well at room temperature for 5 days or can be frozen.

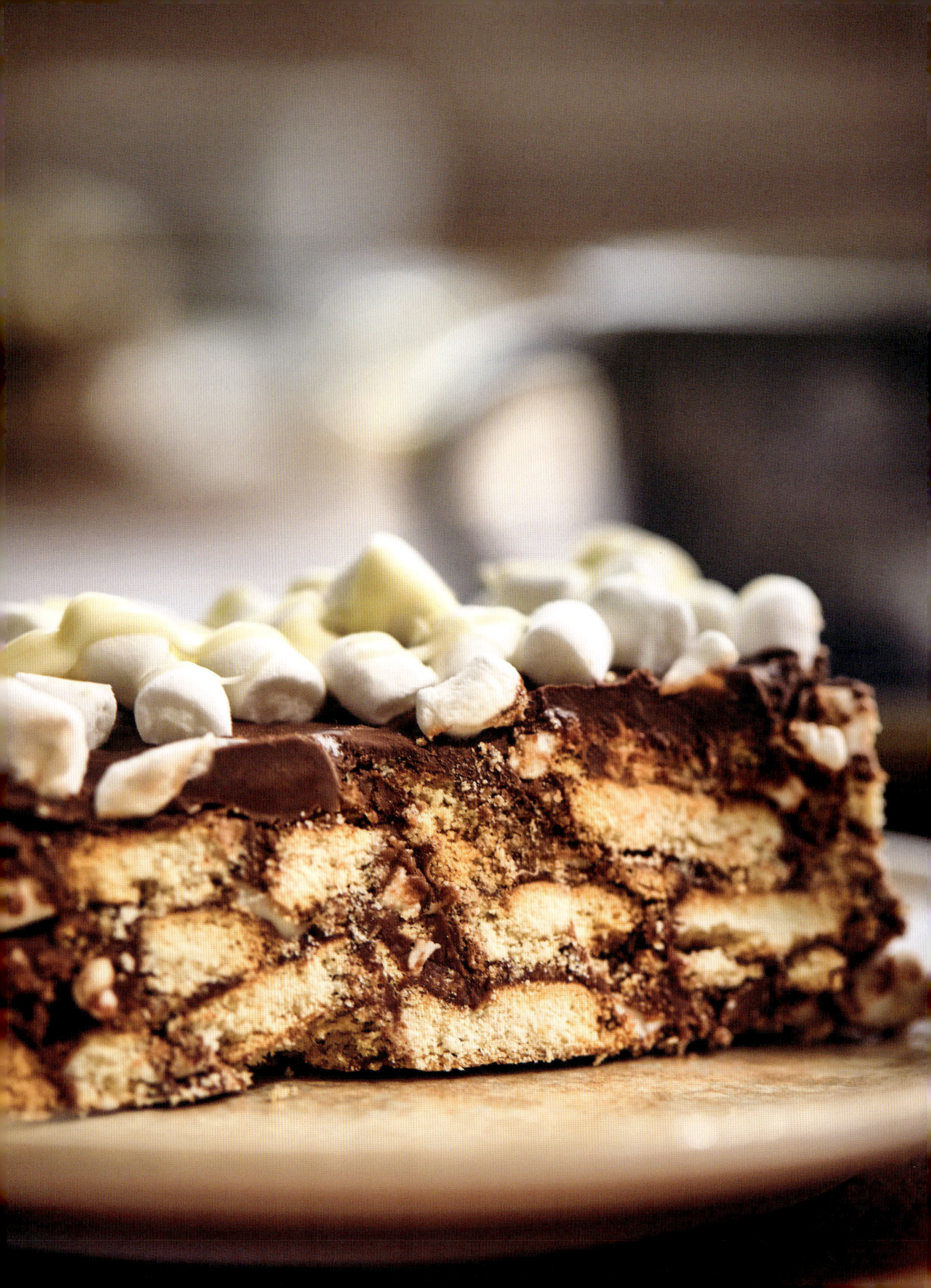

Rocky Road

This is always a hit when we have it on the counter. I have made countless wedding and birthday cakes with this recipe, and it's great to bring to a party or school cake sale. It's simple, as there's no baking involved. The key is to allow it to set completely before slicing or icing.

MAKES 15 SLICES

FOR THE BASE

100g butter, plus extra for greasing
200g milk chocolate
100g dark chocolate, at least 55%
375g biscuits (I use a mix of digestive and rich tea)
397g tin condensed milk
70g mini marshmallows

FOR THE TOPPING

160g milk chocolate
60g dark chocolate, at least 55%
30g mini marshmallows

1. Grease a 32 x 21cm tin or casserole dish. Cut a piece of parchment paper slightly larger than the tin. Using your scissors make a 6cm cut towards the centre from each corner. When you place it in your tin, the paper will sit perfectly into it.
2. To make the base, dice the butter and chop the two types of chocolate into pieces. Place in a microwave-safe bowl and melt on a low setting, stirring frequently. (Or to use the water-bath method instead, see page 124.) Leave aside to cool slightly.
3. Meanwhile, place the biscuits in a freezer bag, close it and crush them by rolling a rolling pin over the bag a few times. Don't overdo it – you want some big chunks, not crumbs.
4. Pour the condensed milk into the melted chocolate mix and stir well using a rubber spatula.
5. Add the crushed biscuits and marshmallows, and mix well. Scoop into the tray and press until evenly distributed.
6. To make the topping, chop and melt your chocolate as you did with the butter and chocolate earlier.
7. Pour it over the base and spread quickly using your palette knife. Sprinkle with the mini marshmallows. Refrigerate for 4 hours or so until completely set.
8. Lift it out of the tray and onto a chopping board. For clean cuts, heat the blade of your chopping knife under a hot tap, quickly wipe it dry with kitchen paper, then slice the rocky road, first lengthways and then across. Repeat the heating of the blade between each cut.
9. These will keep for 2 weeks stored in a cool, dry place in a tin or sealed container between layers of parchment.

Peanut Butter and White Chocolate Powerballs

This is a more luxurious version of its date, coconut and dark chocolate sister (page 102). The white chocolate coating makes them seem more decadent. They're also easier and can be made without a blender.

MAKES ABOUT 20

FOR THE POWERBALLS

120g ground almonds

375g peanut butter

200g desiccated coconut

115ml maple syrup or honey

FOR THE COATING

125g good-quality white chocolate

100–140g desiccated coconut

10g chopped pistachios (optional

1. Mix all the ingredients for the powerballs together. Divide into about 20 pieces and roll into balls. Place in the fridge to chill.
2. To make the coating, first break the white chocolate into pieces. Place in a microwave-safe bowl and melt on a low setting, stirring frequently. Or to use the water-bath method instead, place the chocolate in a glass bowl over a saucepan of warm water on a low heat – the water should not touch the bowl. Stir frequently using a dry, clean spatula. It takes very little heat to melt white chocolate, and it burns easily so watch it carefully. Use a dry tea towel to lift off the bowl once the chocolate has melted, being careful of the escaping steam.
3. Place the coconut on a flat tray.
4. Roll the balls in the melted chocolate using the tips of your fingers – disposable gloves are essential here.
5. Pop each ball onto the tray with the coconut coating, roll gently till well covered, then place on a clean platter. Refrigerate until set (at least 30 minutes) and enjoy!

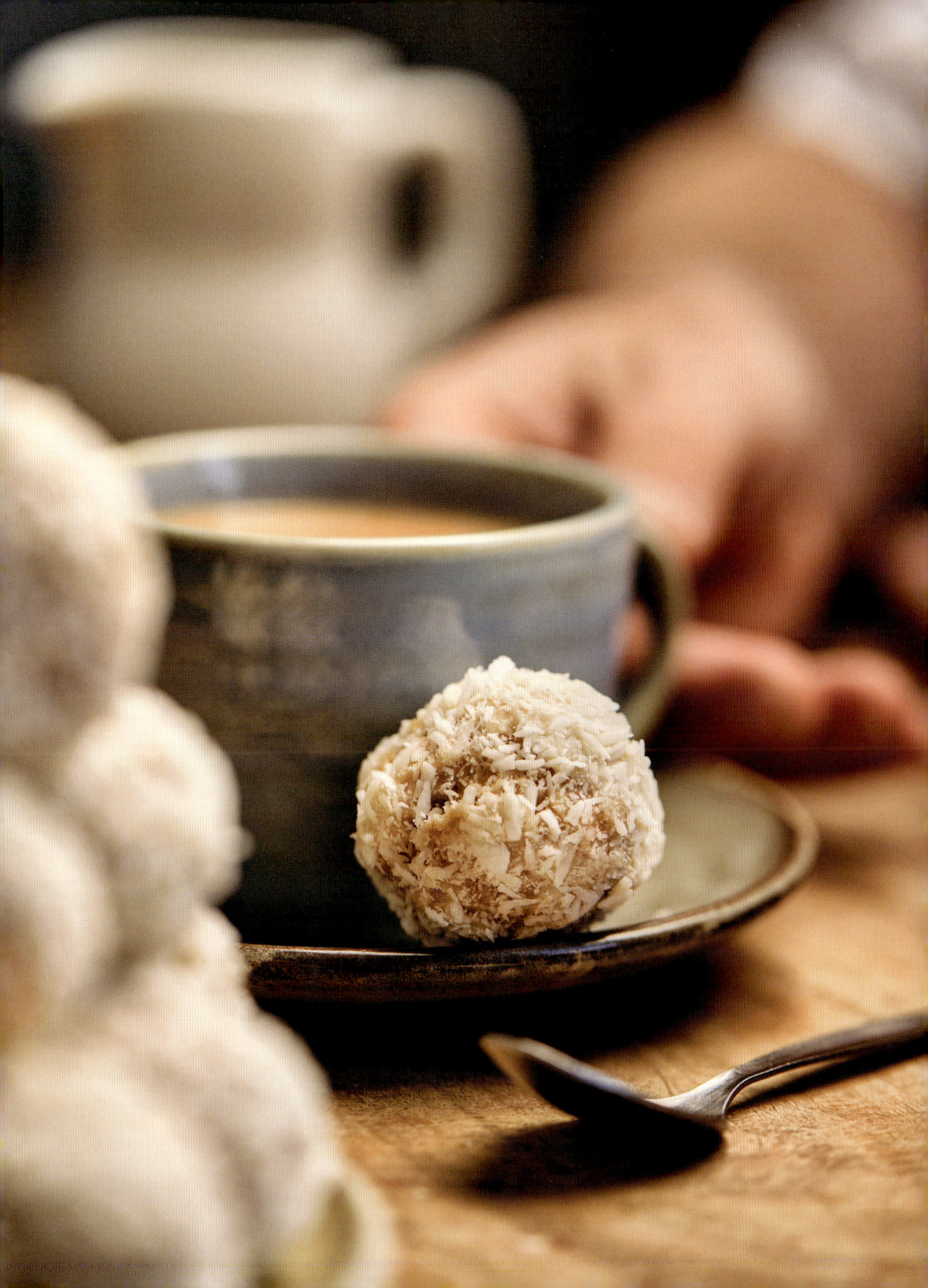

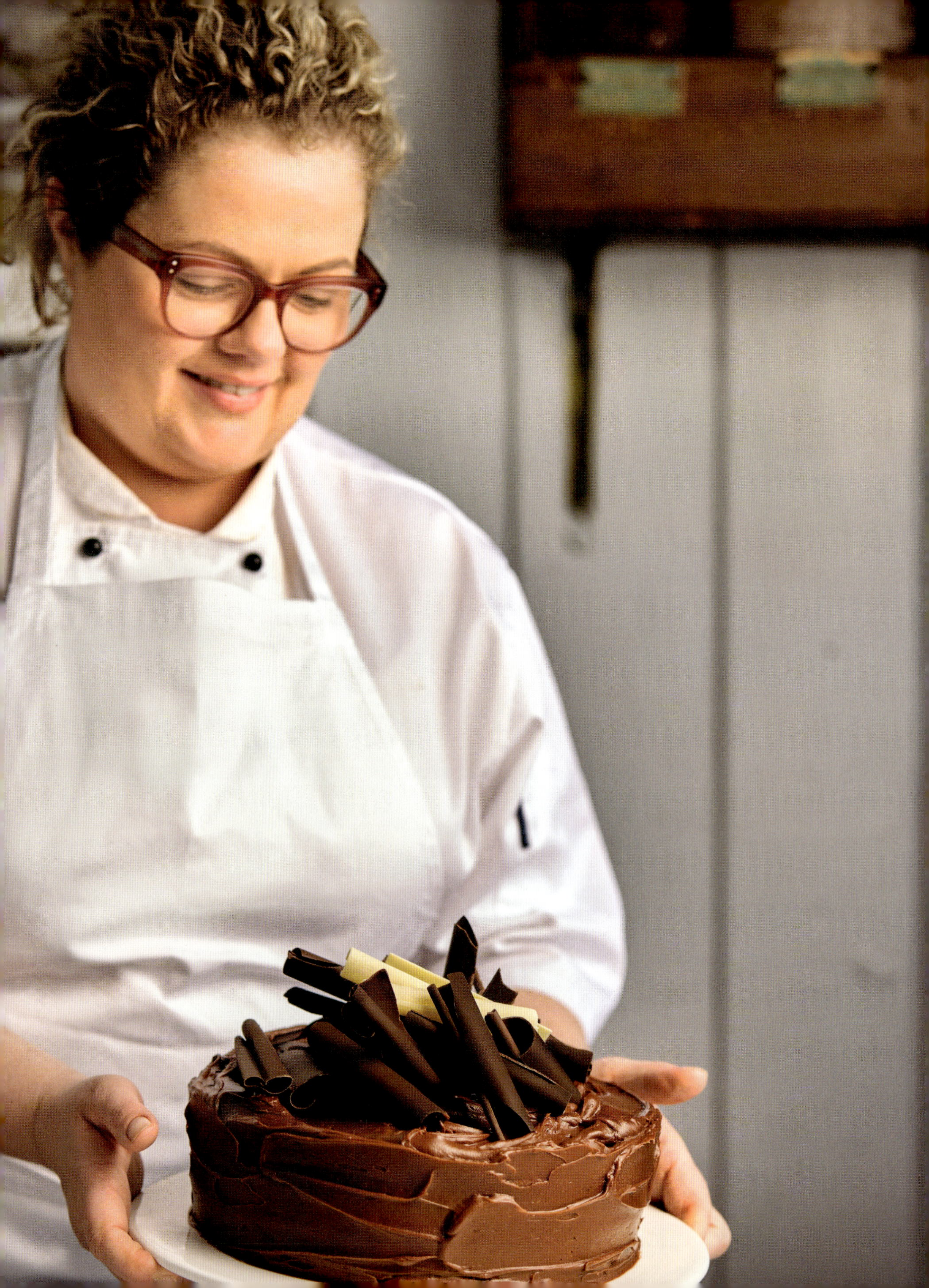

CAKES AND TARTS

This section is all about creating that showstopper, Sunday-lunch dessert or special-occasion treat. Cakes or tarts seem like a lot of effort, but many can be simplified by making a part the previous day. If you're planning to serve the cheesecake, for example, you can make it the day before, refrigerate it and then garnish it just before your event. Tarts are a great way to finish a meal, as they are often lighter than a cake, so bake whatever suits your occasion.

Leaving your cake to cool properly before icing it is essential. Icing takes practice – it's an art all of its own. The internet is full of tips and tricks you can use, often provided by those who have the skills and equipment to make it look easy, right down to the professionally staged images. Your humble attempt at home may taste far better, and family and friends will appreciate your efforts!

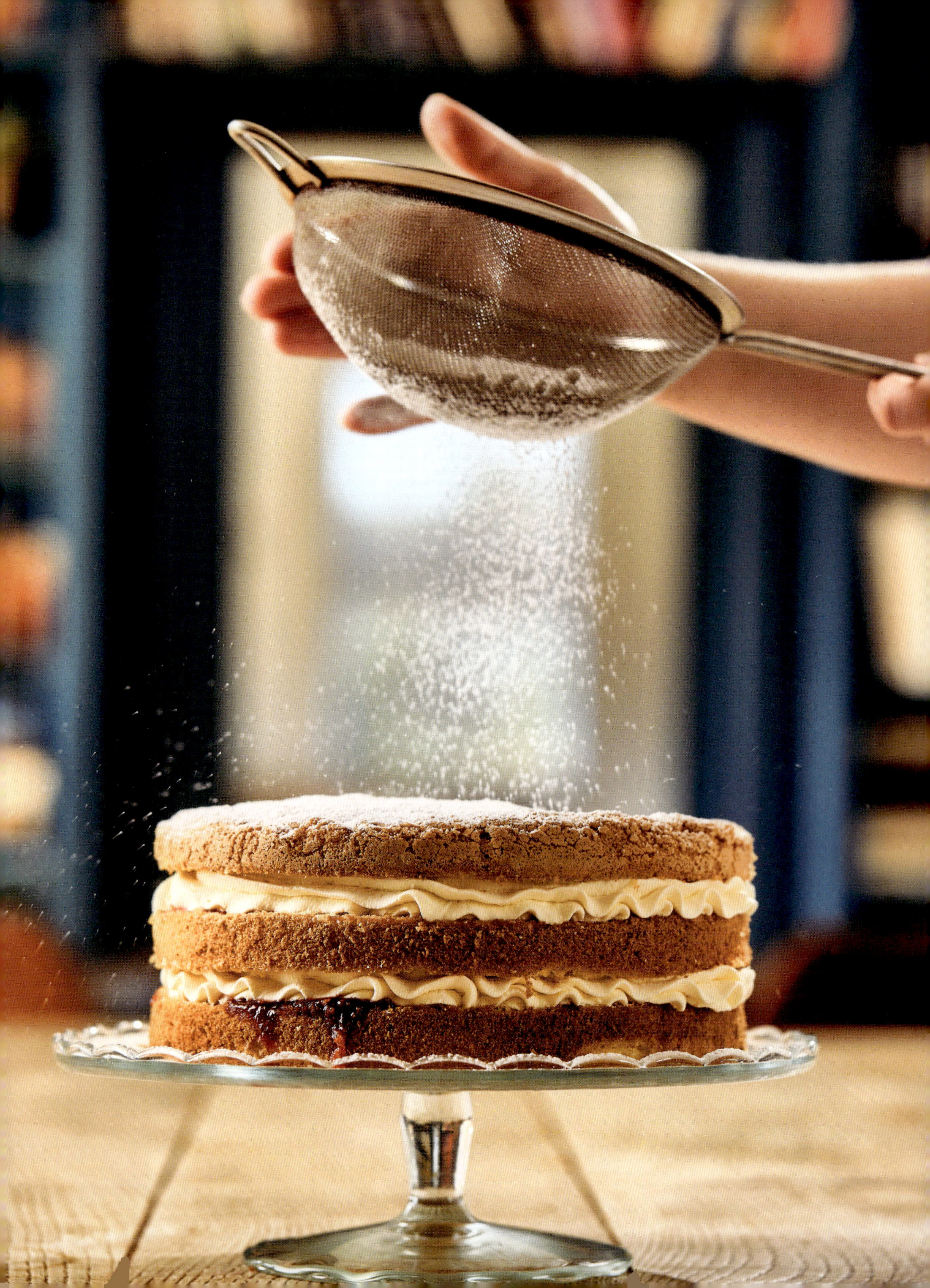

Simple Sponge Cake

This is without doubt our bestselling cake. Some cakes have their moment and it passes, but this one is always there. We layer it with our bestselling rhubarb and strawberry jam and freshly whipped cream. It's everything a sponge should be: light, airy, fluffy and fuss-free. I have made this at home using gluten-free flour and a pinch of xanthan gum, and it is divine also.

SERVES 10

butter, for greasing
200g caster sugar
6 eggs
200g plain flour
300ml fresh cream
250g rhubarb and strawberry jam (page 166) or jam of your choice
50g icing sugar, for dusting

1. Ensure your mixing bowl is well cleaned (no grease) and completely dry.
2. Preheat your oven to 160°C fan/180°C/gas 4. Grease a 23cm loose-bottomed cake tin well, and line the base with a disc of parchment paper.
3. Whisk the caster sugar and eggs on top speed using a hand-held or stand mixer until the mixture doubles in size and is thick and a pale creamy colour. If you lift the whisk, the mix that runs off should leave a ribbon trail on the surface of the mix for a second or two. This will take about 3–8 minutes, depending on the speed and type of your mixer. Give it more rather than less time if you're in doubt. This cake relies on mechanical aeration (whisking), not chemical (no baking powder), so be careful not to bang the bowl when moving it.
4. Hold your sieve filled with flour over the mixing bowl and sieve the flour directly into the egg mix. Gently fold it in by hand, using a large rubber spatula, scraping the bottom of the bowl each time, going under and over the mix in a figure-of-eight motion. Go slowly so you don't knock out all that air. When all the flour is incorporated, gently pour the mix into the cake tin. It will naturally settle.
5. Bake for 35–40 minutes. When pierced with a skewer, it should come out clean, and the cake should have pulled away from the edge of the tin.
6. Place on a wire rack to completely cool. This will take a few hours.

CONTINUED OVERLEAF

7. When the sponge has cooled completely, run a palette knife around the edge of the tin to ensure it hasn't stuck. Lift it out using the loose-bottomed base.
8. Slice the sponge in three horizontally, using a sharp serrated knife.
9. Whip your cream to stiff peaks.
10. Pop the bottom layer of sponge on a cake stand or plate, slather with half of the jam, using a palette knife to spread it and leaving 2cm free around the edge. Spread or pipe half the cream on top of the jam in the same way. Pop on the middle layer of sponge, press lightly, and repeat the jam and cream layers. Pop the top of the cake on, and press lightly – cream and jam should be just peeking out between the layers.
11. Sieve the icing sugar on top and serve.

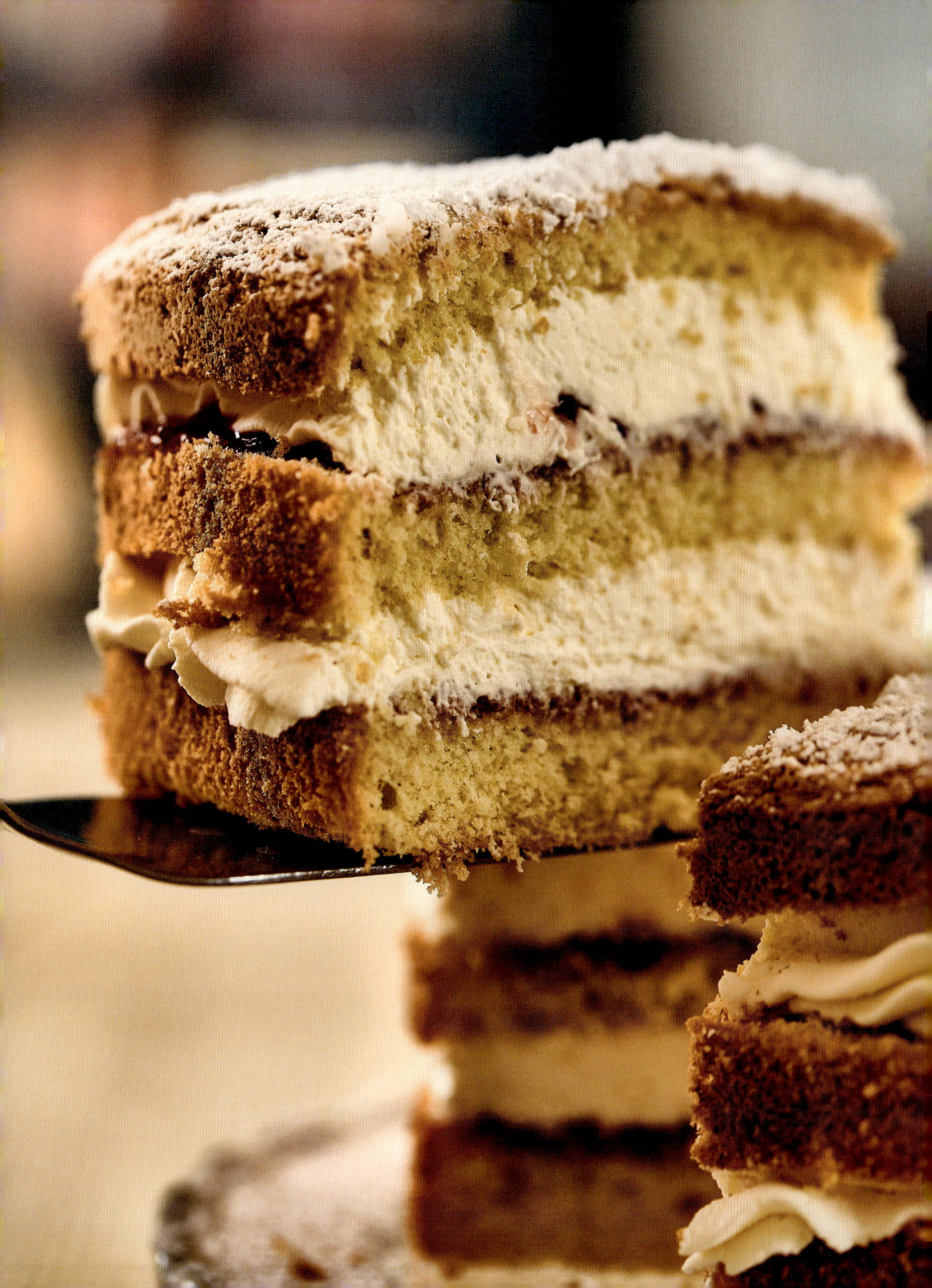

Maple and Pecan Pie

This pie is sweet, nutty and crunchy, with a great texture. Always use real Canadian maple syrup, as the alternatives are just flavoured sugar syrups and your tart will be way too sweet and lack any real depth. Serve with whipped cream.

SERVES 8–10

1 x 28cm sweet pastry case, baked and cooled (page 153)
50g butter
3 eggs
200g soft dark brown sugar
½ tsp vanilla extract
200ml maple syrup
250g whole pecans

1. Preheat your oven to 140°C fan/160°C/gas 3.
2. Melt your butter over a low heat or in the microwave.
3. Using a hand whisk, whisk your eggs, then add the sugar, vanilla and maple syrup, followed by the melted butter, and whisk until combined.
4. Place your sweet pastry base on a tray. Sprinkle the whole pecans on the base and carefully pour in the mix. Make sure the pecans are evenly scattered.
5. Bake for 40–45 minutes, until the mix has set, then allow to cool completely.
6. When the tart has cooled, use a sharp knife to trim off the excess pastry, then lift it out of the tin using the loose base.
7. Using a palette knife or large chopping knife, slide the tart off the base onto a flat plate or cake stand. Slice and serve.

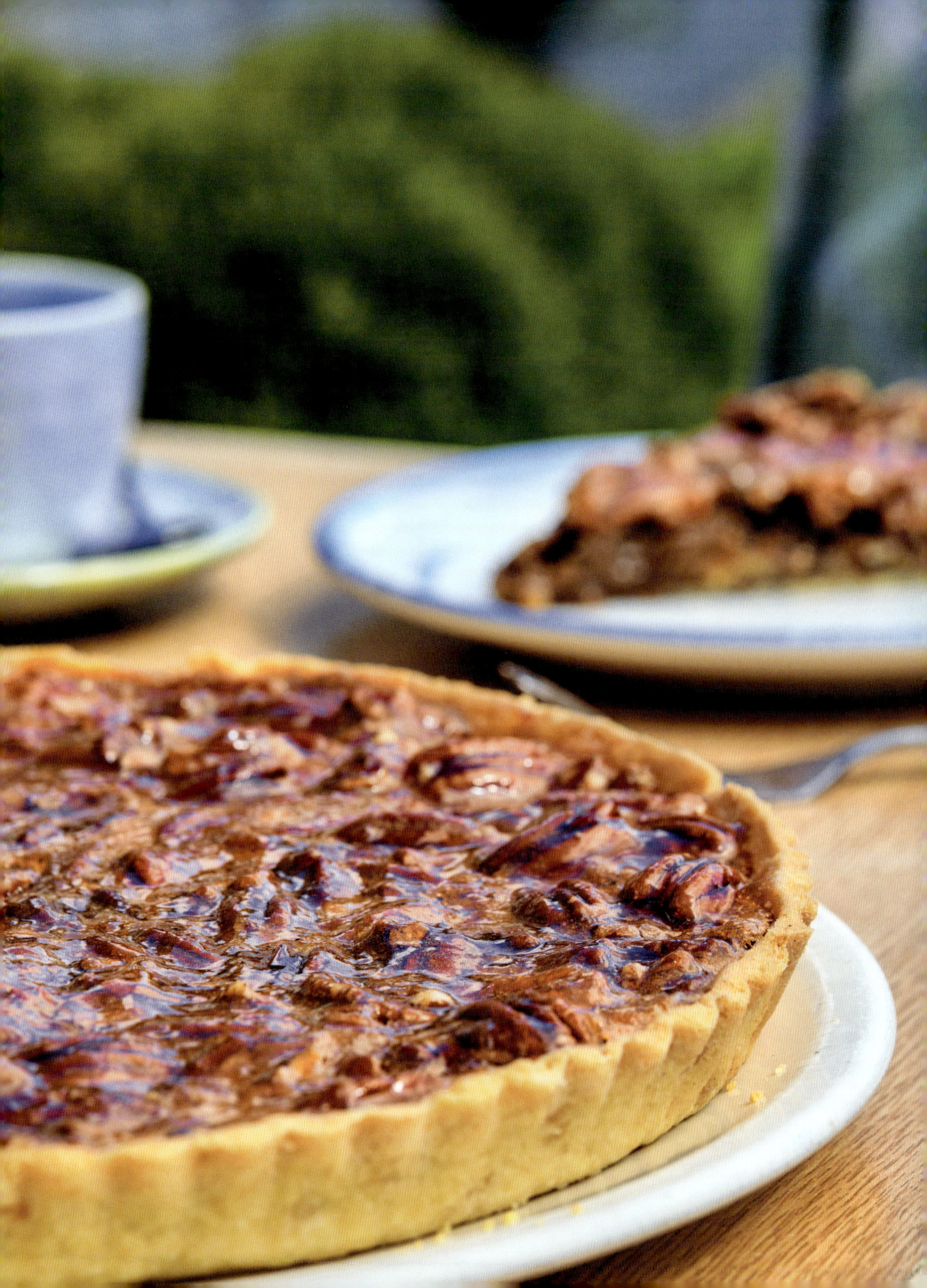

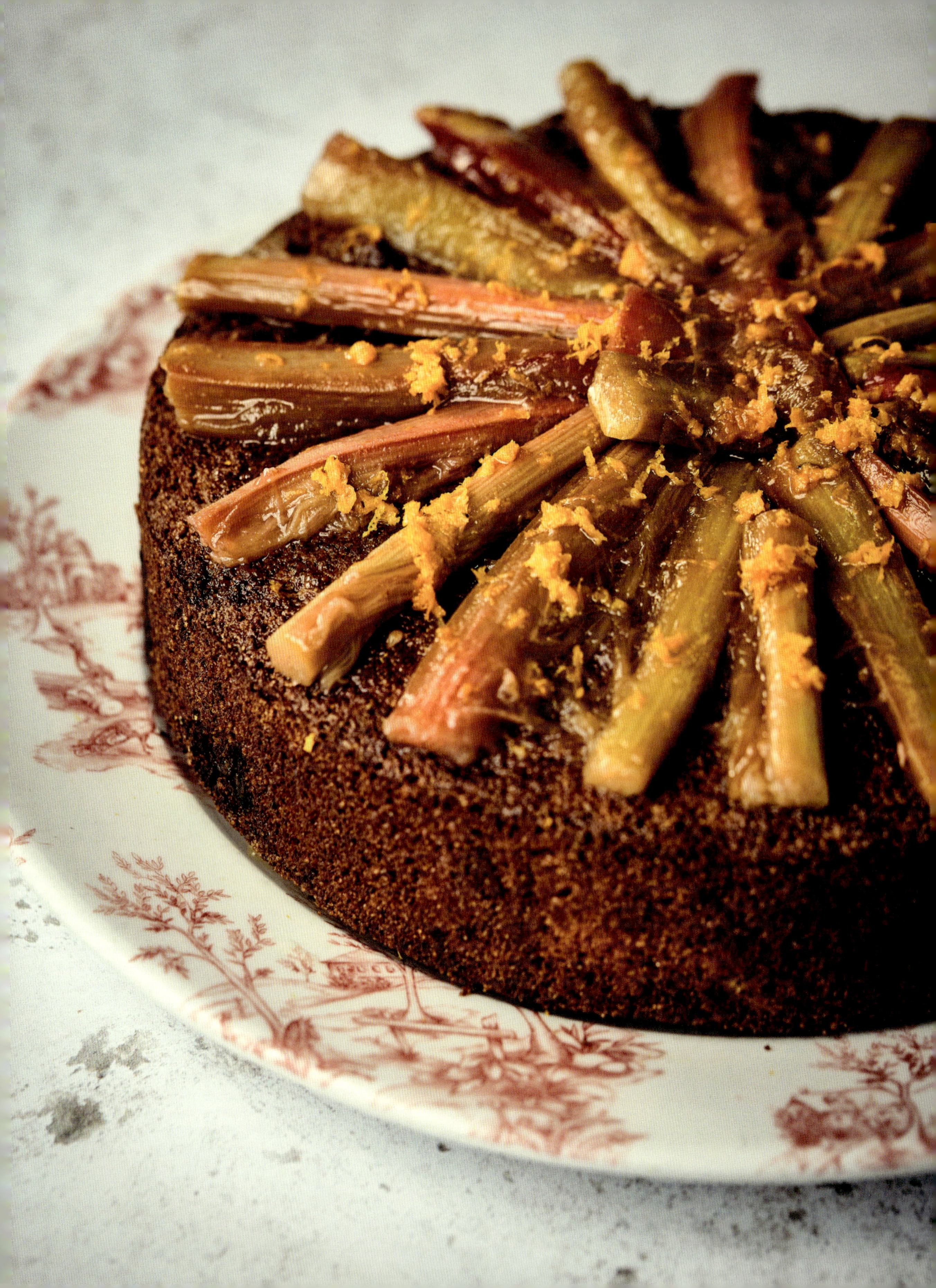

Orange, Polenta and Early Rhubarb Cake

I love this cake, not least because it's gluten-free. It's something different if you want to impress without overdoing it, and it has a great crumbly texture from the polenta. The poached rhubarb for the topping is beautiful. I use it at breakfast with our granola or for dessert with some simple meringues. It is also delicious on a green leaf salad with a drizzle of reduced balsamic vinegar.

SERVES 8–10

FOR THE CAKE

200g rhubarb

250g polenta

zest of 1 orange

250g butter, room temperature, plus extra for greasing

250g caster sugar

4 eggs

100g ground almonds

2½ tsp baking powder

150g yoghurt, natural or Greek

FOR THE POACHED RHUBARB

5 sticks of forced or early rhubarb

1 tbsp caster sugar

juice of 1 orange

a little orange zest, for garnish (optional)

1. Preheat your oven to 160°C fan/180°C/gas 4. Grease a 23cm loose-bottomed cake tin well and line the base with a disc of parchment paper.
2. Top and tail the rhubarb for the cake, wash and pat dry, then chop into 1cm pieces. Toss the diced rhubarb and 50g of the polenta in a bowl together.
3. Wash and zest your orange using a Microplane or the fine side of a grater. Juice the orange. Set zest and juice aside separately.
4. Using a hand-held or stand mixer, cream your butter and caster sugar until pale, light and fluffy.
5. Add your eggs one by one, continuing to mix at full speed and mixing back up to that fluffy stage after each one. This will prevent the batter from splitting – do not rush the process.
6. Turn down the speed to minimum, add the orange zest, the rest of the polenta, the ground almonds and baking powder. Mix for a couple of seconds only.
7. By hand, using a spatula, fold in the yoghurt, making circular motions and ensuring you scrape the bottom of the bowl each time. Be gentle so you don't knock all that precious air out. Before the yoghurt is fully mixed in, stop and add the rhubarb you tossed in polenta earlier. Fold once or twice only.
8. Pour the batter into your lined baking tin and bake for 50–55 minutes. Check if it's baked by piercing with a clean skewer – if it doesn't come out clean, give it another few minutes and recheck.

CONTINUED OVERLEAF

CAKES AND TARTS

9. Place on a wire rack and allow to cool completely. Leave the oven on for the next step.
10. Top and tail, wash and pat dry the rhubarb for the topping. Cut into 6cm/finger-length pieces. Place in a shallow casserole dish or roasting tray lined with parchment paper. Arrange the batons with a little space between each, pour the orange juice from earlier over the rhubarb and sprinkle with the tablespoon of sugar. Cover with tin foil and bake at 160°C for 10 minutes, then remove the foil. Check with a sharp knife – it should be tender, not mushy, and have kept its shape. It may need a further 5–7 minutes, depending on how tough it is. When you're happy, remove it from the oven and cool.
11. Run a palette knife around the edge of the cake tin to ensure it's not stuck. Lift the cake out using the loose bottom, slip a palette knife underneath and slide onto a flat plate or cake stand.
12. Arrange the cooled rhubarb batons around the top of the cake, all pointing to the centre. Layer them until you have used them all up. Drizzle any leftover syrup over the top. If you wish, zest a little orange on top too.

Blueberry and Lemon Polenta Cake (Variation)

To make an equally delicious blueberry and lemon version of this cake, replace the 200g rhubarb with 300g fresh blueberries, and the orange zest with the zest of one lemon, and bake as above. When the cake has cooled, mix 250g of sieved icing sugar with the juice of 1 lemon, a little at a time, till the sugar has dissolved and you have a thick icing. Drizzle the icing over the cake and decorate with a few extra blueberries.

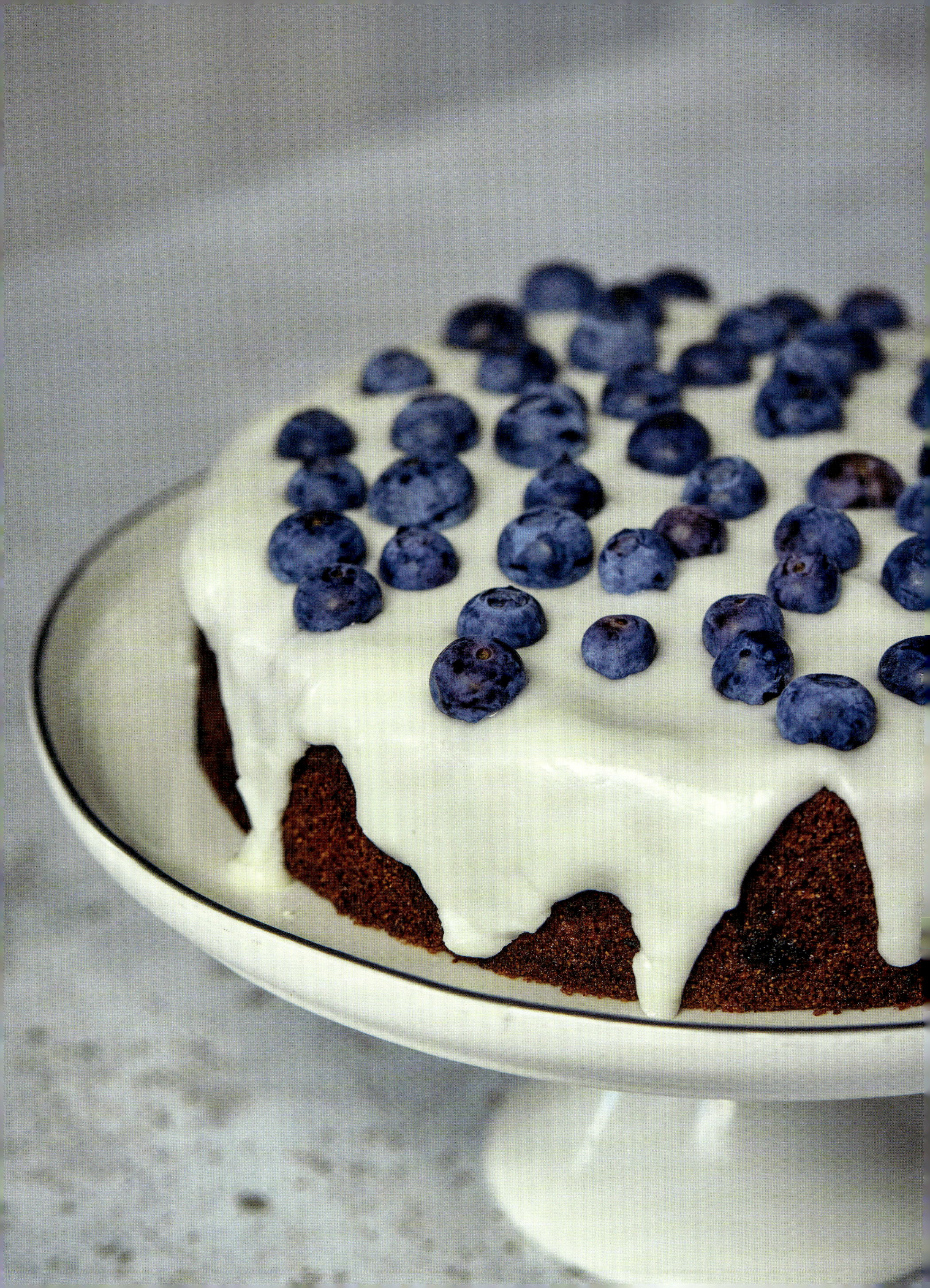

Chocolate Cake with Real Chocolate Frosting

This chocolate cake is rich and moist. It is essential that you use good-quality dark chocolate – I use one with 54% cocoa solids, but anything up to 70% will be fine. This is the perfect birthday cake for the chocolate lover in your life and can be prepared in advance.

SERVES 12

FOR THE CAKE

200g dark chocolate, at least 54%

200g butter

260g caster sugar

7 eggs, separated

170g plain flour

1½ tsp baking powder

dark and white chocolate shavings, to garnish

FOR THE REAL CHOCOLATE FROSTING

120g butter

150g dark chocolate, at least 54%

170g icing sugar, sieved

140g cream

1. Preheat your oven to 160°C fan/180°C/gas 4. Grease a 23cm loose-bottomed cake tin well, and line the base with a disc of parchment paper.
2. Chop your dark chocolate, place in a microwave-safe bowl and melt on a low setting, stirring frequently. Or to use the water-bath method instead, place the chocolate in a glass bowl over a saucepan of warm water – the water should not touch the bowl. Stir frequently using a dry, clean spatula. Use a dry tea towel to lift off the bowl once the chocolate has melted, being careful of the escaping steam. Set aside to cool.
3. Cream your butter and caster sugar using a hand-held or stand mixer until it lightens in colour and becomes light and fluffy. Stop the mixer a couple of times and scrape down the sides so all the butter is incorporated.
4. Add your eggs yolks one by one, continuing to mix at full speed and mixing back up to that fluffy stage after each one. This prevents the batter from splitting, so don't rush the process.
5. Add the melted chocolate and continue mixing until it is all incorporated. Turn down the speed, add the flour and baking powder, and slowly mix until it's all combined.
6. Place the egg whites in a clean bowl and, using a large hand whisk, whisk until the eggs turn white and are light, fluffy and cloud-like.

CONTINUED OVERLEAF

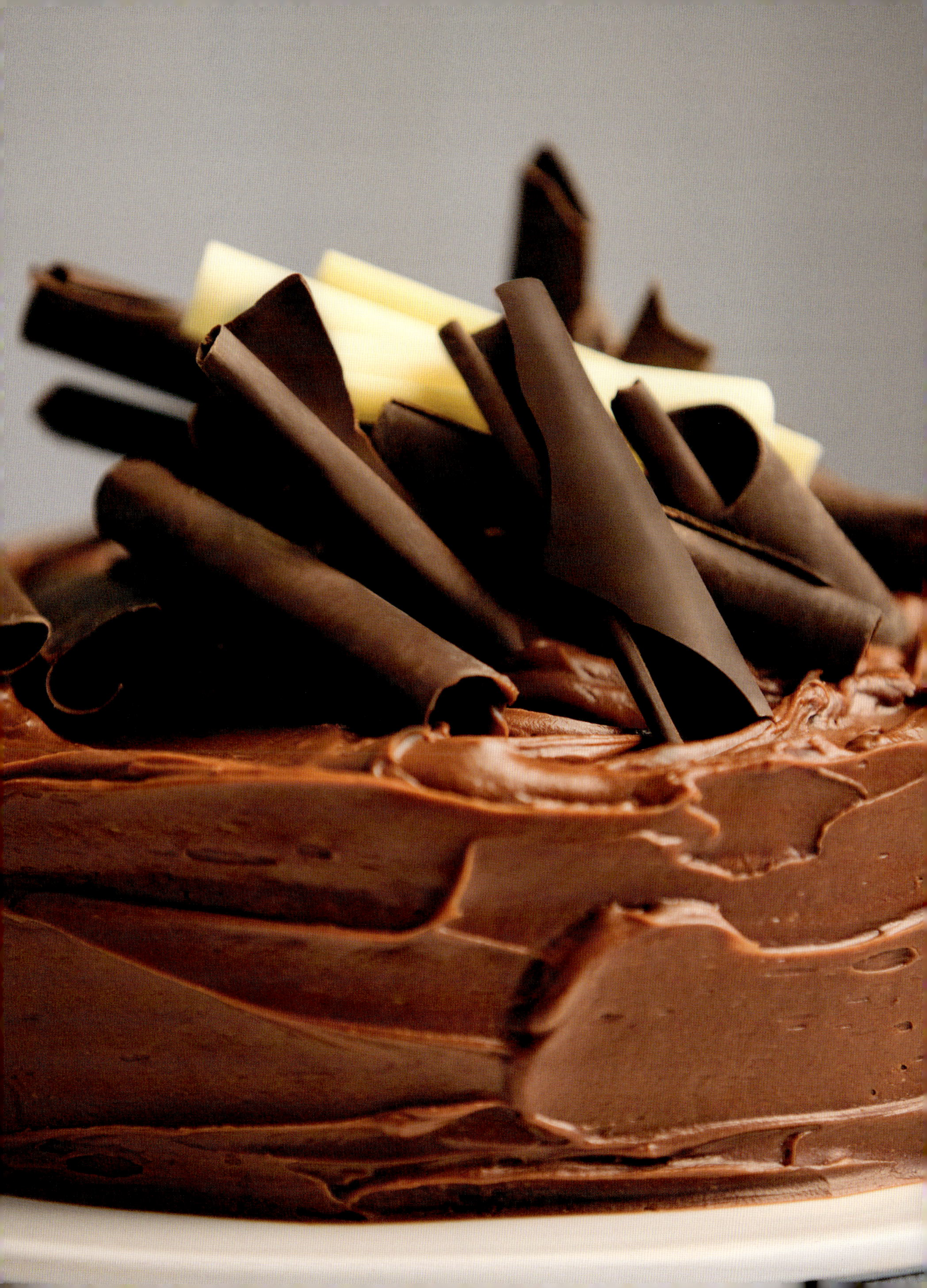

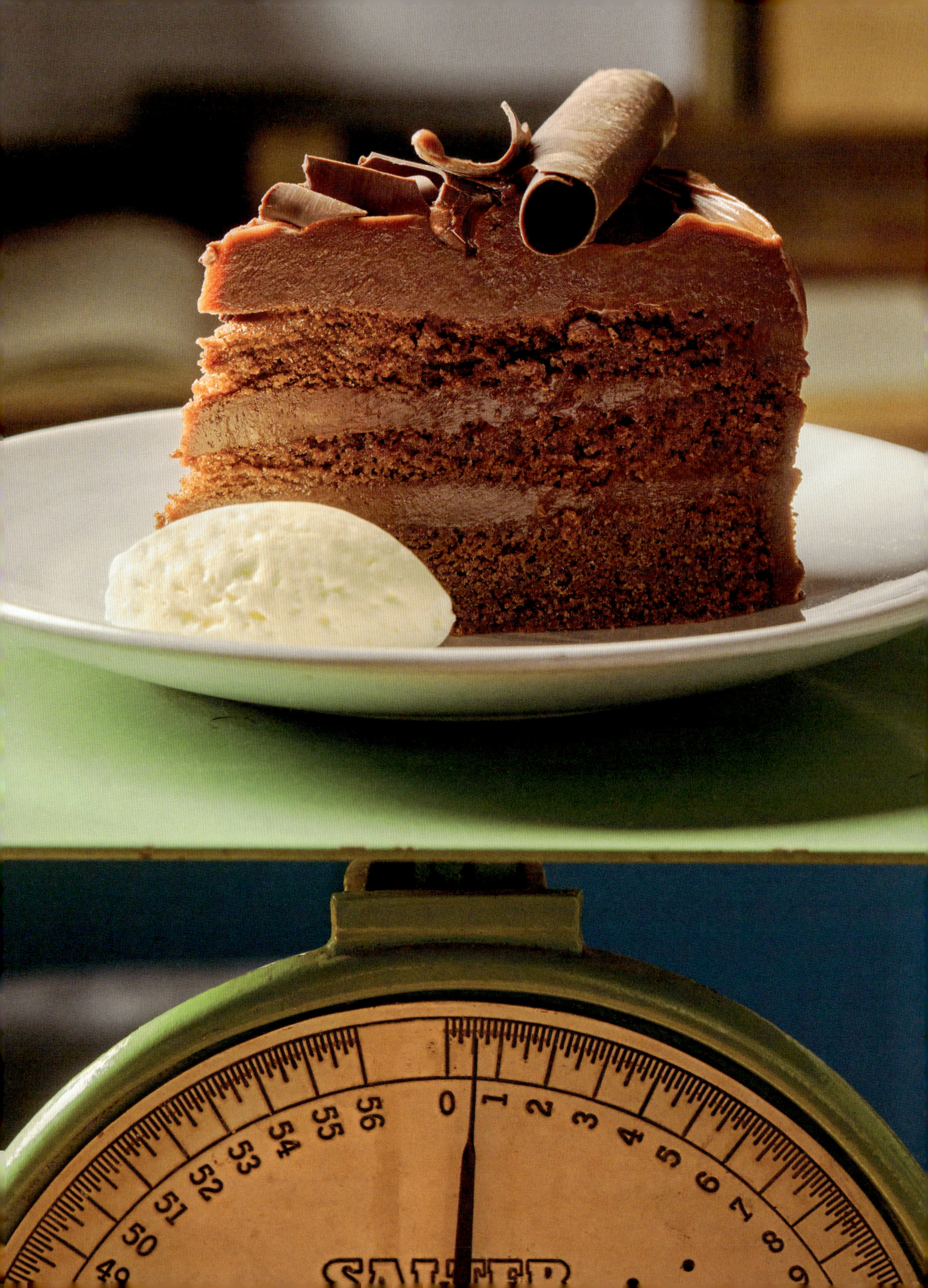
50 51 52 53 54 55 56 0 1 2 3 4 5 6 7 8

7. Using a large rubber spatula, spoon the whisked egg white into the chocolate mix and gently fold it in, ensuring you scrape the bottom of the bowl each time, going under and over the mix in a figure-of-eight motion. Go slowly so you don't knock out all that air.
8. Scrape the mix into the tin and bake for 40 minutes. Check if it's baked by inserting a clean skewer into the centre – if it comes out clean, your cake is ready. If not, bake for a further 10 minutes and recheck. Place on a wire rack to cool completely.
9. To make the frosting, dice the butter and chop the dark chocolate into pieces. Melt as for the chocolate above.
10. Whisk the icing sugar and cream together until smooth. When the chocolate and butter are melted, whisk both mixes together until smooth. Place in the fridge.
11. Run a palette knife around the cake in the tin to ensure it's not stuck. Lift out using the loose base. Slice the cake in three horizontally using a sharp serrated knife.
12. Pop the bottom layer of the cake on a flat plate or cake stand. Spread 2 heaped tablespoons of the frosting on it using a palette knife, leaving 2cm free around the edge. Pop on the middle layer of the cake and repeat this step, then add the top of the cake and press down lightly.
13. Spread the remaining frosting over the top and down the sides of the cake using a palette knife.
14. Garnish with dark and white chocolate shavings.

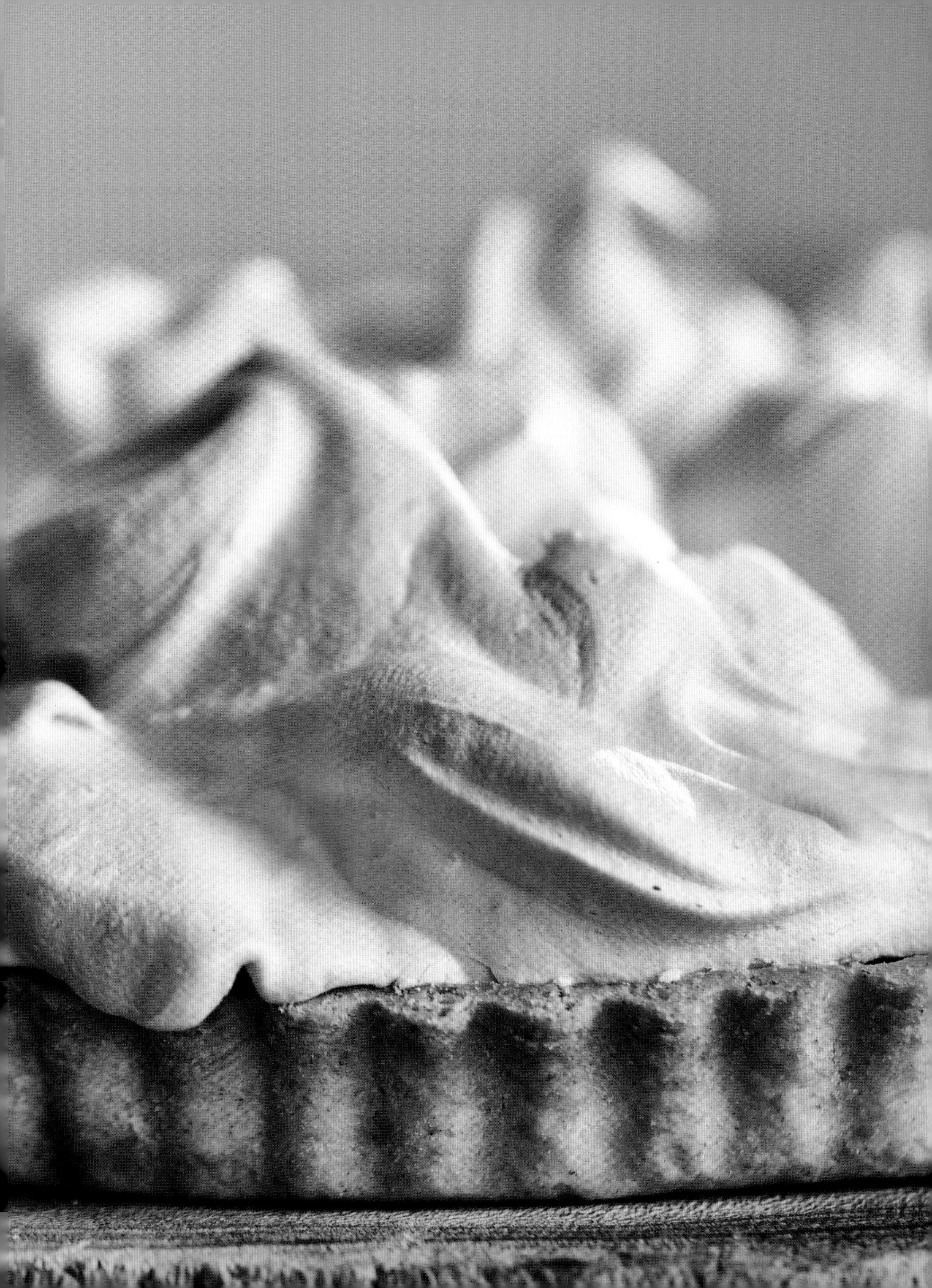

Lemon Meringue Pie

Lemon meringue pie is an absolute favourite of mine. There are a few stages to it, but it's so worth the effort. I use a baked lemon tart as the base, not a curd, as I prefer the lightness of it. You could, of course, skip the meringue, chill the lemon tart and serve with a raspberry compote.

SERVES 10

1 x 28cm sweet pastry case, baked and cooled (page 153)

FOR THE BAKED LEMON FILLING

2 lemons
6 eggs
260g caster sugar
160ml cream

FOR THE MERINGUE

250g egg whites (approximately 7 eggs)
500g caster sugar

1. Preheat your oven to 140°C fan/160°C/gas 3.
2. Zest and juice the lemons. Pass the juice through a sieve to remove any pips.
3. Whisk the eggs and caster sugar in a bowl by hand until just combined. Add the lemon juice, zest and cream. Whisk until fully incorporated and pour the mix into the tart base.
4. Carefully place in the oven and bake for 25 minutes. Wobble the tart tin to see if the custard has set – if not, leave for a further 5 minutes and repeat until fully set. The tart should not take colour – your aim is to just set the custard.
5. Place on a wire rack to cool completely, then use a sharp knife to trim off the excess pastry.
6. Preheat your oven to 150°C fan/170°C/gas 3.
7. Using a hand-held or stand mixer, whisk the egg whites for the meringue until they resemble a fluffy cloud, and the whisk leaves stiff peaks when lifted up.
8. Slow the mixer, add a fifth of the sugar, then turn it up to full speed again until the meringue whips right back up to full peaks. It is important to make these additions gradually. Continue like this, whisking back up for 2–3 minutes between each addition, until all the sugar is incorporated.
9. Using a rubber spatula, scoop the meringue out onto the cooled lemon tart. Using a palette knife, spread the meringue roughly over the tart, leaving peaks with the tip of the knife. Bake for 18–20 mins until the meringue is a light golden-brown colour.
10. Cool the tart for a couple of hours, then lift it out using the loose base.
11. Using a palette knife or large chopping knife, slide the tart off the base onto a flat plate. Slice and serve.

Coffee Cake

Our coffee cake is one of the bestselling cakes we make. It's the espresso-soaked layers that make all the difference. Ireland has fast become a nation of speciality-coffee drinkers, and this cake is inspired by the flavours of a strong simple espresso with a dollop of cream on top.

SERVES 12

FOR THE CAKE

1 shot espresso or 40ml very strong coffee

300g butter, plus extra for greasing

300g soft dark brown sugar

6 eggs

300g plain flour

1¼ tsp baking powder

dark chocolate shavings, to garnish

FOR THE ICING

270g butter

810g icing sugar

250g cream cheese (I use Philadelphia)

3 tbsp coffee extract

FOR THE SOAKING SYRUP

160ml boiling water

3 shots espresso or 120ml very strong coffee

2 tsp coffee extract

1. Preheat your oven to 160°C fan/180°C/gas 4. Grease a 23cm loose-bottomed cake tin well, and line the base with a disc of parchment paper. Make your espresso or strong coffee and set aside to cool.

2. Cream your butter and soft dark brown sugar using a stand or hand-held mixer, until the mix lightens in colour and becomes light and fluffy. Stop the mixer a couple of times and scrape down the sides to ensure all the butter is incorporated.

3. Add your eggs one by one, continuing to mix at full speed and mixing back up to that fluffy stage after each one. This will prevent the batter from splitting, so don't rush the process.

4. Add the flour, baking powder and cooled espresso and slowly continue to mix until fully incorporated. Use a rubber spatula to give it a final mix by hand, ensuring it scrapes the bottom of the bowl, before scooping the mix into the tin.

5. Bake for 1 hour 5 minutes. Insert a clean skewer into the centre of the cake – if it comes out clean, your cake is ready. If not, bake for a further 5 minutes and recheck. Place on a wire rack to cool completely, ideally overnight.

6. To make the icing, beat the butter and icing sugar using a hand-held or stand mixer. Increase the speed gradually, stopping and scraping down the sides of the bowl regularly, until the mix becomes light and fluffy. Only then add the cream cheese.

7. Continue mixing until the cheese is full incorporated, stopping to scrape down the bowl a couple of times, then add the coffee extract, and mix well. The icing should be firm, shiny and smooth. Pop it in the fridge for 30 minutes or so.

8. Meanwhile, mix the ingredients for the soaking syrup together in a jug. Set aside to cool.

CONTINUED OVERLEAF

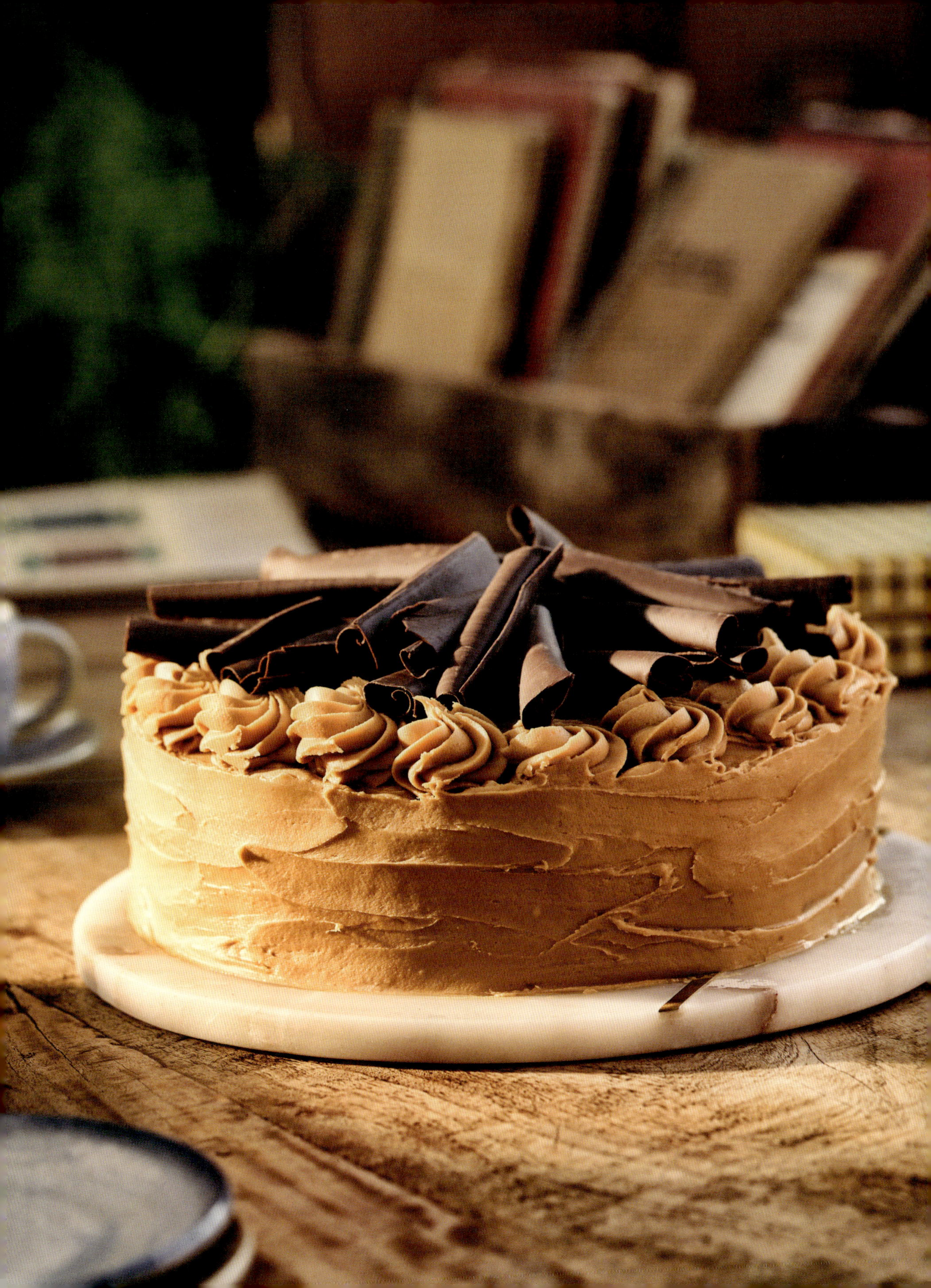

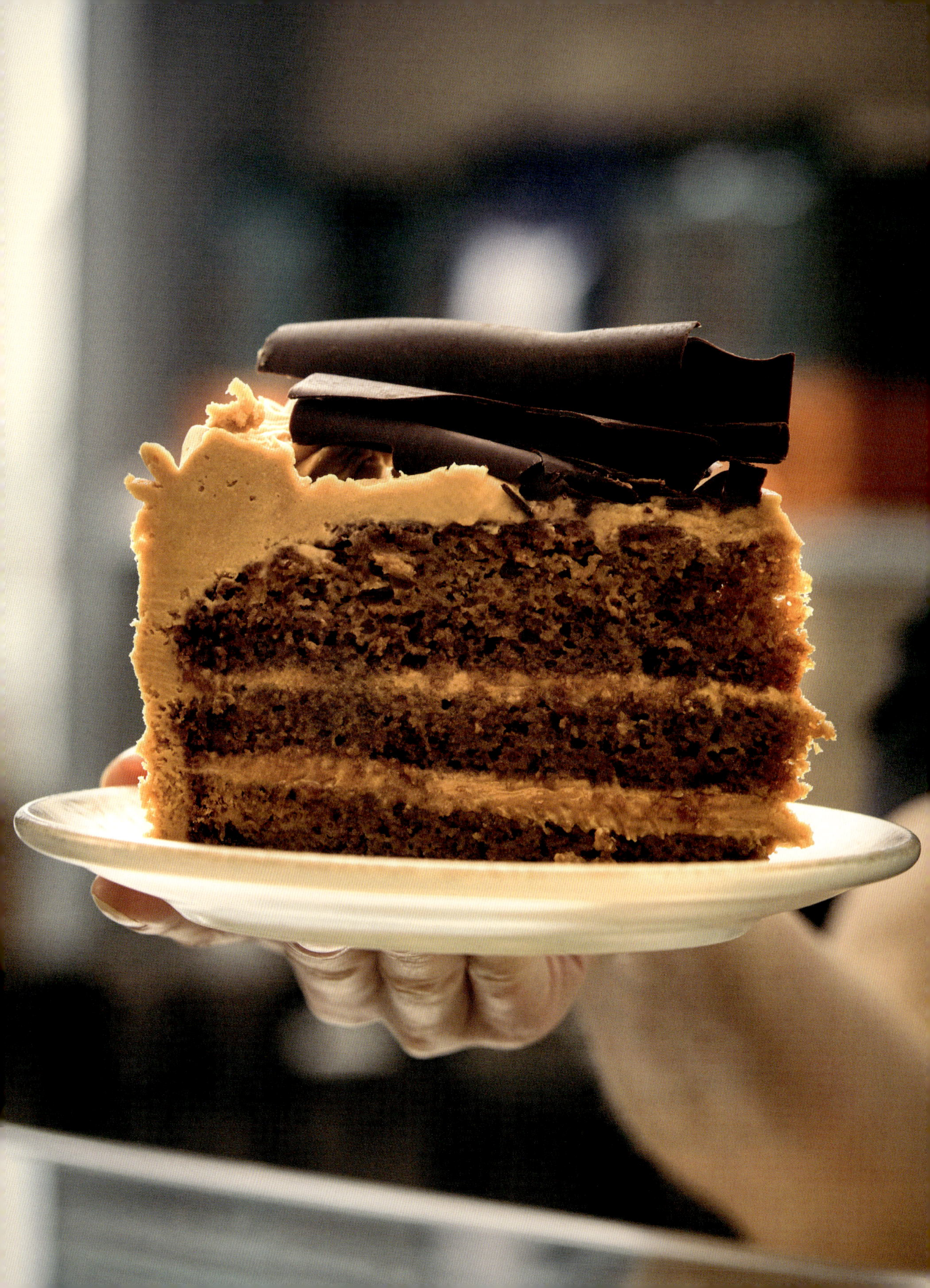

9. Run a palette knife around the edge of the cake in the tin to ensure it's not stuck. Lift out using the loose base. Slice in three horizontally, using a sharp serrated knife.
10. Pop the bottom layer of the cake on a flat plate. Using a pastry brush, dab the bottom layer with syrup until ⅓ is gone. Carefully spoon on 3 heaped tablespoons of the icing and use a palette knife to spread it, leaving 2cm free around the edge of the cake. Pop on the middle layer of the cake, press lightly, and repeat the syrup and icing as for the first layer. Turn the top layer of the cake cut side upwards on the countertop and soak the inside with the remaining syrup. Then carefully turn it baked side up, pop it on top of the cake and press down lightly. I put the cake in the freezer at this stage for about 30 minutes to set it a little before icing the outside.
11. Finally, scoop the remaining icing on top of the cake and spread over the top and down the sides using a palette knife. Garnish with some dark chocolate shavings.

Brown Sugar Meringue Roulade

Brown sugar gives meringue a delicious caramel flavour. It's so different from the usual white one. I love using autumnal fruits with it, and it makes a super-light Christmas dessert also.

SERVES 6

butter, for greasing
125g egg whites (from about 4 eggs)
250g soft dark brown sugar
1 large or 2 small Bramley apples
½ tbsp water
½ tbsp sugar
½ tsp ground cinnamon
250ml cream
1 orange
dehydrated orange slices, to garnish (page 174)

1. Preheat your oven to 160°C fan/180°C/gas 4. Grease a shallow rectangular baking tray (32 x 21cm), then cut a piece of parchment slightly larger than the tin. Using your scissors, cut a 6cm slit towards the centre from each corner. When you place it in your tin, the paper will sit into it perfectly.
2. Using a hand-held or stand mixer, whisk the egg whites for the meringue. This will take some time depending on your mixer. The egg whites should resemble a fluffy cloud, and the whisk should leave stiff peaks in the mix when lifted up.
3. Slow the mixer, add a fifth of the dark brown sugar, then turn it up to full speed again until the meringue whips right back up to full peaks. It is important to make these additions gradually. Continue like this, whisking back up for 2–3 minutes between each addition, until all the sugar is incorporated.
4. Scoop the meringue onto the tray using a rubber spatula. Spread evenly, finally running your palette knife lengthways back over the meringue to leave tracks.
5. Bake for 8 minutes. Open the oven to release the heat, turn the temperature down to 140°C fan/160°C/gas 3, then bake for a further 10 minutes.
6. Place the tray on a wire rack to cool.
7. Meanwhile wash, peel and roughly chop the apples.
8. Place them in a small saucepan with the water, sugar and cinnamon over a medium heat, stirring regularly until the apple begins to break down. Leave some chunks – don't cook it to a purée. Scoop it out onto a flat dish and allow it to cool. I prefer to leave this quite tart, as the meringue is so sweet, so don't be tempted to add too much sugar, even if the apples are sour.
9. Whip the cream to stiff peaks.

CONTINUED OVERLEAF

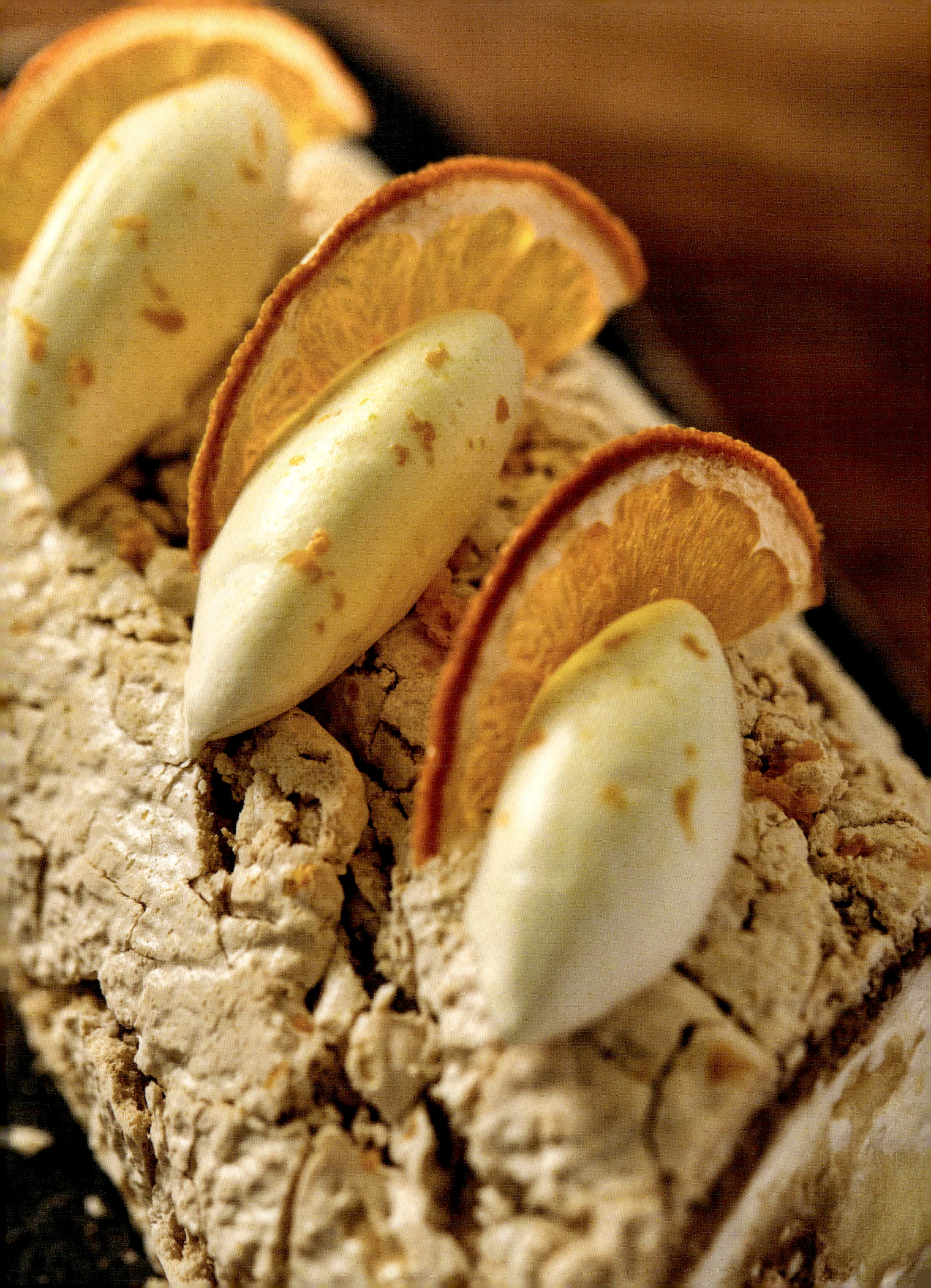

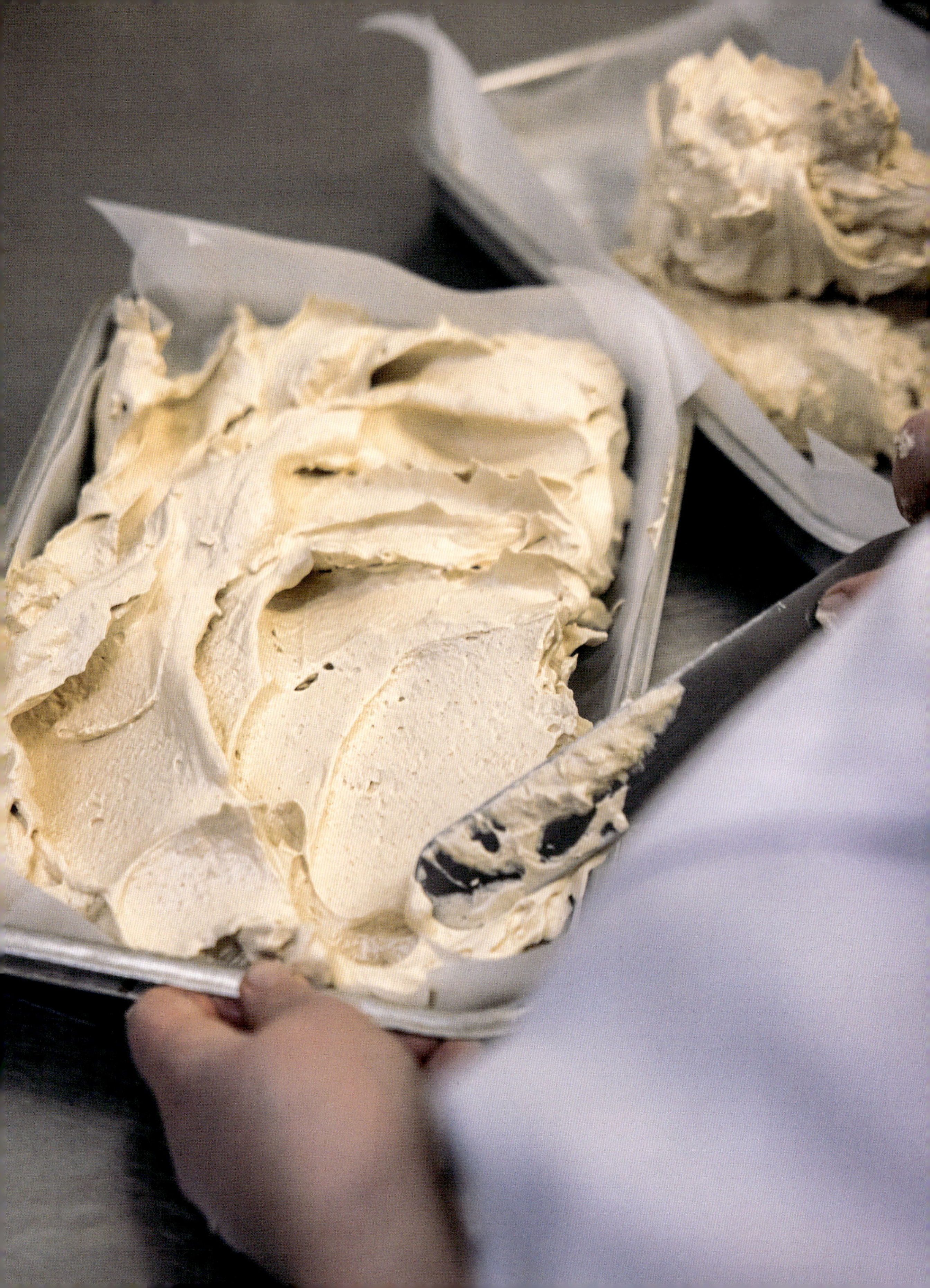

10. Place a piece of parchment on a tray of similar size to the one the meringue is in, and turn this on top of the meringue, then flip over the trays. Hold the edge of the paper under the meringue and carefully remove the tray, so your meringue is now upside down in front of you on the clean parchment. Pull away the parchment paper the meringue was baked on.
11. Spread most of the whipped cream over the meringue, leaving 2.5cm free on all sides. Spoon the cooled compote lengthways along the centre.
12. Roll the meringue up from the long end, as tightly as possible, using the paper underneath to help. Wrap in parchment and refrigerate.
13. When you are ready to serve, decorate the top with the reserved cream (I use a spoon dipped in hot water to make little quenelles, but you could also pipe some rosettes). Then zest the orange, using a Microplane, directly on top and garnish with some dehydrated orange slices (page 174).

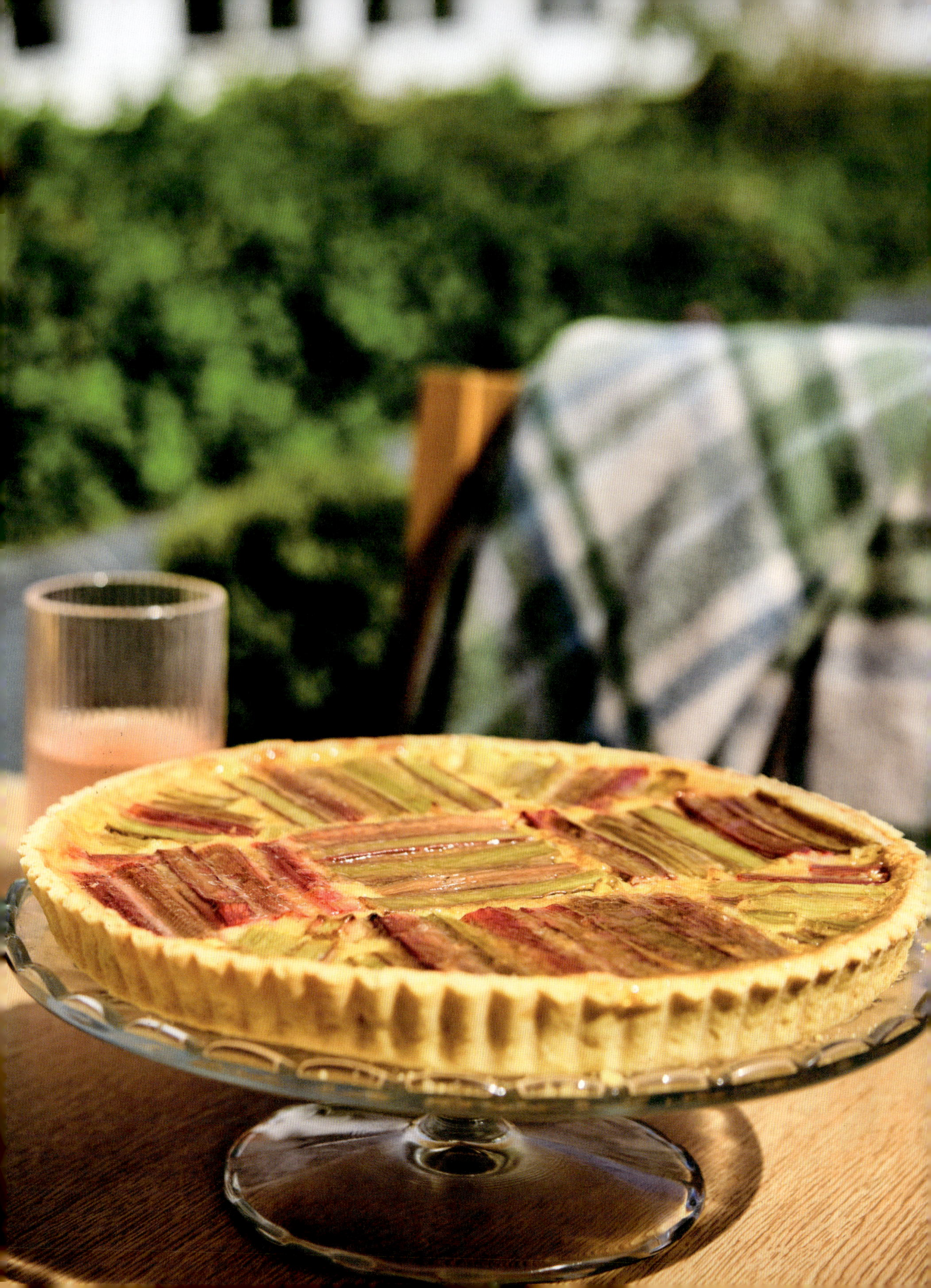

Rhubarb and Custard Tart

We make this tart at the start of rhubarb season, using early or forced rhubarb, and again when rhubarb is widely available. We use different fresh fruits in this tart throughout the year too – it works best with the tarter berries. It can take longer to bake if the fruit has a higher water content, like strawberries, but it's so worth it. I also like to mix rhubarb and fresh strawberries in this tart.

SERVES 8

FOR THE SWEET PASTRY CASE

100g butter, plus extra for greasing
50g caster sugar
1 egg
20ml cold water
210g plain flour

FOR THE FILLING

3–4 skinny sticks of rhubarb
6 eggs
260g caster sugar
drop of vanilla extract
160ml cream

FOR THE GLAZE

2 heaped tbsp apricot jam
2 tsp water

FOR THE SWEET PASTRY CASE

1. Grease a 28cm fluted loose-bottomed tin well and line the base with a disc of parchment paper.
2. To make the pastry, beat the butter and sugar using a hand-held or stand mixer until well mixed and creamy in texture. Add the remaining ingredients and mix on the lowest speed until it comes together.
3. Remove the pastry from the bowl and knead gently on a very lightly floured surface until it's smooth and forms a ball. Keep the mixing and kneading to a bare minimum, as it can make the pastry tough and elastic, which will cause it to shrink when rolling and baking. Wrap in cling film or a sealed container (a glass or plastic lunchbox) and pop it in the fridge for half an hour.
4. Lightly flour your rolling surface and rolling pin. Roll out your pastry until the disc is slightly bigger than the tin. Only roll in one direction, back and forward, never side to side (this prevents the pastry from stretching and contracting) – turn the pastry rather than the rolling pin.
5. Roll the pastry back over the rolling pin to help lift it over the tart tin. Gently sit the pastry into the tin, then, using your thumbs, press it all the way round into the sides of the tin. The pastry should be falling over the edge of the tin and will be rough around the edges, which is fine. Place in the freezer for an hour.
6. Preheat your oven to 160°C fan/180°C/gas 4.

CONTINUED OVERLEAF

7. Pop a disc of parchment 5cm bigger than the tin on top of the pastry and fill with beans for baking blind (I use dried chickpeas or rice).
8. Bake for 30 minutes until the pastry is golden brown at the edges.
9. Place on a wire rack and carefully lift off the disc of parchment with the beans inside. Store the beans for next use, and allow the tart to cool completely.

FOR THE FILLING

1. Preheat your oven to 140°C fan/160°C/gas 3.
2. Wash your rhubarb, chop off the ends, and dice the sticks into 2cm pieces. Pat dry. Place in the cooked pastry base. It should be one layer and completely cover the pastry.
3. Crack your eggs into a mixing bowl. Add your sugar and vanilla and whisk until well mixed. Then add your cream, and whisk again until it's all incorporated.
4. Pour the custard mix into the tart base over the rhubarb.
5. Carefully place in the oven and bake for 30 minutes. Wobble the tart tin to see if the custard has set – if not, leave for a further 5 minutes, and repeat until it has fully set. The tart should not take colour – your aim is to just set the custard.
6. Place on a wire rack to cool completely.
7. When the tart has cooled, use a sharp knife to trim off the excess pastry, then lift the tart out using the loose bottom. Slip a palette knife or large chopping knife underneath and slide the tart onto a flat plate or cake stand.
8. To glaze the tart, place your apricot jam and water in a saucepan over a medium heat and allow the jam to dissolve – it should be syrup-like. Strain to remove any bits. Using a pastry brush, lightly brush the syrup over the tart – do not re-brush any area, as the glaze will just become sticky and lose its shine.
9. Slice and serve.

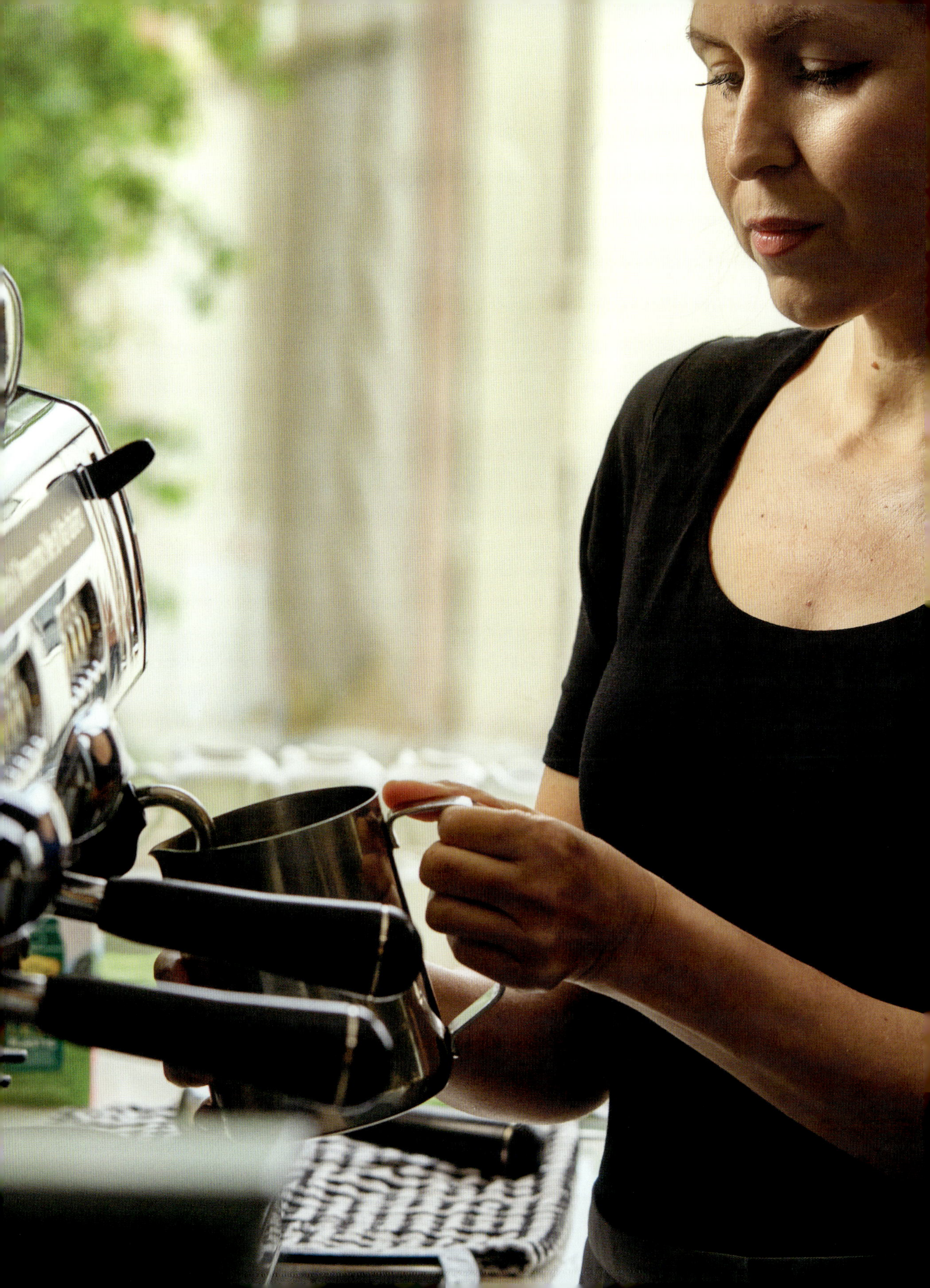

White Chocolate and Cranberry Cheesecake

This cake is quite the festive showstopper, but it's great all year round with different toppings. The cake itself can be prepared well in advance and even frozen. Pile fresh berries or peaches on top with some chocolate shavings, or spread some lemon or passion fruit curd over the top. It is light and sweet, so the topping should be tart. Biscuit bases can also be varied – I prefer to use digestives or gingernuts because of their naturally grainy texture and slight saltiness.

SERVES 10–12

FOR THE BASE
170g butter
350g digestive biscuits

FOR THE CAKE
400g cream cheese (I use Philadelphia)
drop of vanilla extract (optional)
160g caster sugar
15g leaf gelatine
500ml cream
70g white chocolate

FOR THE CRANBERRY SAUCE
250g fresh cranberries
50g sugar
¼ orange, zest and juice, plus extra zest to serve
1 star anise
¼ lemon, zest only

FOR THE BASE
1. Line the base and sides of a 25cm loose-bottomed cake tin with parchment paper. I don't grease cheesecake tins, as it leaves a residue on the cake, so dampen the underside of the parchment with water to keep it in place.
2. Melt the butter in the microwave or a saucepan over a low heat.
3. Pop your digestive biscuits into a plastic bag and, using a rolling pin, crush them until they are well crumbled.
4. Mix the butter and biscuit crumbs together well, ensuring all the biscuit is coated in the butter, then press into the base of the tin until well compacted. Pop in the fridge while you make the cake mix.

FOR THE CAKE
1. Place the cream cheese, vanilla (if using) and sugar in a bowl and mix using a spatula.
2. Soak the gelatine leaves in ice-cold water for about 5 minutes.
3. Meanwhile, whisk the cream to soft peaks using a hand-held or stand mixer.
4. Check the gelatine is soft and jelly-like. Squeeze the water out well. Place in a saucepan over a low heat, and add 3 tablespoons of the whipped cream. Warm the mix until the gelatine has dissolved to a liquid.

CONTINUED OVERLEAF

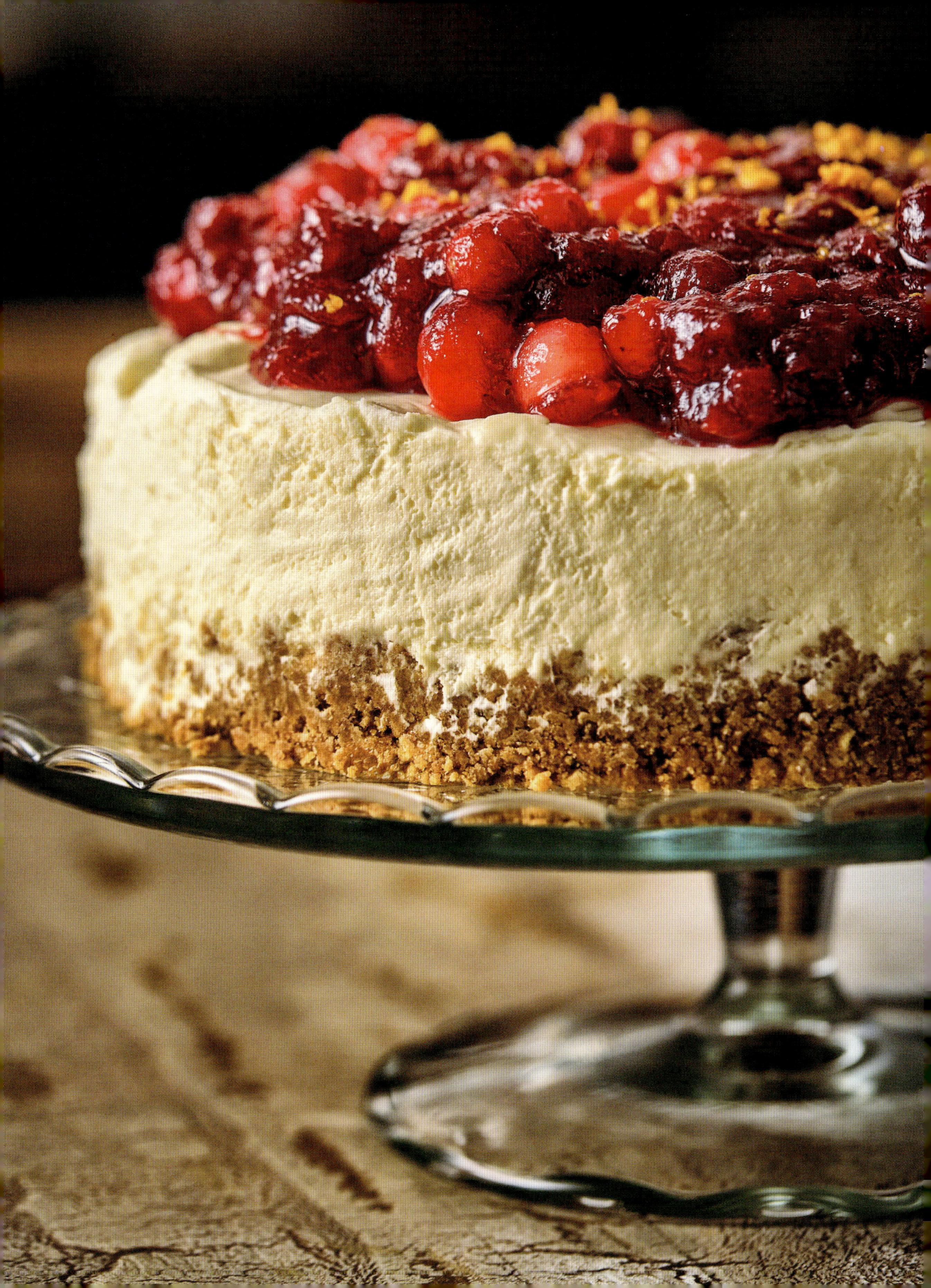

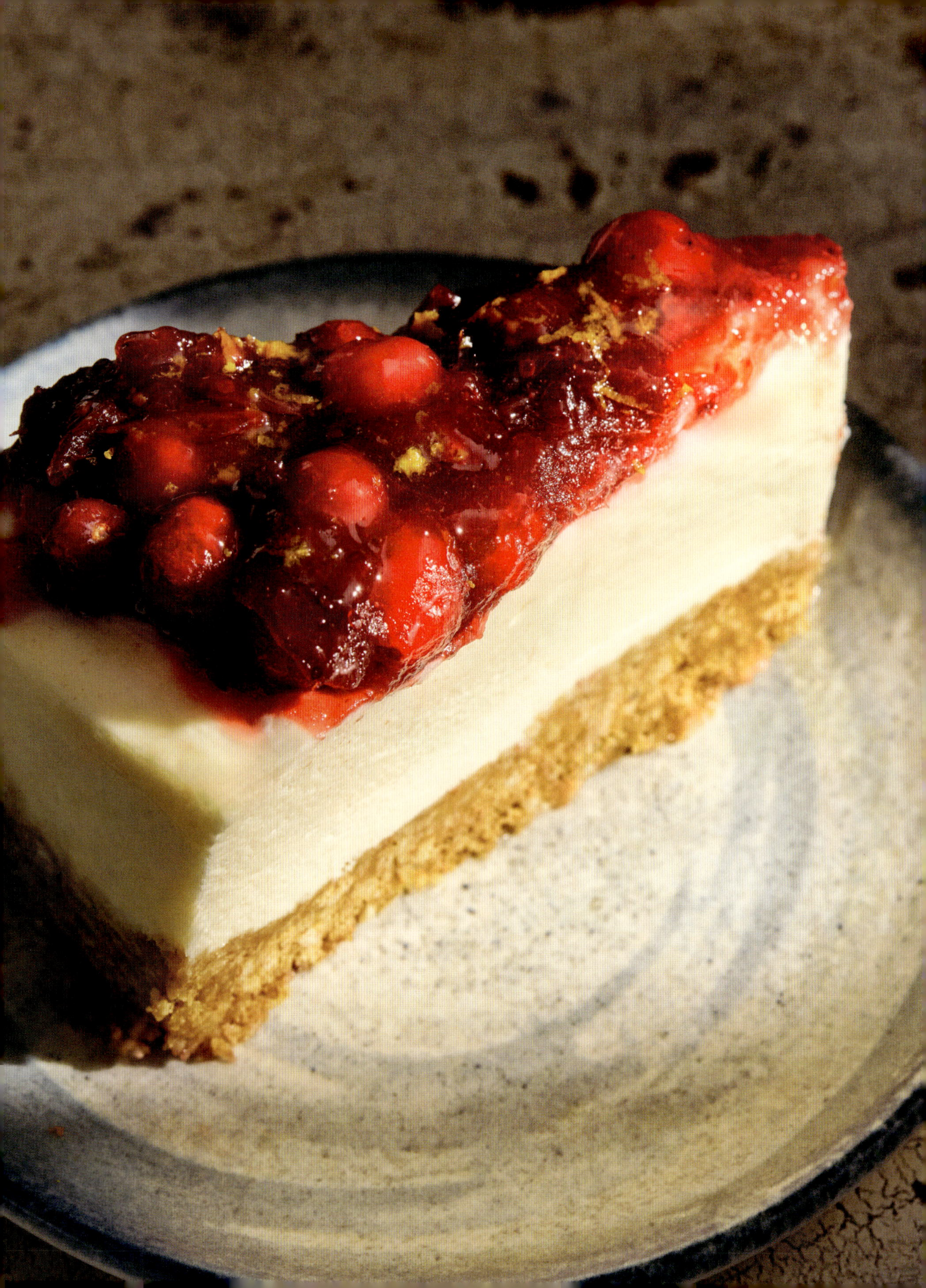

5. Chop the white chocolate into pieces. Place in a microwave-safe bowl and melt on a low setting, stirring frequently. Or to use the water-bath method instead, place the chocolate in a glass bowl over a saucepan of warm water on a low heat – the water should not touch the bowl. Stir frequently using a dry, clean spatula. Use a dry tea towel to lift off the bowl once the chocolate has melted, being careful of the escaping steam.
6. Using a spatula, fold the whipped cream into the cream-cheese mix.
7. Whisk the melted gelatine quickly into your chocolate. Add a third of the cream-cheese mix to this and whisk quickly so the chocolate does not set once it hits the cold cream. Finally, fold in the rest of the cream-cheese mix using a spatula.
8. Pour onto the biscuit base and allow to set overnight in the fridge.

FOR THE CRANBERRY SAUCE

1. You can also make the sauce the night before. Place all the ingredients in a saucepan, and bring to the boil slowly. Simmer until the berries are soft and begin to break down.
2. Remove from the heat and cool completely. Keep in the fridge until you're ready to use it.

TO SERVE

1. Remove the cake from the tin, pull off the parchment and place it on your selected plate or stand. Spoon the cooled cranberry sauce over it, grate some orange zest on top and serve.

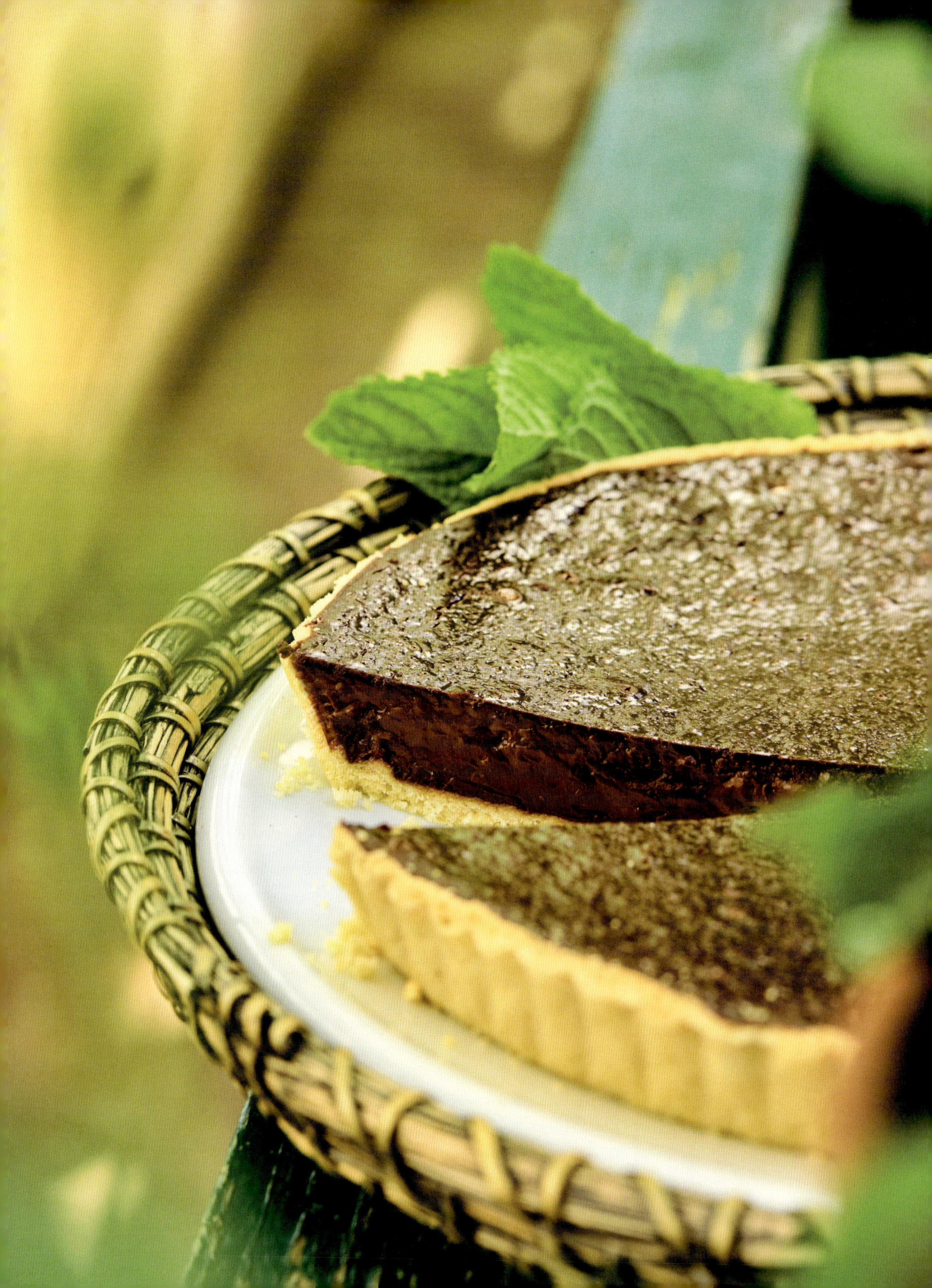

Baked Chocolate and Mint Tart

If you love real dark, rich chocolate, this is the tart for you. The mint is optional, so you could leave it out. For a chocolate and raspberry version, sprinkle fresh raspberries on the base before you pour on the chocolate mixture.

SERVES 8-10

1 x 28cm sweet pastry case, baked and cooled (page 153)
500g dark chocolate, at least 55%
3 eggs
300ml cream
200ml milk
25g fresh mint, plus extra to garnish

1. Preheat your oven to 140°C fan/160°C/gas 3.
2. Chop your chocolate and place in a mixing bowl. Crack your eggs into a small bowl.
3. Place your cream, milk and mint (including stalks) in a heavy-based saucepan and bring to the boil. Remove from the heat, then blend the cream and mint mix slightly using a stick blender. It doesn't have to be completely blended – it just helps extract more flavour from the mint. The cream will turn slightly green, but should still be hot – this should only take 30 seconds or so.
4. Place a sieve over the bowl of chocolate and pour the cream over, straining out the mint pieces. Whisk by hand until the chocolate dissolves, then whisk in the eggs until they're incorporated. The mix should be glossy and shiny.
5. Using a rubber spatula, scrape into the tart base.
6. Bake for 25–30 minutes until the mix has just set – it doesn't need to take colour and it's fine if it has a slight wobble.
7. Remove from the oven, and allow to cool completely.
8. When the tart has cooled, use a sharp knife to trim off the excess pastry, then lift it out of the tin using the loose base and slide it onto a stand or plate. Garnish with sprigs of fresh mint.
9. Serve at room temperature with real vanilla-bean ice cream or whipped cream.

Spicy Tomato Relish
HANDMADE AT FOXFORD, COUNTY MAYO
FOXFORD cafe
Mango Chutney
Pickled Sour Cherries
Irish Whiskey Orange Marmalade
Raspberry Jam
Sweet Chilli Sauce
250kg
550lb

FOXFORD CAFE PANTRY

The food product range, developed by Kathleen and produced in the cafe kitchen in the mill, is available to buy in the cafe, online and in FOXFORD'S other retail outlets.

This range of artisanal food has become the fulcrum of my own pantry – it's filled with so many essentials that I now can't live without.

I start my day with Kathleen's homemade granola: hazelnuts, almonds, sunflower seeds and a smidge of honey. It's delicious with natural yoghurt and fruit – you can almost feel this breakfast doing you good!

For an appetiser or dinner-party starter, I often serve her pickled cherries with a semi-soft cheese like burrata or the pickled pears, thinly sliced on a bed of rocket, with generous chunks of Stilton or Cashel Blue, scattered with chopped walnuts and dressed with Kathleen's honey and pink peppercorn dressing. The pickled pears and cherries are also excellent accompaniments to lamb, duck or pork, whether served hot or cold. And you can liven up any cheeseboard – or even a charcuterie board – with Kathleen's beetroot orange chutney.

The clean, modern packaging on all the pantry products makes them perfect for gifting. A set of three jams always goes down well, as does a package of cranberry and orange biscotti.

And now, by sharing some of her pantry recipes, Kathleen is giving you the opportunity to make these delicious products at home, to gift, to share or to keep all for yourself. They're sure to become essential parts of your own pantry – those extra touches that truly elevate the everyday.

Helen McAlinden
Designer, FOXFORD

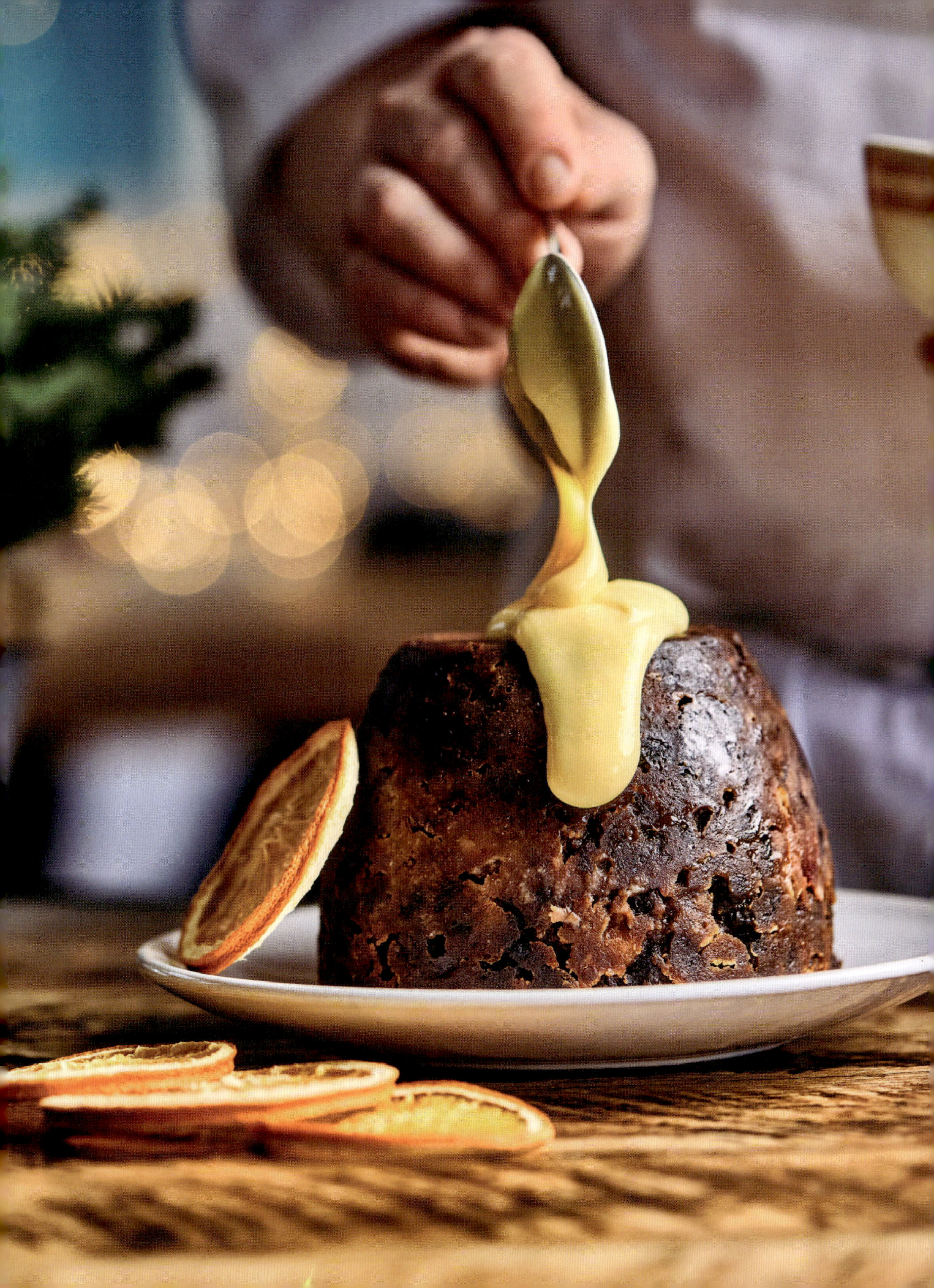

Foxford Cafe Christmas Pudding

Christmas pudding is a slow task but so worth doing. It also keeps for up to a year when stored correctly. If you are coeliac, use gluten-free breadcrumbs, gluten-free flour and butter, not suet. Also leave out the Guinness and increase the whiskey a little.

MAKES 2 PUDDINGS

FOR PART 1

340g sultanas
450g raisins
230g currants
115g mixed peel
115g glacé cherries
2 tsp mixed spice
1 tsp ground cinnamon
zest of ¼ orange
zest of ½ lemon
170ml Guinness
80ml Irish whiskey

FOR PART 2

butter, for greasing
2 large carrots
1 cooking apple
60g treacle
4 medium free-range eggs
90g plain white flour
170g vegetable suet or grated butter
90g fresh breadcrumbs
170g soft dark brown sugar

PART 1

1. Place all the ingredients for part 1 in a large bowl, and stir with a rubber spatula, making sure all the fruit is coated in the spices and alcohol. Cover with cling film or a lid, and leave at room temperature to soak for 1–2 weeks.

PART 2

1. Grease 2 plastic or glass 2lb pudding bowls.
2. Peel, grate and weigh your carrot and apple – you must end up with 100g carrot and 170g apple.
3. In a large bowl, mix all of the ingredients from parts 1 and 2 together thoroughly.
4. Divide the mix between the pudding bowls. Cover with a double thickness of parchment paper, and tie under the rim of the bowl with cotton twine, making a handle for ease of lifting.
5. Steam in a covered saucepan of water for 6 hours. The water should come halfway up the bowl and should be topped up every hour or so, so it doesn't boil dry.
6. Remove the puddings and allow them to cool completely.
7. Re-cover with fresh parchment paper, and then wrap in tin foil and store in a cool, dry place.
8. To serve the pudding, steam for 1½–2 hours until hot throughout. Turn out onto a plate, and decorate with holly and some dehydrated orange slices (page 174). I serve it with lots of custard and whipped cream.
9. If you don't want to eat the whole pudding, slice off as much as you want, put it in a bowl and heat as above (re-cover and store the unheated portion). A microwave can be used to reheat portions, but beware you don't overheat it and ruin your hard work!

Foxford Jams

I love the idea of preserving the seasons, and making your own jam is a great way to do this. You can use frozen berries also – no need to defrost – but they will contain more water so you will need to cook the jam out a little more. There is no comparison between commercial and homemade preserves – even if they don't set perfectly, they will still taste great.

MAKES 7 X 340G JARS

FOR EACH JAM

1,450g jam sugar

35ml lemon juice

RHUBARB AND STRAWBERRY JAM

725g rhubarb

725g strawberries

Boil for 10 minutes

BLACKBERRY JAM

1,450g blackberries

Boil for 6 minutes

MIXED BERRY AND SPICE JAM

1,450g mixed berries (strawberries, redcurrants, blackcurrants, cherries, raspberries, blackberries)

1 star anise

Boil for 6 minutes

RASPBERRY JAM

1,450g raspberries

Boil for 5 minutes

1. Wash your fruit, remove any stalks and pat dry. If using rhubarb, chop into 2cm pieces, and halve any strawberries.
2. Wash your jars with soapy water, rinse and dry. Place them in the oven at 140°C fan/160°C/gas 3 for 20 minutes. Turn off the oven and leave the jars inside until the jam is ready. Place 3 small plates in the freezer, for testing.
3. Place the prepared fruit for your chosen jam in a large heavy-based saucepan with a splash of water and stir continuously over a medium heat. You need to cook the fruit until it softens and the juices run. Then add your jam sugar and lemon juice. If the mix comes more than halfway up the pot, it is not big enough.
4. Stir using a heatproof spatula until all the sugar has dissolved.
5. Bring to a rolling boil on a high heat for several minutes (see ingredients lists for timings), stirring occasionally. Then take off the heat. Remove your jars from the oven.
6. Place a few drops of jam on a cold plate, and leave for a minute. Run your finger through the jam – if it's tacky and not runny on the plate, it's ready. If not, boil for a further 2 minutes and check again with another plate.
7. Remove any scum with a clean metal spoon. (For the mixed berry and spice jam, also remove the star anise.)
8. Pour the hot jam into the jars using a clean ladle and a jam-potting funnel. Place the lids on immediately and carefully turn upside down for 20 seconds. Label and store in a cool, dry place away from direct sunlight.
9. If stored correctly, they should last up to a year unopened. Once opened, store in the fridge and use within a month.

Raspberry Jam
HANDMADE AT FOXFORD, COUNTY MAYO
FOXFORD cafe
Mixed Berry & Spice Jam
Fine Cut Orange Marmalade

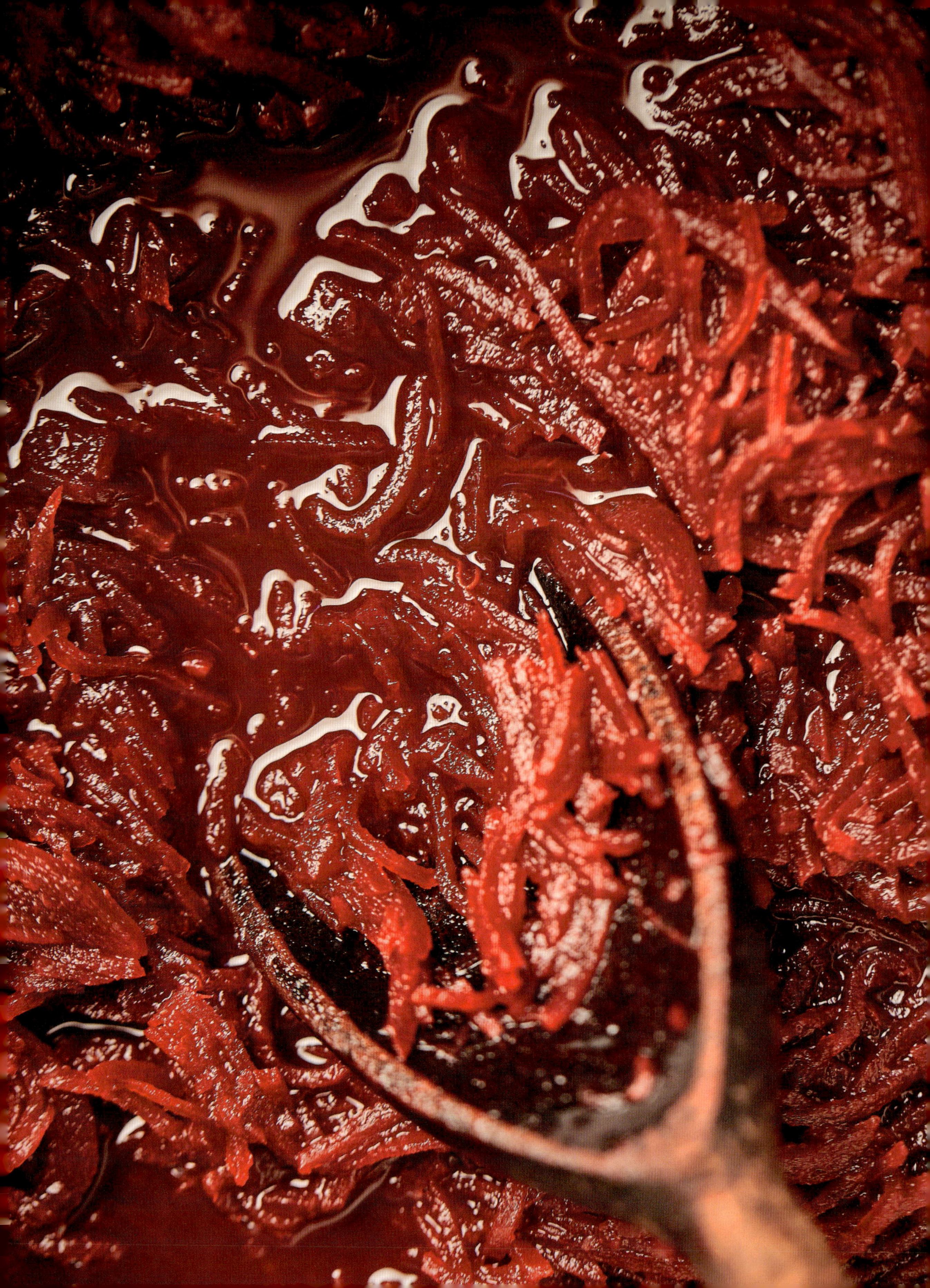

Beetroot Orange Chutney

A good chutney is a great addition to your kitchen cupboard. If you are a gardener, it's a delicious way of preserving gluts of vegetables and fruits so you can enjoy them all year round. This flavoursome chutney is delicious with a cheeseboard or a simple ham or cheese sandwich. It also pairs well with our sausage (page 75) and veggie (page 90) rolls.

MAKES 5-6 X 340G JARS

10-11 medium beetroot
3-4 cooking apples
400g red onion
510ml cider vinegar
420g granulated sugar
30g orange zest
2 tsp mustard seeds
1 tsp mixed spice
½ tsp ground coriander

1. Wash, peel and grate the beetroot and cooking apple – you'll need to end up with 1,020g beetroot and 600g apple.
2. Peel, half and slice the red onions.
3. Place all the ingredients in a heavy-based saucepan.
4. Bring to the boil slowly, stirring frequently so nothing sticks and the apples begin to break down. Allow to simmer uncovered for 2-3 hours. The chutney is ready when it becomes thick and rich in colour and has reduced well.
5. Meanwhile, wash your jars with soapy water, rinse and dry.
6. When your chutney is almost ready, place your dry jars in the oven at 140°C fan/160°C/gas 3 for 20 minutes, then leave in the oven until the chutney is ready.
7. Pot the chutney while hot, using a clean ladle and a jam-potting funnel, filling your jars to the brim. Place the lids on immediately and carefully turn upside down for 20 seconds. Label and store in a cool, dry place away from direct sunlight.
8. If stored correctly, it should last up to a year unopened. Once opened, store in the fridge and use within a month.

Homemade Granola

A simple granola is a great start to any day. This one, which is very popular with our customers, can be made using gluten-free or regular oats. The whole hazelnuts and flaked almonds add texture as well as flavour, and the naturally sour dried cranberries complement the sweetness of the honey.

MAKES ABOUT 700G

60g butter
75g honey
½ tsp vanilla extract
400g oat flakes
25g pumpkin seeds
25g sunflower seeds
25g whole hazelnuts
25g flaked almonds
100g dried cranberries

1. Melt the butter, honey and vanilla extract together in the microwave or on the hob.
2. Preheat your oven to 150°C fan/170°C/gas 3. Line a large baking tray with baking parchment.
3. Place the rest of the ingredients, except the cranberries, in a mixing bowl.
4. Pour the melted butter mix over the dry ingredients and stir thoroughly until everything is lightly coated.
5. Spread evenly onto the lined trays and bake for 15 minutes. Stir with a metal spoon and toast for another 6 minutes. Stir and return to the oven again for a further 6 minutes or until the granola is a light golden brown – not dark.
6. Remove from the oven and allow to cool on the trays. Add your cranberries, mix through and place in a clean Kilner jar or an airtight container.
7. If stored in a cool, dark place away from direct sunlight, it should last up to 6 months unopened. Use within 1 month once opened.

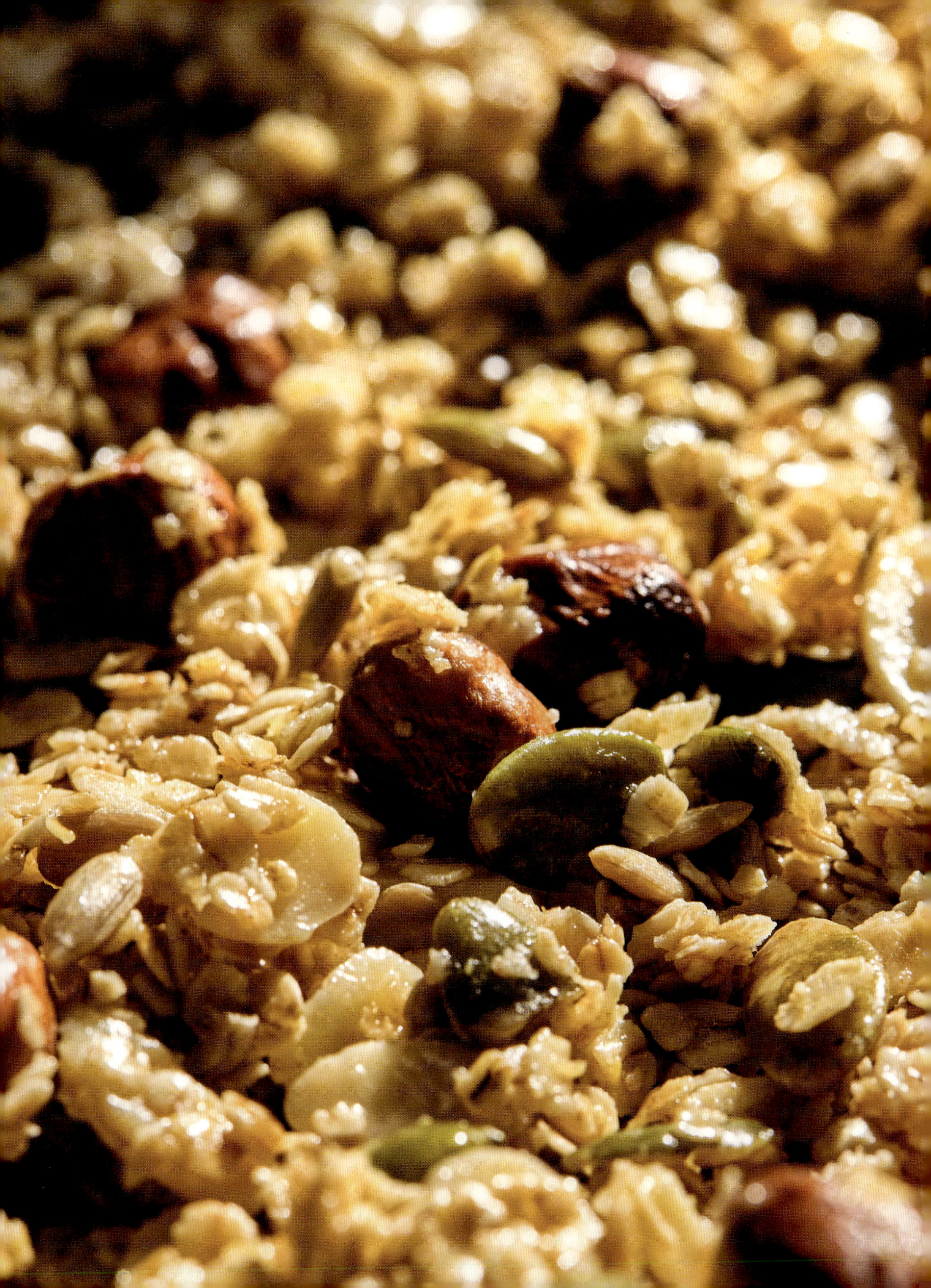

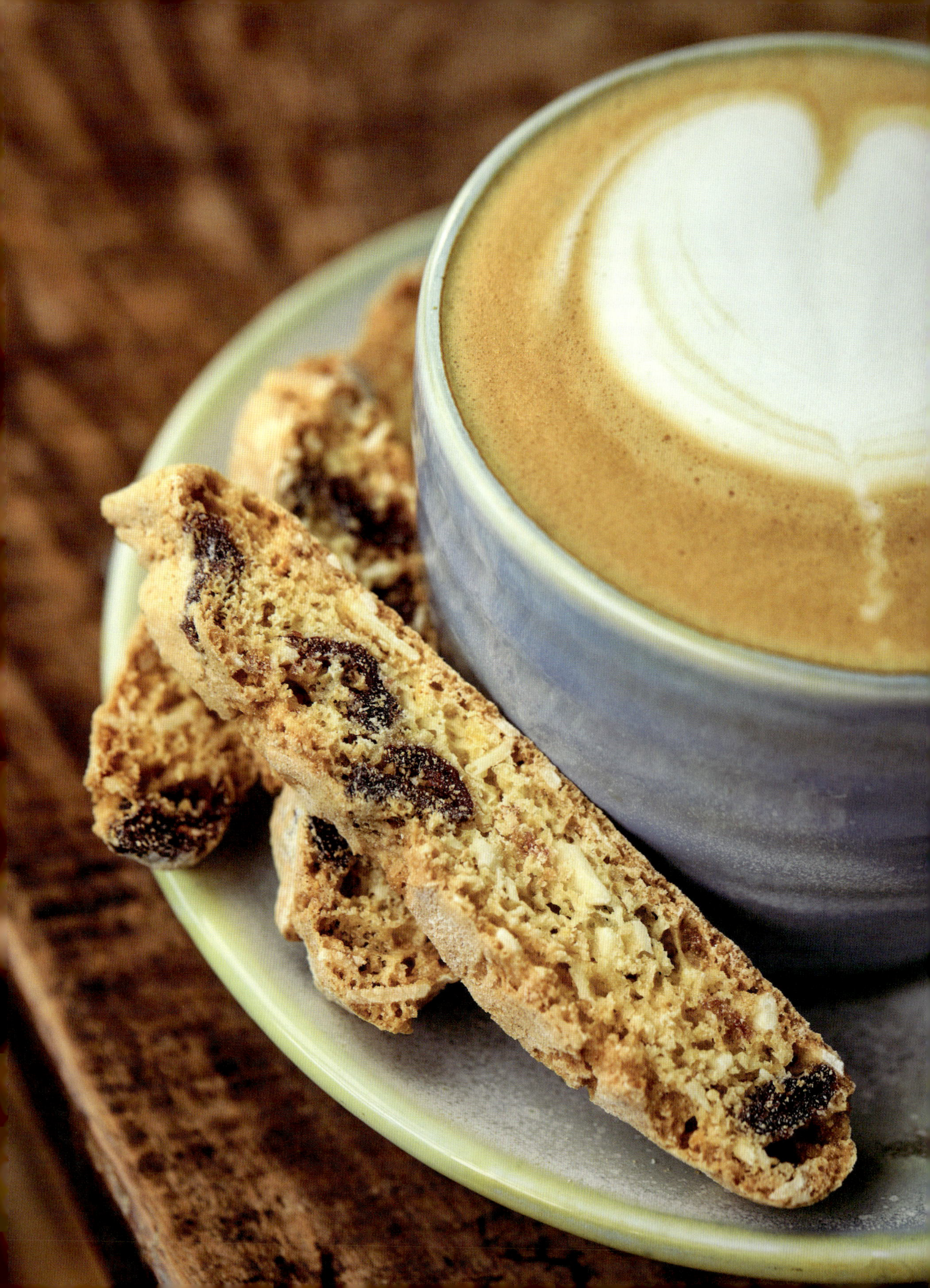

Cranberry Orange Biscotti

Biscotti are twice-baked Italian biscuits. The Italians have them with an espresso, and tend to dip them in to soften. I think they are also delicious with a cup of tea. As they are baked twice, they are fully dried so they will keep for ages. Make a batch and you'll have a month's supply!

MAKES 60

250g plain flour
250g caster sugar
1½ tsp baking powder
3 eggs
zest of 1 orange
200g dried cranberries
100g flaked almonds

1. Preheat your oven to 160°C fan/180°C/gas 4. Line a 37 x 26cm baking sheet with parchment paper.
2. Place the flour, caster sugar and baking powder in a mixing bowl and stir.
3. Whisk your eggs, and mix in your orange zest. Add your egg mix to the dry ingredients and mix by hand with a rubber spatula. When the mix has almost come together as a dough, add your dried cranberries and flaked almonds. Mix for a few minutes, then turn out onto a lightly floured surface.
4. Divide the mix into 3. Knead each portion into a ball and roll into a log, about 30 x 3cm. Place on the lined baking sheet approximately 6cm apart.
5. Bake for 25–30 minutes until golden brown.
6. Leave for 10 minutes to cool slightly. Turn the oven down to 120°C fan/140°C/gas 1.
7. Place each log on a chopping board and, using a sharp knife, slice in 1cm slices at an angle. Place the slices on their side on the tray, tightly packed together. (You may need to bake these in batches or use a second tray.)
8. Bake for 12 minutes. Remove, turn each piece over, then return to the oven for a further 10 minutes. They should be dry and pale in colour.
9. Allow to cool completely. Place in Kilner jars or sealed cellophane pouches with a ribbon for gifting. If they are for you, pop in a sealed tin or plastic container and store in a cool, dry place for up to 6 months. Once opened, use within 1 month.

Dehydrated Orange Slices

These slices take time but have all sorts of uses and, I think, are absolutely worth it. I have even had customers buy them for wreath making! We use them in our mulled wine spice mix and as garnishes for cakes, like the rich fruit loaf cake (page 112) and brown sugar meringue roulade (page 148). They can be used in cocktails too.

MAKES 10–12 SLICES

1 large orange

1. Wash and dry your orange. Cut horizontally into 3mm slices. Place in a single layer in a clean air fryer, with the slices touching, to fit as many as possible.
2. Set the air fryer at 70°C for 3½ hours. Turn the slices after 2 hours and again after 3.
3. Remove the slices, place on a wire rack and cool completely, then place in sealed glass Kilner jars.
4. Store in a cool, dark place away from direct sunlight – they should last up to a year unopened.

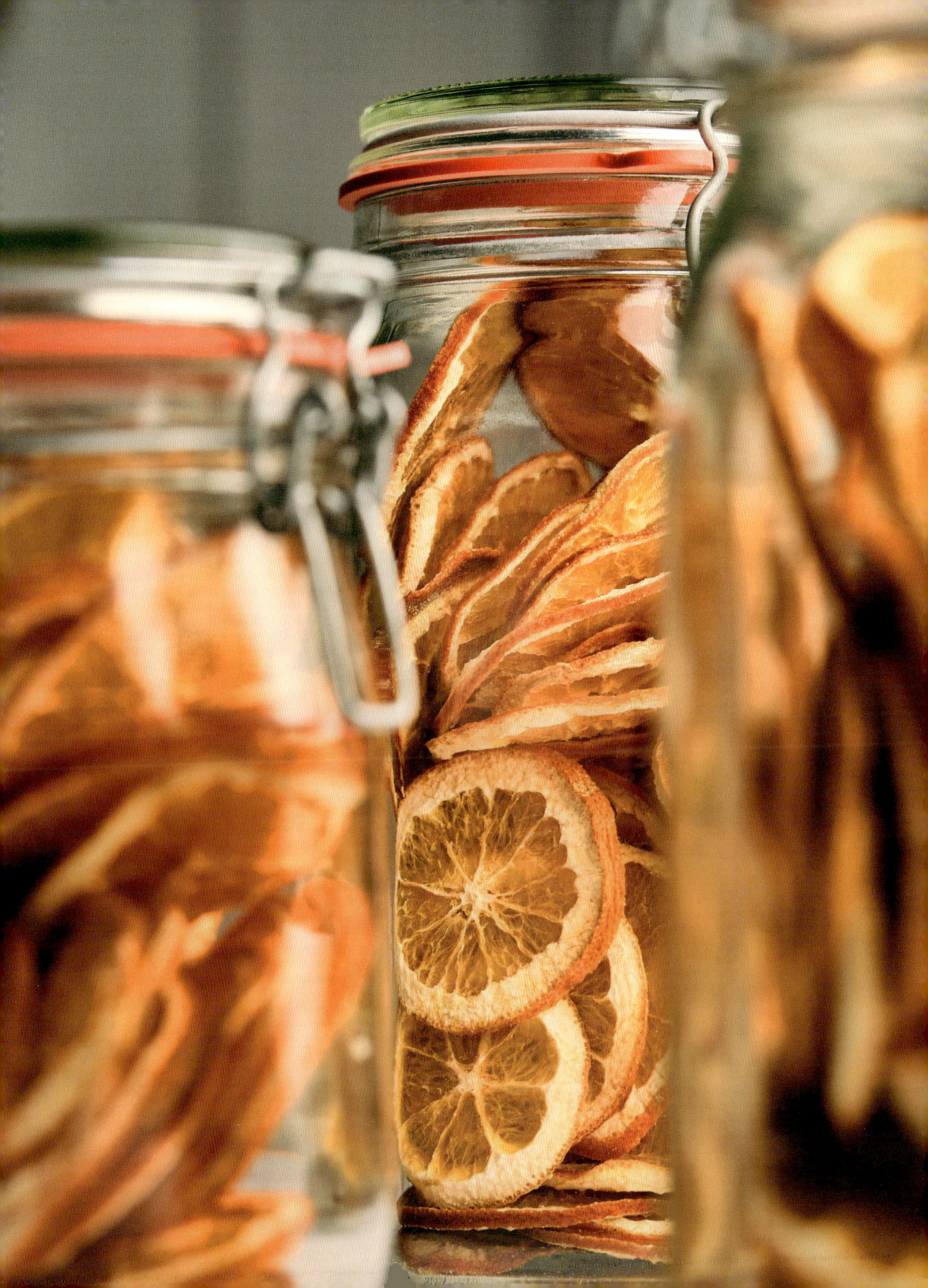

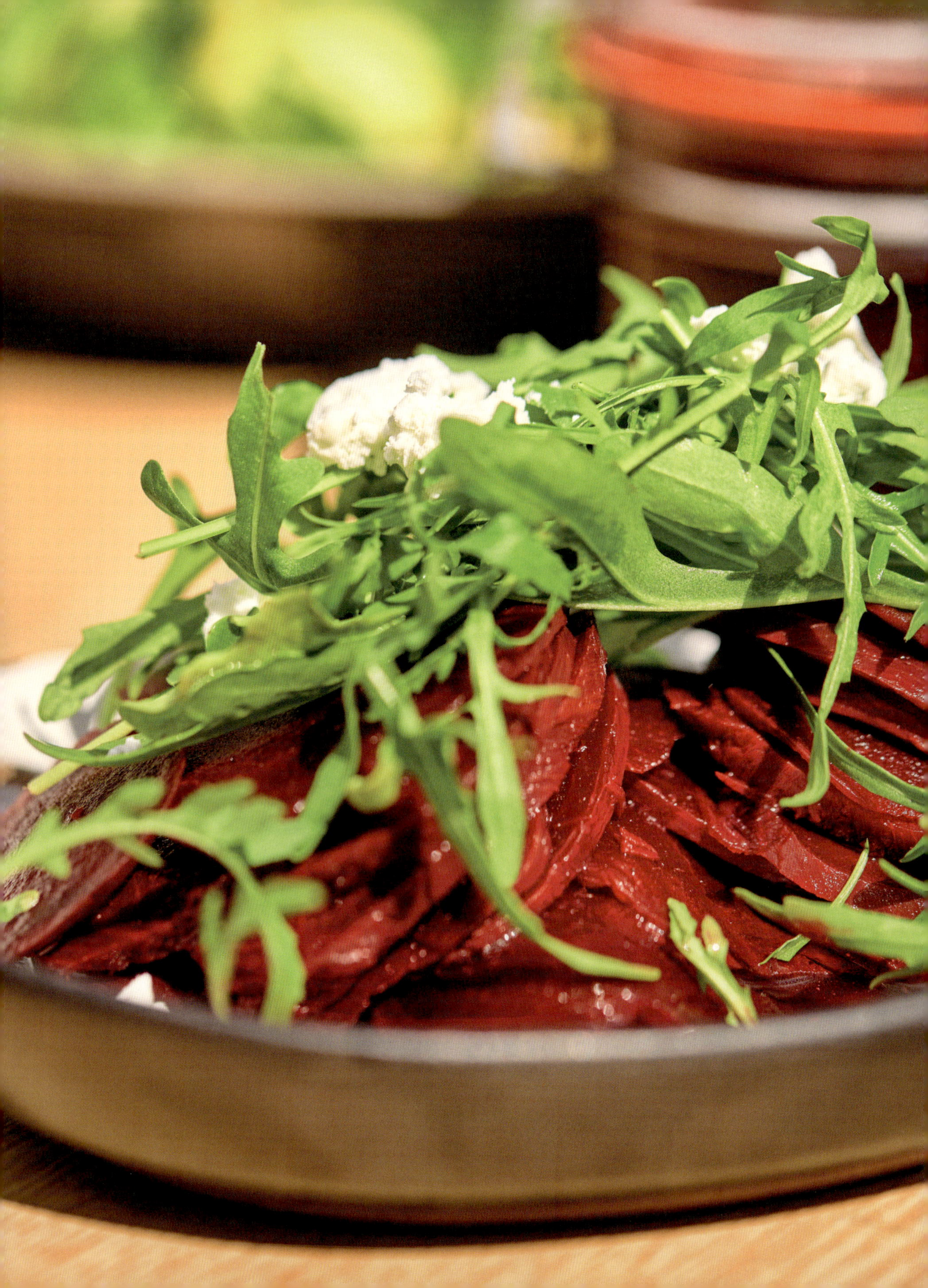

Pickled Beetroot

Pickling beetroot is a core food memory from my childhood. I remember the earthy smell of them cooking so vividly. Then they were sliced thickly and pickled in whatever vinegar was available, with minimal sugar. I prefer to use cider vinegar, as it's not so sharp, and to lightly spice the pickle. I often serve this as a salad, garnished with some fresh leaves and a sprinkle of soft goat's cheese.

MAKES 6-7 X 340G JARS

1kg fresh beetroot

700ml cider vinegar or white wine vinegar

100g granulated sugar

½ tbsp black peppercorns

½ tbsp mustard seeds

5 cloves

1 star anise

1 bay leaf

pinch of chilli flakes (optional)

1. Using a sharp knife, trim off the tops of the beetroot at the end of the stalk and any hanging roots – do not cut into the flesh, as this will cause the beetroot colour to bleed. Wash well.
2. Place in a pot, cover with cold water and a pinch of salt and bring to the boil. Cover, turn down the heat and simmer until the beetroot is cooked. This could take 30–45 minutes depending on their size. They should be tender when pierced with a knife. Drain and set aside to cool slightly.
3. Meanwhile, wash your jars with soapy water, rinse and dry. Place in the oven at 140°C fan/160°C/gas 3 for 20 minutes. Turn off the oven and leave the jars inside until the beetroot is ready to slice.
4. Wearing disposable gloves, peel the beetroot while still warm – slice off the top and root, and the skin should just push off with your fingers. Slice as thinly as possible using a mandolin or a sharp knife, then pack the beetroot into the sterilised jars.
5. Place all the other ingredients into a saucepan and bring to the boil. Place a sieve on top of a measuring jug and pour the pickling liquid inside, removing the spices.
6. Carefully pour the strained liquid on top of the beetroot and fill the jars to the brim, covering the beetroot completely. Place the lids on immediately and carefully turn upside down for 20 seconds. Label and store in a cool, dry place away from direct sunlight.
7. It should last up to a year unopened. Once opened, store in the fridge and use within a month.

Pickled Pears

These were inspired by a fresh pear and bacon sandwich I had on a visit to a local cafe in Sligo. I loved the idea but the season is so short that, in order to prolong it, I naturally turned to pickling. These beauties feature in many a salad on our menu and are a key ingredient in the fresh fig and pickled pear salad on page 13.

MAKES 4 X 340G JARS

10 medium pears
600ml cider vinegar
800g granulated sugar
2 x 3cm pieces of cinnamon stick
1 tsp cloves
2 star anise

1. Wash your jars with soapy water, rinse and dry. Place in the oven at 140°C fan/160°C/gas 3 for 20 minutes. Turn off the oven and leave the jars inside until the pears are cooked.
2. Wash your pears, slice in half and, using a melon baller, scoop out the seeds and cores.
3. Place all the ingredients except the pears in a heavy-bottomed wide saucepan, and bring the liquid to the boil.
4. Pop the pears into the boiling liquid, turn the heat down and cover with a piece of parchment (this allows some steam to escape while still keeping the pears submerged; it prevents excess evaporation and helps the pears to cook evenly). Simmer until the pears are soft and translucent – 10–20 minutes, depending on how hard the pears are.
5. Spoon the pears into the jars and top up with the poaching liquid (including the spices). Place the lids on immediately and carefully turn upside down for 20 seconds. Label and store in a cool, dry place away from direct sunlight.
6. If stored correctly, they should last up to a year unopened. Once opened, store in the fridge and use within a month.

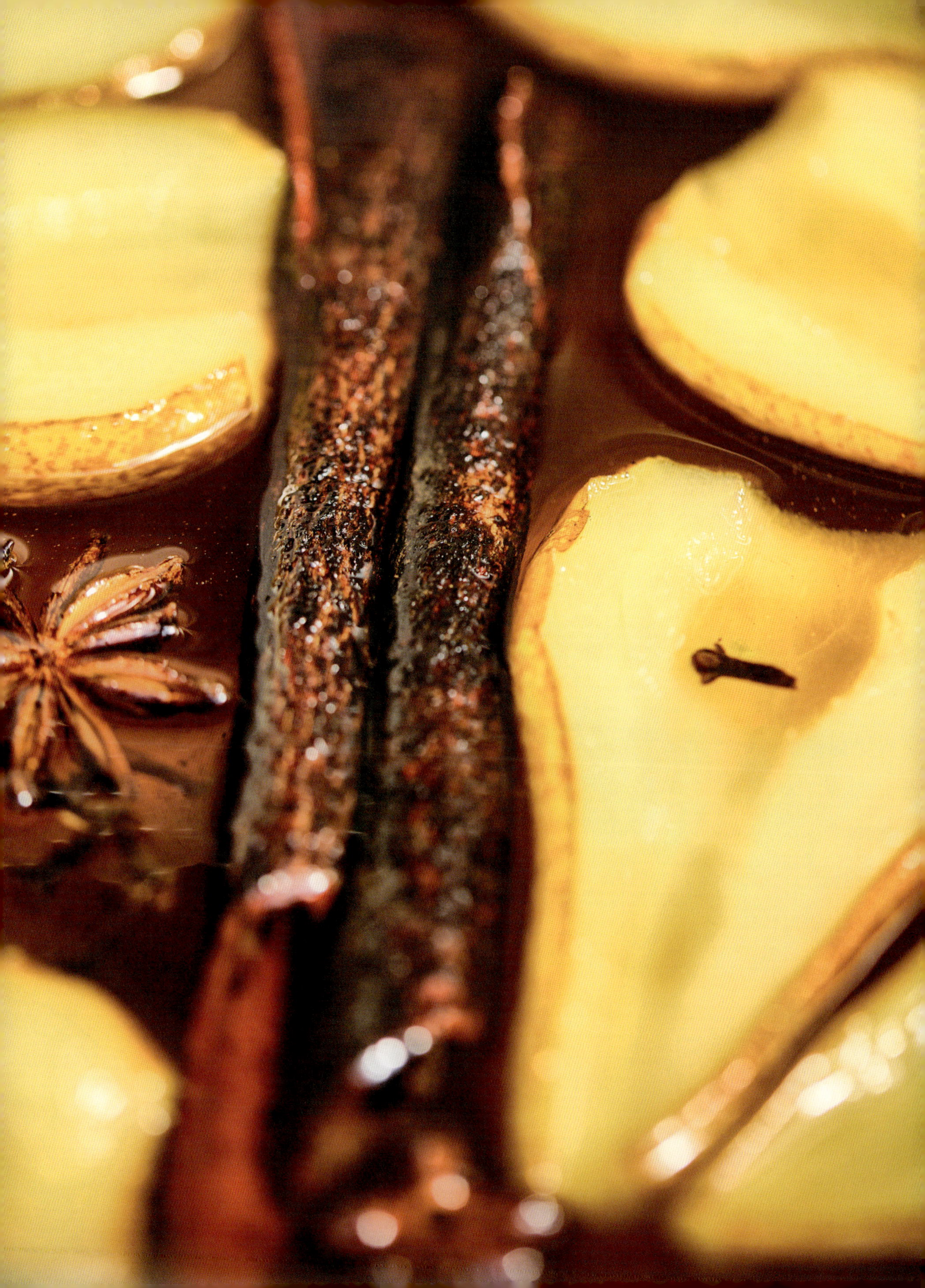

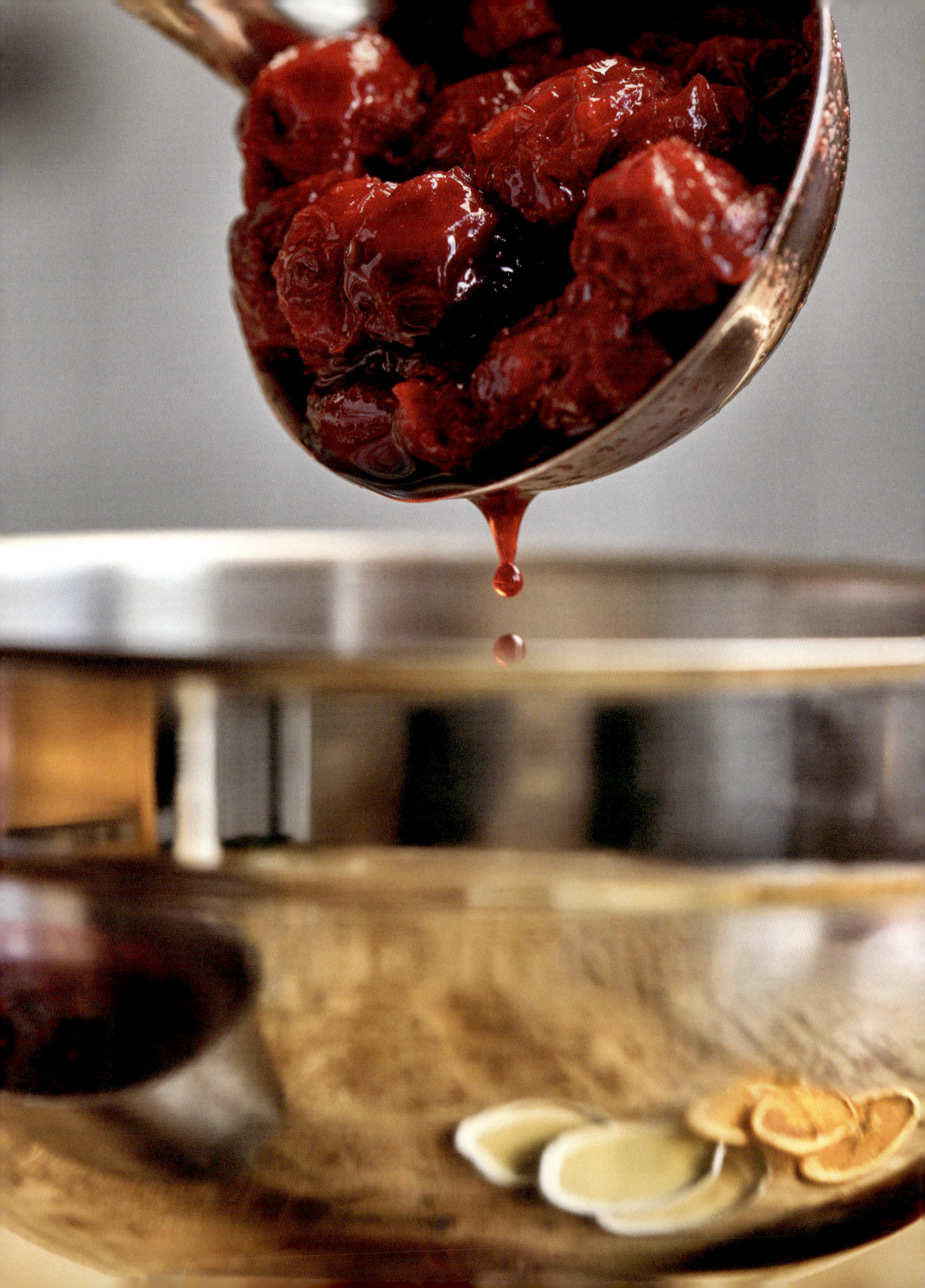

Pickled Cherries

I like to use sour cherries in this recipe, but you can also use sweet. They are a super addition to a winter leaf salad and pair beautifully with creamy goat's cheese. They are also great on a cheeseboard or mezze platter.

MAKES 4 X 340G JARS

1kg fresh sour cherries
300ml cider vinegar
1 x 3cm piece of cinnamon stick
zest of ½ orange
375g white sugar
1 star anise

1. Wash your jars with soapy water, rinse and dry. Place in the oven at 140°C fan/160°C/gas 3 for 20 minutes. Turn off the oven and leave the jars inside until the cherries are ready.
2. Wash your cherries and, using a cherry pitter, remove the stones. (If you don't possess a cherry pitter, use a metal drinking straw: hold the cherry between your two fingers on a board, push the straw through the stem end and dislodge the pit, being careful not to lose lots of the flesh. Mind your fingers.)
3. Place all the remaining ingredients in a saucepan and bring to the boil. Add the cherries, then turn down the heat and simmer for 3–4 minutes. The cherries are ready when they are soft but not breaking up.
4. Immediately spoon the cherries into the jars, then top up the jars with the pickling liquid. Place the lids on immediately and carefully turn upside down for 20 seconds. Label and store in a cool, dry place away from direct sunlight.
5. If stored correctly, they should last up to a year unopened. Once opened, store in the fridge and use within a month.

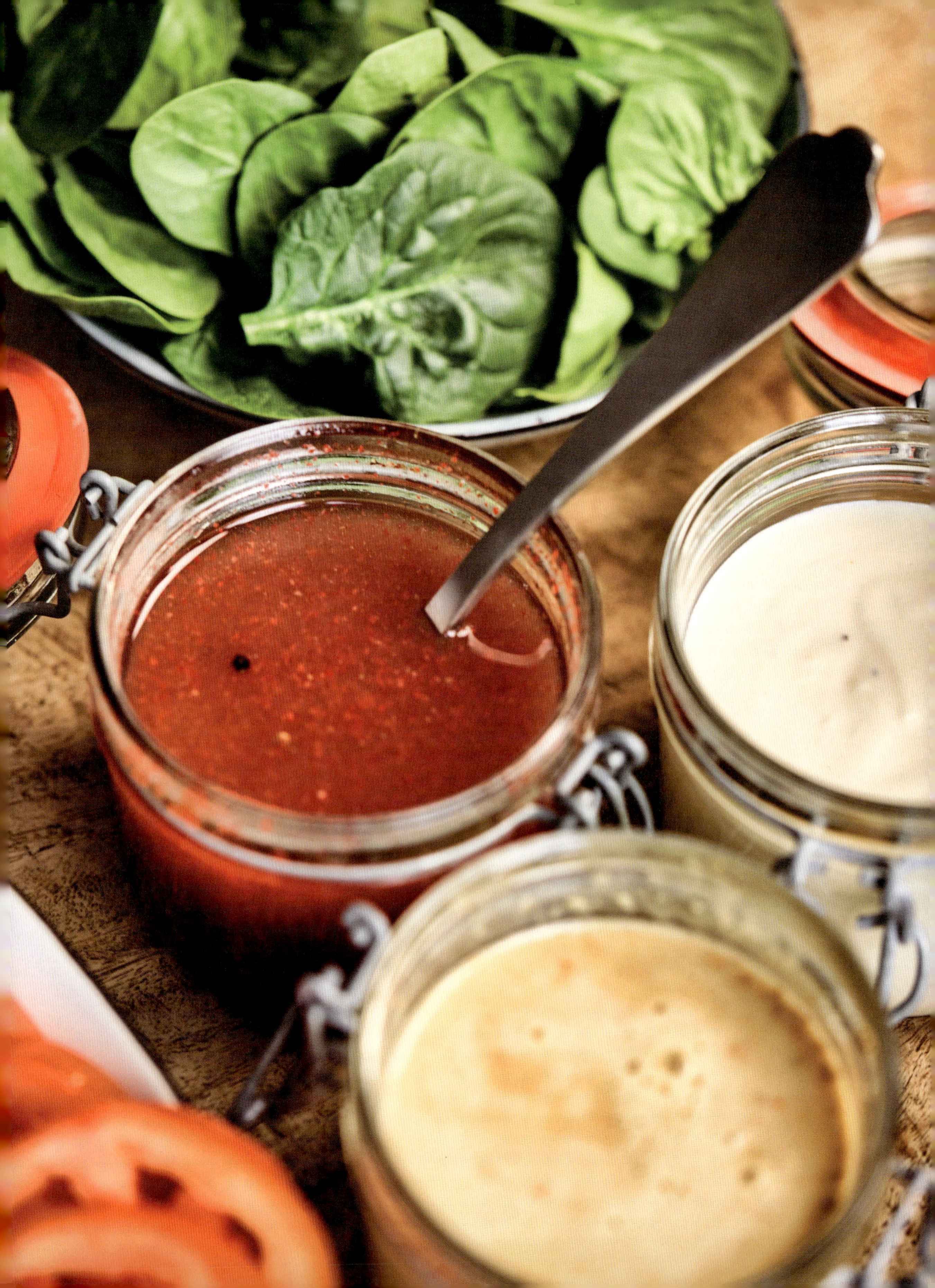

DRESSINGS

A good dressing or sauce can elevate any dish or salad. Here are a few of my favourites – they're a versatile bunch. There's something for everyone, whether creamy dressings are your thing or if lighter vinaigrettes do it for you. I love the pink peppercorn one in salads with fruits, like the tomato and strawberry platter on page 29. Our house dressing is great on a shredded carrot salad. The buttermilk dressing packs a punch and is a great dip – we serve it with our fishcakes (page 83) and on our cauliflower tacos (page 84). The maple tahini is
great with kale (page 34).

Honey and Pink Peppercorn Dressing

MAKES 225ML

3 tbsp pink peppercorns
2 tbsp honey
2 tbsp lemon juice
150ml light olive oil

1. Crush your pink peppercorns using a pestle and mortar or pulse them a couple of times in a spice grinder.
2. Place in a bowl with the remaining ingredients and whisk until combined.
3. Using a funnel, pour your dressing into a glass bottle.
4. This will keep for up to 3 months in the fridge. Shake well before use.

Maple Tahini Dressing

MAKES 170ML

3 tbsp cider vinegar
3 tbsp light olive oil
3 tbsp real Canadian maple syrup
1 heaped tbsp tahini paste
pinch each of sea salt and cracked black pepper

1. Place all the ingredients in a bowl and whisk until combined.
2. Using a funnel, pour your dressing into a glass bottle.
3. This will keep for up to 3 months in the fridge. Shake well before use.

House Dressing

MAKES 230ML

6 tbsp light olive oil
3 tbsp vegetable oil
3 tbsp cider vinegar
1 tbsp honey
1 heaped tsp Dijon mustard
1 clove of garlic
¾ tsp salt
pinch of cracked black pepper

1. Place all the ingredients except the vegetable oil in a jug.
2. Place your vegetable oil in a saucepan over a low heat for 1 minute to warm it a little. Turn off the heat.
3. Using a stick blender, blend all the ingredients in the jug until smooth and combined. Then slowly drizzle in the warmed vegetable oil while still blending. This will help keep your dressing from separating for a little longer.
4. Using a funnel, pour your dressing into a glass bottle.
5. This will keep for up to 3 months in the fridge. Shake well before use.

Ginger and Sesame Dressing

MAKES 190ML

FOR THE PICKLED GINGER

60g fresh ginger

4 tbsp cider vinegar

2 tbsp sugar

¼ tsp salt

FOR THE DRESSING

60g pickled ginger

1 small clove of garlic

2 tbsp lime juice

3 tbsp light olive oil

2 tsp tahini paste

1½ tbsp maple syrup

1 tbsp soy sauce (GF or regular)

2 tsp water

pinch of sea salt

1. To make the pickled ginger, peel and finely slice the ginger. Mix with the rest of the pickling ingredients and pop in the fridge. Leave to sit for a minimum of 3 hours before using.
2. To make the dressing, drain the pickled ginger and place in a jug with the rest of the dressing ingredients. Blend until smooth using a stick blender.
3. Using a funnel, pour your dressing into a glass bottle.
4. This will keep for up to 3 months in the fridge. Shake well before use.

Buttermilk Dressing

MAKES 250ML

140g mayonnaise

60g yoghurt

3 tbsp cultured buttermilk

2 tsp white wine vinegar

3 small cloves garlic

tiny pinch each of sea salt and cracked black pepper

1. Place all the ingredients in a jug and blend using a stick blender until the garlic cloves are well creamed.
2. Store in the fridge in a sealed jar, where it will keep for 3 days. Stir before use.

Our Suppliers

A special word of thanks must go to our local producers and suppliers. Their passion for and dedication to what they do is evident in every interaction we have with them, and we are grateful for their continued support. So thank you to:

Clive and staff – Clives Butcher Shop, Foxford
John and staff – Clarkes Salmon Smokery, Ballina
Michael and the team – Falcon Fruits, Ballina
Sarah – Willow & Wild Farm
Danilo and Helen – Dozio Cheese, Carracastle
Liz Courtie – local fig grower
Paul – B & B foods
West-A-Wake eggs, Kiltimagh
O'Haras of Foxford
Taste the View, Irish artisan product supplier
Martin – Foxford Honey
Keith – Knocknarea Honey
Jude – Nephin Honey
David and Martina – Richmount Cordial
The O'Malley family – Achill Island Seasalt
Fox & Co. Coffee, Foxford
Matt, George and team – Coffee.ie and Geometry Coffee
John – Aurivo
Aghna Flynn – shortbread
The Chocolate Garden of Ireland
Deborah and Rob – Van Velze's Chocolates
Sysco
Tuffy's Cash & Carry
Oliver Kelleher Castlebar
Bunzl McLaughlin
HiFive Clothing
JJ O'Toole Packaging
Berlin Packaging Ireland/Alpack

Acknowledgements

This book could not have happened without a few key people, and at the top of that list is Seamus Doherty, our sous-chef, who uses these recipes daily and tested them with me. Rachel Jackson, our restaurant manager, who keeps the show on the road. Joe Queenan, our managing director here at FOXFORD, who pushes us all to do better and gives us the opportunity to develop and improve. Helen McAlinden, our designer, for her honest and always on-the-money advice and guidance. Thank you to our wonderful suppliers. Thank you to our talented photographer Christopher Heaney. Thanks to our marketing and social media team. I owe a great deal of gratitude to our editor, Emma Dunne, and the team at The O'Brien Press – Ivan, Kunak, Ruth, Emma, Lir, Brenda, Gabbie, Joana and Paula – for their patience and guidance. To the customers of our Foxford Cafe, without whom none of this would exist.

Finally, to all our cafe staff, past and present, who have contributed to the life of the Foxford Cafe. Thank you.

Index

A
Aioli, Lemon Caper, **26**, 84
almonds **see** nuts
apples
    Apple Bakewell Slices, 118
    Brown Sugar Meringue Roulade, 148
    Pork and Apple Sausage Rolls, 75

B
Baked Chocolate and Mint Tart, 161
Basil Pesto, **30**, 47
BBQ Smoked Salmon Fishcakes, 83
beetroot
    Beetroot Orange Chutney, 75, 80, **169**
    Beetroot Patties with Roast Carrot Hummus, 76
    Diced Beetroot and Orange Salad, 38
    Pickled Beetroot, 177
Biscotti, Cranberry Orange, 173
Blackberry Jam, 166
Blueberry and Lemon Polenta Cake, 136
Bombay Roast Potatoes, 18
broccoli
    Broccoli, Potato and Spinach Soup, 52
    Garlic Roasted Broccoli with Romesco Sauce and Toasted Almonds, **17**, 84
Brown Soda Bread, 55, **60**
Brown Sugar Meringue Roulade, 148
Brown Treacle Scones, 101
Brown Treacle Soda Bread, 63
Brownies, 117
Buttermilk Dressing, 83, 84, 185

C
cabbage: Winter Slaw with Ginger and Sesame Dressing, 33
caramel: Gluten-Free Millionaire's Shortbread, 109
carrots
    Beetroot Patties with Roast Carrot Hummus, 76
    Carrot, Ginger and Coconut Soup, 43
    Carrot and Parsnip Soup, 55
    Roast Carrot and Chickpea Rolls, 90
Cashel Blue cheese
    Fresh Fig and Pickled Pear Salad with Cashel Blue Cheese, 13
    Cashel Blue and Spinach Frittata, 72
    Mixed Leaves with Maple-Glazed Peach or Nectarine, Toasted Pecans and Cashel Blue Cheese, **25**, 79
cauliflower
    Cauliflower Cheese Soup, 56
    Cauliflower Tacos, 84
    Curried Cauliflower and Coconut Soup, 48
    Roast Cauliflower Salad with Pearl Couscous and Zhoug, **37**, 79
    Roasted Cauliflower with Parmesan, 22
Cheddar and Ham Quiche, 87
cheese
    Cashel Blue and Spinach Frittata, 72
    Cauliflower Cheese Soup, 56
    Fresh Fig and Pickled Pear Salad with Cashel Blue Cheese, 13
    Goat's Cheese and Pepper Frittata, 72
    Goat's Cheese Tartlets with Red Onion Marmalade, 93
    Ham and Cheddar Quiche, 87
    Mixed Leaves with Maple-Glazed Peach or Nectarine, Toasted Pecans and Cashel Blue Cheese, **25**, 79
    Roasted Cauliflower with Parmesan, 22
    Rocket with Pickled Cherries, Orange and Crumbled Goat's Cheese, 25
    Smoked Salmon and Parmesan Frittata, 72
    Watermelon Salad with Honey and Pink Peppercorn Dressing with Feta, **21**, 79
Cheesecake, White Chocolate and Cranberry, 156
Cherries, Pickled, 25, **181**
chickpeas
    Beetroot Patties with Roast Carrot Hummus, 76
    Falafels, 80
    Roast Carrot and Chickpea Rolls, 90
chocolate
    Baked Chocolate and Mint Tart, 161
    Chocolate Brownies, 117
    Chocolate Cake with Real Chocolate Frosting, 138
    Chocolate Chip Cookies, 106
    Date, Coconut and Dark Chocolate Powerballs, 102
    Gluten-Free Millionaire's Shortbread, 109
    Peanut Butter and White Chocolate Powerballs, 124
    Rocky Road, 123
    White Chocolate and Cranberry Cheesecake, 156
Christmas Pudding, Foxford Cafe, 165
Chutney, Beetroot Orange, 75, 80, **169**
coconut
    Carrot, Ginger and Coconut Soup, 43
    Curried Cauliflower and Coconut Soup, 48
    Date, Coconut and Dark Chocolate Powerballs, 102
Coffee Cake, 144
Cookies, Chocolate Chip, 106
Couscous, Pearl, with Roast Cauliflower Salad and Zhoug, **37**, 79
cranberries
    Cranberry Orange Biscotti, 173
    Homemade Granola, 170
    White Chocolate and Cranberry Cheesecake, 156
cream
    Brown Sugar Meringue Roulade, 148
    Simple Sponge Cake, 129
Creamy Mushroom and Spinach Soup, 44

cucumbers
    Cucumber Pickle, **14**, 83
    Lamb Koftas with Tzatziki, 79
Curly Kale with Maple Tahini Dressing and Pickled Red Onion, 34
Curried Cauliflower and Coconut Soup, 48
Custard and Rhubarb Tart, 153

D
Date, Coconut and Dark Chocolate Powerballs, 102
Dehydrated Orange Slices, 112, 148, 165, **174**
Diced Beetroot and Orange Salad, 38
dried fruit
    Foxford Cafe Christmas Pudding, 165
    Fruit Scones, 99
    Fruity Soda Bread, 64
    Rich Fruit Loaf Cake, 112

E
eggs
    Free-Range Egg Quiche Three Ways, 87
    Goat's Cheese and Pepper Frittata, 72
    Ham and Cheddar Quiche, 87
    Rhubarb and Custard Tart, 153
    Smoked Salmon and Parmesan Frittata, 72
    Smoked Salmon Quiche, 87
    Veggie Quiche, 87

F
Falafels, 80
Feta, Watermelon Salad with Honey and Pink Peppercorn Dressing with, **21**, 79
Fig, Fresh, and Pickled Pear Salad with Cashel Blue Cheese, 13
fish
    BBQ Smoked Salmon Fishcakes, 83
    Seafood Chowder, 51
    Smoked Salmon and Parmesan Frittata, 72
    Smoked Salmon Quiche, 87

Focaccia, 67
Foxford Cafe Christmas Pudding, 165
Foxford Jams, 166
frangipane: Apple Bakewell Slices, 118
Free-Range Egg Quiche Three Ways, 87
Fresh Fig and Pickled Pear Salad with Cashel Blue Cheese, 13
frittatas
    Cashel Blue and Spinach Frittata, 72
    Goat's Cheese and Pepper Frittata, 72
    Smoked Salmon and Parmesan Frittata, 72
Fruit Scones, 99
Fruity Soda Bread, 64

G
Garlic Roasted Broccoli with Romesco Sauce and Toasted Almonds, **17**, 84
ginger
    Ginger and Sesame Dressing, 33, **185**
    Carrot, Ginger and Coconut Soup, 43
gluten free
    Gluten-Free Millionaire's Shortbread, 109
    Blueberry and Lemon Polenta Cake, 136
    Chocolate Brownies, 117
    Foxford Cafe Christmas Pudding, 165
    Homemade Granola, 170
    Iced Lemon Loaf, 105
    Orange, Polenta and Early Rhubarb Cake, 135
    Simple Sponge Cake, 129
goat's cheese
    Goat's Cheese and Pepper Frittata, 72
    Goat's Cheese Tartlets with Red Onion Marmalade, 93
    Rocket with Pickled Cherries, Orange and Crumbled Goat's Cheese, 25
Granola, Homemade, 170

H
Ham and Cheddar Quiche, 87
Homemade Granola, 170

Honey and Pink Peppercorn Dressing, 21, 29, **184**
House Dressing, 184
Hummus, Roast Carrot, 76

I
Iced Lemon Loaf, 105
Iced Lemon Scones, 100

J
jam
    Blackberry Jam, 166
    Mixed Berry and Spice Jam, 166
    Raspberry Jam, 166
    Rhubarb and Strawberry Jam, 166
    Simple Sponge Cake, 129

K
kale: Curly Kale with Maple Tahini Dressing and Pickled Red Onion, 34

L
lamb
    Lamb Koftas with Tzatziki, 79
    Spiced Lamb and Potato Parcels, 71
layer cakes
    Chocolate Cake with Real Chocolate Frosting, 138
    Coffee Cake, 144
    Simple Sponge Cake, 129
lemons
    Blueberry and Lemon Polenta Cake, 136
    Iced Lemon Loaf, 105
    Iced Lemon Scones, 100
    Lemon Caper Aioli, **26**, 84
    Lemon Meringue Pie, 143
Lime and Mint Watermelon Salad, 21
loaf cakes
    Iced Lemon Loaf, 105
    Rich Fruit Loaf Cake, 112

M
Maple and Pecan Pie, 132
Maple Tahini Dressing, 34, **184**

INDEX 189

meringue
    Brown Sugar Meringue Roulade, 148
    Lemon Meringue Pie, 143
Minestrone Soup, 59
mint
    Baked Chocolate and Mint Tart, 161
    Mint and Lime Watermelon Salad, 21
Mixed Berry and Spice Jam, 166
Mixed Leaves with Maple-Glazed Peach or Nectarine, Toasted Pecans and Cashel Blue Cheese, **25**, 79
Mushroom and Spinach Soup, Creamy, 44
mussels: Seafood Chowder, 51

N

nectarine: Mixed Leaves with Maple-Glazed Peach or Nectarine, Toasted Pecans and Cashel Blue Cheese, **25**, 79
New Season Baby Potatoes with Lemon Caper Aioli, **26**, 84
nuts
    Garlic Roasted Broccoli with Romesco Sauce and Toasted Almonds, **17**, 84
    Homemade Granola, 170
    Maple and Pecan Pie, 132
    Mixed Leaves with Maple-Glazed Peach or Nectarine, Toasted Pecans and Cashel Blue Cheese, **25**, 79

O

Onion, Pickled Red, **34**, 84
oranges
    Diced Beetroot and Orange Salad, 38
    Orange, Polenta and Early Rhubarb Cake, 135
    Rocket with Pickled Cherries, Orange and Crumbled Goat's Cheese, 25
    Beetroot Orange Chutney, 75, 80, **169**
    Cranberry Orange Biscotti, 173
    Dehydrated Orange Slices, 112, 148, 165, **174**

P

Pappardelle Pasta with Pesto, 30
Parmesan, Roasted Cauliflower with, 22
Parsnip and Carrot Soup, 55
pasta
    Minestrone Soup, 59
    Pappardelle Pasta with Pesto, 30
peach: Mixed Leaves with Maple-Glazed Peach or Nectarine, Toasted Pecans and Cashel Blue Cheese, **25**, 79
Peanut Butter and White Chocolate Powerballs, 124
pears
    Fresh Fig and Pickled Pear Salad with Cashel Blue Cheese, 13
    Pickled Pears, 178
pecans *see* nuts
peppers
    Goat's Cheese and Pepper Frittata, 72
    Tomato and Roast Pepper Soup, 47
pesto
    Basil Pesto, **30**, 47
    Wild Garlic Pesto, 30
pickles
    Cucumber Pickle, **14**, 83
    Pickled Beetroot, 177
    Pickled Cherries, 25, **181**
    Pickled Pears, 13, **178**
    Pickled Red Onion, **34**, 84
pies *see* tarts
Plain Scones, 99
Polenta
    Blueberry and Lemon Polenta Cake, 136
    Orange, Polenta and Early Rhubarb Cake, 135
Pork and Apple Sausage Rolls, 75
potatoes
    Bombay Roast Potatoes, 18
    Broccoli, Potato and Spinach Soup, 52
    New Season Baby Potatoes with Lemon Caper Aioli, 26
    Spiced Lamb and Potato Parcels, 71
powerballs
    Date, Coconut and Dark Chocolate Powerballs, 102
    Peanut Butter and White Chocolate Powerballs, 124
Pudding, Foxford Cafe Christmas, 165
puff pastry
    Pork and Apple Sausage Rolls, 75
    Roast Carrot and Chickpea Rolls, 90

Q

quiche
    Ham and Cheddar Quiche, 87
    Smoked Salmon Quiche, 87
    Veggie Quiche, 87

R

Raspberry Jam, 166
Red Onion Marmalade with Goat's Cheese Tartlets, 93
rhubarb
    Orange, Polenta and Early Rhubarb Cake, 135
    Rhubarb and Custard Tart, 153
    Rhubarb and Strawberry Jam, 166
Rich Fruit Loaf Cake, 112
Roast Carrot and Chickpea Rolls, 90
Roast Cauliflower Salad with Pearl Couscous and Zhoug, **37**, 79
Roasted Cauliflower with Parmesan, 22
Rocket with Pickled Cherries, Orange and Crumbled Goat's Cheese, 25
Rocky Road, 123
Romesco Sauce, **17**, 84
Roulade, Brown Sugar Meringue, 148

S

Sausage Rolls, Pork and Apple, 75
scones
    Brown Treacle Scones, 101
    Fruit Scones, 99
    Iced Lemon Scones, 100
    Plain Scones, 99

Seafood Chowder, 51
Sesame and Ginger Dressing, 33, **185**
Shortbread, Gluten-Free Millionaire's, 109
Simple Sponge Cake, 129
Slaw, Winter with Ginger and Sesame Dressing, 33
smoked salmon
    Smoked Salmon and Parmesan Frittata, 72
    Smoked Salmon Quiche, 87
    BBQ Smoked Salmon Fishcakes, 83
soda bread
    Brown Soda Bread, 55, **60**
    Brown Treacle Soda Bread, 63
    Fruity Soda Bread, 64
Spiced Lamb and Potato Parcels, 71
spinach
    Broccoli, Potato and Spinach Soup, 52
    Cashel Blue and Spinach Frittata, 72
    Creamy Mushroom and Spinach Soup, 44

strawberries
    Rhubarb and Strawberry Jam, 166
    Tomato and Strawberry Salad, 29
sweet pastry
    Apple Bakewell Slices, 118
    Baked Chocolate and Mint Tart, 161
    Lemon Meringue Pie, 143
    Maple and Pecan Pie, 132
    Rhubarb and Custard Tart, 153

T

Tacos, Cauliflower, 84
Tahini Maple Dressing, 34, **184**
tarts
    Baked Chocolate and Mint Tart, 161
    Goat's Cheese Tartlets with Red Onion Marmalade, 93
    Lemon Meringue Pie, 143
    Maple and Pecan Pie, 132
    Rhubarb and Custard Tart, 153

tomatoes
    Tomato and Roast Pepper Soup, 47
    Tomato and Strawberry Salad, 29
Tzatziki, 79

V

Veggie Quiche, 87

W

watermelon
    Mint and Lime Watermelon Salad, 21
    Watermelon Salad with Honey and Pink Peppercorn Dressing with Feta, **21**, 79
White Chocolate and Cranberry Cheesecake, 156
Wild Garlic Pesto, 30
Winter Slaw with Ginger and Sesame Dressing, 33

Z

Zhoug, Roast Cauliflower Salad with Pearl Couscous and, 37, 79

First published 2025 by
The O'Brien Press Ltd,
12 Terenure Road East, Rathgar,
Dublin 6, D06 HD27, Ireland.
Tel: +353 1 4923333
E-mail: books@obrien.ie
Website: obrien.ie

The O'Brien Press is a member of Publishing Ireland.

ISBN: 978-1-78849-620-9

Text © Foxford Cafe and Kathleen Flavin 2025
The moral rights of the author have been asserted.
Editing, design and layout © The O'Brien Press 2025
Cover and text design by Emma Byrne
Photography by Christopher Heaney, North Harbour Productions

All rights reserved. No part of this publication may be reproduced or utilised in any form or by any means, electronic or mechanical, including for text and data mining, training artificial intelligence systems, photocopying, recording or in any information storage and retrieval system, without permission in writing from the publisher.

8 7 6 5 4 3 2 1
29 28 27 26 25

Printed and bound by EDELVIVES, Spain.
The paper in this book is produced using pulp from managed forests.

To the best of our knowledge, this book complies in full with the requirements of the General Product Safety Regulation (GPSR). For further information and help with any safety queries, please contact us at productsafety@obrien.ie.

Published in:

DUBLIN
UNESCO
City of Literature

Enjoying life with
O'BRIEN
obrien.ie